Thoreau in His Own Time

WRITERS IN THEIR OWN TIME

Joel Myerson, *series editor*

THOREAU

in His Own Time

A BIOGRAPHICAL

CHRONICLE OF HIS LIFE,

DRAWN FROM RECOLLECTIONS,

INTERVIEWS, AND

MEMOIRS BY FAMILY,

FRIENDS, AND

ASSOCIATES

EDITED BY

Sandra Harbert Petrulionis

University of Iowa Press
Iowa City

University of Iowa Press, Iowa City 52242
Copyright © 2012 by the University of Iowa Press
www.uiowapress.org
Printed in the United States of America

The University of Iowa Press is a member of Green Press Initiative
and is committed to preserving natural resources.

Printed on acid-free paper

Library of Congress Cataloging-in-Publication Data

Thoreau in his own time: a biographical chronicle of his life, drawn from
recollections, interviews, and memoirs by family, friends, and associates /
edited by Sandra Harbert Petrulionis.
p. cm.—(Writers in their own time)
Includes bibliographical references and index.
ISBN-13: 978-1-60938-087-8, ISBN-10: 1-60938-087-8 (pbk)
ISBN-13: 978-1-60938-097-7, ISBN-10: 1-60938-097-5 (ebook)
1. Thoreau, Henry David, 1817–1862. 2. Thoreau, Henry David, 1817–1862—
Friends and associates. 3. Authors, American—19th century—Biography.
4. Intellectuals—United States—Biography. 5. Naturalists—United
States—Biography. I. Petrulionis, Sandra Harbert, 1959–
PS3053.T497 2012
818'.309—dc23 [B] 2011035855

TO MY AMERICAN STUDIES STUDENTS IN 2010
AT FRIEDRICH SCHILLER UNI, IN JENA,
WITH GRATITUDE AND ADMIRATION

Contents

CONTENTS

CONTENTS

[ix]

Introduction

Our woods and waters will always be different because of this man.
—EDWARD EMERSON

Thoreau had a manifest reason for living.
—WILLIAM ELLERY CHANNING

"I AM A SCHOOLMASTER—a Private Tutor, a Surveyor—a Gardener, a Farmer —a Painter, I mean a House Painter, a Carpenter, a Mason, a Day-Laborer, a Pencil-Maker, a Glass-paper Maker, a Writer, and sometimes a Poetaster."[1] So did Henry Thoreau, at age thirty, unwittingly spawn what became the time-honored assessment of his standing—he was an author *and* many other things as well. Indeed, more than other Transcendentalists, Thoreau embodied the full complement of the movement's ideals and vocations— author, advocate for self-reform, stern critic of his society, abolitionist, philosopher, naturalist. Regardless of how whimsical he may have been in laying out these assorted vocations in response to a Harvard alumni questionnaire, Thoreau's legacy in the nineteenth century and since has always been enmeshed with multiple identities.

In *our* own time, of course, Thoreau has inspired generations to step to the beat of "a different drummer," to "advance confidently in the direction of . . . [their] dreams," "to live the life . . . [they have] imagined," to "beware of all enterprises that require new clothes," to "simplify, simplify." He's taught us that "the universe is wider than our views of it," that "there is more day to dawn," that "in Wildness is the preservation of the world."[2] He has been cited as not only the founding tree-hugger but the inspirer of civil disobedience acts large and small, whether antiwar protests on a global scale or gay rights sit-ins at local high schools. Thoreau authority Walter Harding noted decades ago that "there is hardly an ism of our times that has not attempted to adopt Thoreau."[3] But these Thoreaus did not exist in the nineteenth century. *His* audience had not achieved any consensus on his appeal, his worth, his legacy. If, as Robert Sattelmeyer surmises, the conundrum over how (or whether) to value Thoreau results from a "contrariness [that] is expressive of one-half of a deep-seated antiphony in American culture," then this was a trend that most certainly began in Thoreau's time. Not only did critics disagree over the genre, quality, and originality of his writing, they differed on how to classify Thoreau himself and considerably amplified his own list: poet, prose writer, naturalist, poet-naturalist, humorist, artist, scientist, "consecrated crank," hermit, philosopher, stoic, cynic, transcendentalist, idealist, wild man, pantheist, misanthrope, heretic, disciple, "one of the Concord oddities," "one of the eccentric literary geniuses who seem to swarm in Old Concord," "one of the old Concord Mutual Admiration Society," "a crooked genius," "a wayward genius," "an extraordinary 'man of letters,'" and, most prophetically, "one of those singular characters about whom very sincere people will honestly differ." To one or more of his contemporaries, Henry David Thoreau was all of these. For every critic who praised his humor in *Walden,* another lamented his lack thereof. For every resident who decried his reclusiveness, a townsman thought him "neighborly always."[4]

Being revered most by ordinary readers, neighbors, and students—rather than critics or fellow authors—is a consistent thread in any study of Thoreau's reception. Few may have agreed with the *Christian Register*'s pronouncement in May 1862 that with Thoreau's death "has passed away one of the most original thinkers our country has produced," yet this paper's tribute reflects the homage Thoreau had begun to receive from those who envied his example of leading an unconventional life. In the nineteenth century it was, not surprisingly, those who knew him personally, such as educator E. Harlow Russell, rather than contemporary literati, who most prized Thoreau's example: "To have lived in the same age and country with Thoreau, and to have walked for more than thirty years—however far behind—in the effulgence of his genius," wrote Russell, was one of his "greatest privileges."[5] Nonetheless, as Thoreau's renown increased, many who had not known him well penned quite detailed accounts of their supposed relations with the man. In several nineteenth-century reminiscences concerning the major Concord authors—Thoreau, Nathaniel Hawthorne†, and Ralph Waldo Emerson†—Thoreau appears frequently in familiar and sometimes apocryphal scenes: Emerson visiting Thoreau in jail, orthodox neighbors rebuking Thoreau for going fishing rather than attending church, others ridiculing him for reversing the order of his first and middle names or for standing motionless for hours on end observing tadpoles in a bog. Such accounts typically emphasize Thoreau the misanthrope, the hermit, the nonconformist—extremes that elide his membership in the community of Concord as well as his engagement with the national crises of antebellum America.

How can we disentangle Henry Thoreau from the myriad causes and ideas now synonymous with his name? From the daunting stature and accumulated, often fanciful lore of his reputation? To begin answering these questions, *Thoreau in His Own Time* presents remembrances from men and women who lived with, argued with, loved, and read Thoreau over the course of the nineteenth century. Those who knew him during his life reveal Thoreau as young man and college student; teacher, lecturer and author; naturalist and explorer; and, finally, acclaimed writer. In these often disparate individual recollections and published critiques, Thoreau emerges as a warm and generous teacher, friend, author, and family member as well as an occasionally diffident neighbor whose insatiable desire for solitude and lifelong commitment to "live deliberately" could interfere with the best of his intentions and the closest of his relationships.

Any study of Henry Thoreau in the nineteenth century must begin with his profound connection to his native Concord. In Thoreau's words, the place was "the old coat that I wear. . . . is my morning robe and study gown, my working dress and suit of ceremony, and my night-gown after all. . . . Home—home—home." His relations with Concord neighbors, on the other hand, have been persistently cast in pejorative terms, despite the work of a few critics, most notably Mary Elkins Moller, in recovering Thoreau's keen appreciation of the "true *community*" in which he lived. Waldo Emerson told those gathered at Thoreau's funeral that a "dangerous frankness" had given rise to the appellation "that terrible Thoreau," a phrase that for over a century has taken on a life of its own. Despite the lack of attribution—Emerson never names the coiner of the phrase—scholars have for years repeated the truism that neighbors regarded Thoreau "as a crank and did not hesitate to tell him so to his face." These blanket assertions, along with specific incidents of understandable local ire, as when Thoreau and Edward Hoar† accidentally set hundreds of acres of Concord woods on fire in 1844, have morphed over the years into absolutes, even in critical discourse, such as "Henry David Thoreau was not an easy man to like," and Thoreau "didn't like the neighbors."[6]

Without a doubt those most critical were the businessmen, town leaders, and religious figures who recognized themselves as the targets of Thoreau's pronouncement that "the greater part of what my neighbors call good I believe in my soul to be bad." Predictably, such neighbors reacted testily when a young townsman with no clear vocation despite his Harvard pedigree announced a goal of waking them up in order to point out that most were caught fast in "lives of quiet desperation." Concord physician and historian Edward Jarvis judged that Thoreau's "ideal of the social relation was very different from that generally entertained. Absolutely honest and conscientious, he had no confidence in his fellow-men, nor in their business habits, or the system of trade and finance prevalent in the world." Moller reminds us, however, that Thoreau engaged in a lifelong habit of serving and educating his community: as lyceum organizer and lecturer, as displayer of his natural history collections, as locator of the annual town hall Christmas tree—activities that display his "appreciative awareness of a community esprit," and examples of which abound in Thoreau's journal.[7]

Few reminiscences of Thoreau as a child or school pupil are extant. One fellow schoolboy known only as J. H. idealizes his classmate: "No profane or vulgar words did I ever hear, or know, to come from his mouth, and in all his intercourse with his mates he was always gentle and obliging. He never engaged in any of the sports or games that boys of his age delighted in, but preferred to stand still and look on, which he did with an indifference that to us boys was perfectly unaccountable and disgusting."[8] A more dynamic figure emerges from the diary of Concord lawyer John Shepard Keyes, who depicts his teenage rivalry with Thoreau for the attentions of young women. Keyes describes his infatuation in 1839 with Ellen Sewall, who a year later turned down marriage proposals from both Henry and his brother, John; in 1841, Keyes competes with Thoreau to spend time with Mary Russell:

> Talked with Miss [Mary] Russell about several things and had a rich time. . . .
> [We had] some real conversation about "love and friendship" (Mr. Emerson's essay[s]) such as I seldom engage in, when that odious Henry Thoreau called to invite the girls to go to sail. They had promised before but went, but Henry after thinking he could row them alone at last flatly refused to let me go at Mary

Russell's request—Cool—Transcendental—Independence now & forever. Hurrah. Whew T was so damnably impudent however that I could not be mad although I knew it was affectation and done because I left his boat at the cliffs.

On a later evening Keyes outsmarted Thoreau: "Completely cut out 'Henry David,' and made another 'vain striving' to be added to his list, by going home with Mary Russell."⁹ Keyes's jibe at his Transcendentalism likely calls attention to the local perception of Thoreau as Emerson's protégé and a *Dial* contributor.

His Harvard classmates remember Thoreau for traits marked in his later years: seriousness of purpose and preference for solitary nature outings. He "walked in his own ways often, instead of those prescribed for him" recalled Henry Williams, while David Greene Haskins phrases it less generously: "In college Mr. Thoreau had made no great impression. He was far from being distinguished as a scholar. . . . [He] was of an unsocial disposition and kept himself much aloof from his classmates." Amos Perry blames his association with the Transcendentalists for derailing Thoreau's academic focus:

> He was during more than two years a diligent student, bright and cheerful. I consulted him more than once about the translations of some of Horace's odes. In his junior year he went out to Canton to teach school. There he fell into the company of Orestes A. Brownson, then a transcendentalist. He came back a transformed man. He was no longer interested in the college course of study. The world did not move as he would have it. While walking to Mt. Auburn with me one afternoon, he gave vent to his spleen. He picked up a spear of grass, saying: "Here is something worth studying; I would give more to understand the growth of this grass than all the Greek and Latin roots in creation." The sight of a squirrel running on the wall at that moment delighted him. "That," said he, "is worth studying." The change that he had undergone was thus evinced. At an earlier period he was interested in all our studies.¹⁰

As Thoreau transitioned in the fall of 1837 from Harvard student to classroom teacher, this divergence of opinion continued. Particularly in contrast to his fellow instructor and brother, John Thoreau, some of their students characterized Henry as a "merciless," "rigidly exacting" disciplinarian, despite the fact that rather than administer corporal punishment he famously resigned from his first teaching job in Concord, as confirmed by family friend Prudence Ward: "The committee think that a school cannot be governed without occasional resort to corporal punishment—& H[enry] whipped one or two—but finding it against his conscience, & thinking the surveillance of such a Committee wouldn't be comfortable as it would be impossible at first, & perhaps never—to keep the school as *still* as they would require on his plan—he gave up, & means to get an academy or private school where he can have his own way—."[11]

Former pupils recall Thoreau's lesson on the absurdity of profanity: "'Boys, if you went to talk business with a man, and he persisted in thrusting words having no connection with the subject into all parts of every sentence—Boot-jack, for instance,—would n't you think he was taking a liberty with you, and trifling with your time, and wasting his own?' He then introduced the 'Boot-jack' violently and frequently into a sentence, to illustrate the absurdity of street bad language in a striking way."[12] Other Concord youngsters faulted Thoreau for keeping nature's secrets to himself: "He never will tell a fellow anything unless it is in his lectures," scoffed John Pratt. Annie Sawyer Downs recalls an incident of this kind that reveals another Concord naturalist sharing in Thoreau's game:

> No entreaties ever induced him to show us where his rare floral friends made their homes. He had no secrets, however, from Mr. Minot Pratt, and only a couple years before his death I had an amusing interview with him. Mr. Pratt had promised to take me to the only place in Concord where the climbing fern could be found. I had given my word of honor that I would not tell, and in due season we were on the ground. In the midst of our enjoyment we heard a snapping of twigs, a brisk step, in the bordering thicket, and in a second Mr. Thoreau's spare figure and amazed face confronted us. Mr. Pratt answered for my trustworthiness, and so won over Mr. Thoreau by representing what a deed of charity it was to enlighten my ignorance that he climbed with us into our clumsy vehicle and by circuitous ways took us to the haunt of a much rarer plant which he said nobody else in Concord had ever found. I was sincerely grateful and not backward in telling him so. But noticing an odd twinkle in Mr. Pratt's eye, I asked him later what it meant. He told me he had known of the plant years before Mr. Thoreau found it, and that the spot was not half a mile from where Mr. Thoreau discovered us. He had doubled and redoubled upon his track to puzzle and prevent my ever finding the place again.[13]

Some childhood memories, such as that of Sarah Ripley's grandson, Edward Simmons, proved amazingly resilient but unforgiving:

Like all boys, I was intensely interested in birds and animals. One day I was playing in the grass in front of the Old Manse, when I suddenly looked up to see a short man with a blond beard leaning over me.

"What have you there, Eddie?"

"A great crested flycatcher's egg," I replied.

This was a very rare find.

He wanted me to give it to him, but I would not. Then he proposed a swap.

"If you will give it to me, I will show you a live fox," he said. This was too much to resist. We made a rendezvous for the next Sunday.

Although descended from a line of parsons, I had already learned that Sunday was, for me, merely a holiday, and it was evidently the same for him. This man was Henry W. [*sic*] Thoreau.

Accordingly, the following Sabbath I trudged down to his place at Walden Pond, and he, who had "no walks to throw away on company," proceeded to devote his entire afternoon to a boy of ten. After going a long way through the woods, we both got down on our bellies and crawled for miles, it seemed to me, through sand and shrubbery. But Mr. Fox refused to show himself—and worse luck than all, I never got my egg back! I have always had a grudge against Thoreau for this.[14]

Such images, however, diverge from those of children vying to hold Henry Thoreau's hand, expectant for his stories as they walked home from school, or that of Louisa May Alcott†, who fondly remembers Thoreau bidding her to regard a spiderweb on the morning grass as a "handkerchief dropped by a fairy."[15] Similarly, for years afterward, George Carr credited Thoreau for helping him overcome his fear of snakes:

I used to work, when a boy at Sam Barrett's mill, . . . and Thoreau used to come in there quite often. He was in one day when some boys were there, and they asked me if I was going swimming, I said, no, I was afraid of the water snakes. Thoreau said they would not hurt me, and asked if there was any chance of one being out . . . and we went up the brook, found one about three feet long, when Thoreau went up carefully, picked up the snake, and showed us that it had no sting in its tail, and no bones in its head, that would give it power to bite, & that it was perfectly harmless, and since that time, . . . I lost all fear of the snakes.[16]

Annie Sawyer Downs repeats what had become by the late nineteenth century a standard impression of Thoreau:

[He] was good-naturedly laughed at in Concord when I was a child. Perhaps that is the reason, while doing full justice to his rare genius, that I find it difficult to judge him without prejudice even now. His retirement at Walden was generally looked on as a whim. . . . It was commonly said, "Anybody could live on six cents a day when mother's cupboard was close at hand and well stocked." . . . Doubtless this gossip did him injustice and I have no longer any doubt of his sincerity. But he was not agreeable.

Behavior that struck some as foolish, however—Thoreau's spending hours stock still in a swamp to observe wildlife—held others, like school-girl Abigail Hosmer, spellbound:

"We children saw Mr. Thoreau standing right down there across the road near the Assabet. He stood very still, and we knew he was watching something in the water. But we knew we must not disturb him, and so we stayed up here in the dooryard. At noontime he was still there, watching something in the water. And he stayed there all afternoon.

At last, though, along about supper time, he came up here to the house. And then we children knew that we'd learn what it was he'd been watching. He'd found a duck that had just hatched out a nest of eggs. She had brought the little ducks down to the water. And Mr. Thoreau had watched all day to see her teach those little ducks about the river."

And while we ate our suppers there in the kitchen, he told us the most wonderful stories you ever heard about those ducks.

Edith Emerson Forbes† and Ellen Emerson† as well as their mother recount their pleasure in Thoreau's playfulness and parent-like affection. Ellen describes Thoreau's "glorious plans for my delight. He meant some day to build me a house with 'interspiglions,' which was something very stately and attractive evidently in his imagination[.] No one knew exactly what the word meant; it was of his own invention. He moreover planned a clock for me which he said when it struck would 'be heard all over the house, all over the yard, all over the world,' and he seemed to be listening in his imagination to its strong tones." During her toddler years, Thoreau penned "To Edith" for the youngest Emerson child, a poem whose opening lines instantiate not only Edith's importance to him but reflect one of the most commonly mentioned traits of Thoreau's interactions with children—his treatment of and discourse with them as equals:

Thou little bud of being, Edith named,
With whom I've made acquaintance on this earth,

Who knowest me without impediment,
As flowers know the winds that stir their leaves,
And rid'st upon my shoulders as the sphere,
Turning on me thy sage reserved eye.[17]

Ellen mentions Thoreau being "in great demand" during the spring months, when "we are, as usual at this season, interested especially in flowers and birds." This observation, regarded with other similar reminiscences, sustains Moller's contention that as an informal natural history educator Thoreau nurtured a "subcommunity" of students, a process that also worked in reverse, as farmers such as George Melvin shared with Thoreau their findings of the elusive *azalea nudiflora,* and as African Americans such as Jennie and Elisha Dugan and Peter Hutchinson talked to him about snapping turtle eggs, the different bark of various oak species, and other natural phenomena. As Moller notes, Thoreau regularly names in his journal those who instructed him; in this way, acquaintances such as Stedman Buttrick, the Dugans, Reuben Rice, Hutchinson, George Minott, Noah Wheeler, and others become characters in a Concord natural history narrative.[18]

A recurring feature of nineteenth-century commentary on Thoreau calls attention to his affinity with Native Americans. Many echo John Burroughs† in reckoning Thoreau himself "a man in whom the Indian reappeared on the plane of taste and morals." Although Maine naturalist Fanny Eckstorm† confirms the accuracy of Thoreau's portrayal of Indian culture in *The Maine Woods,* at times the Concord writer's connection with Native Americans is absurdly inflated, as with George Bartlett's depiction of Thoreau in *The Concord Guide Book* (1880): "Often he wandered alone through these grand old primeval forests; at other times he took an Indian guide or joined some roving band of savages who welcomed him as a lover of nature, and taught him their simple woodcraft, sometimes gliding for days in a birch canoe like an autumn leaf on the gentle lakes, or down the foaming rapids, and sometimes climbing rough mountain sides or scaling dangerous precipices." Recent scholarship by Joshua Bellin accurately notes that Thoreau's "lifelong fascination with" Native Americans never translated into activism on their behalf or real sympathy for their situation, but his contemporaries—who shared to various degrees Thoreau's nineteenth-century ethnocentrism and stereotyping of the "noble savage"—found persuasive Thoreau's acknowledgment "of our obligations to them, and our ingratitude," as editor George William Curtis† judged:

> Thoreau so ingeniously traced our debts to the aborigines that the claims of civilization for what is really essential palpably dwindled. He dropped all manner of curious and delightful information as he went on. . . .
>
> His talk of the Indians gave an impression entirely unlike that of the Cooper novel and the red man of the theatre. It was untouched by romance or sentimentality. They appeared a grave, manly race, intimately familiar with nature, with a lofty scorn of feebleness. The sylvan shade and the leafy realm and Arden and pastoral poetry were wholly wanting in the picture he drew, quite as much as the theory that they are vermin to be exterminated as fast as possible. He said that the pioneers of civilization, as it is called, among them are purveyors of every kind of mischief. We graft the sound native stock with a sour fruit, then denounce it bitterly and cut it down. . . . Thoreau acknowledged that the Indian was not only doomed, but, as he gravely said, damned, because his enemies were his historians; and he could only say, "Ah, if we lions had painted the picture!"[19]

Naturally, many Concord youngsters listened in rapt attention to Thoreau's Indian tales. Frederick Willis remembers that Thoreau "told us stories of the Indians that 'long ago' had lived about Walden and Concord." Sarah Hosmer Lunt is one of many who recalls Thoreau's uncanny knack of finding Indian relics: "When a young student during a walk with Thoreau asked him where he would be likely to find Indian arrow-heads, Thoreau looked down, saying 'Here is one.' He frequently gave my brothers the arrow heads which he found in his rambles, and they are still kept at the old home in Concord." In a similar vein John Weiss† cites Waldo Emerson's amazement "that Thoreau could always find an Indian arrowhead in places that had been ploughed over and ransacked for years. 'There is one,' he would say, kicking it up with his foot." Thoreau's own excitement at these discoveries is recalled by David Atwood Wasson: "'When I come upon these things,' he said, 'I feel that I have indeed found something! This is genuine and unmistakable; there is Nature in it, no cant, nor artifice, nor make-belief; it is solid and real as rock; and with such relics before me I could lose the houses of the village, the shops, the churches, and the post office, without missing them.'"[20]

Thoreau's insistence on poeticizing nature likewise enraptured child and adult alike. Similar to Louisa May Alcott's reflections of the forest visits that Thoreau had beguiled her with as a child are the memories of Harvard Divinity School student Moncure Conway†, who recalls that Thoreau "by his scientific talk [would] guide us into the water-lilies' fairyland," always "taking care to explain the scientific secret inside each fairy-tale." This insistence on the duality of science and poetry did not detract from the value that professional scientists and naturalists placed on Thoreau's contributions to their fields. Ironically, even as literary critics denigrated Thoreau's scientific pursuits as those "of a fairly intelligent schoolboy—a counting of birds' eggs and a running after squirrels," his inimitable knowledge and collection of Concord's natural history garnered the respect of esteemed professionals. In *The Annual of Scientific Discovery*, "American naturalist" Henry D. Thoreau appears among the "Men Eminent in Science" who died in 1862. In the tribute published in *Proceedings of the Boston Society of Natural History*, Dr. Charles Jackson†, Lidian Emerson's brother, judged that Thoreau's research had "promised important acquisitions to science." Entomologist and Harvard librarian Thaddeus William Harris, whose *Report on the Insects of Massachusetts* Thoreau had reviewed in "Natural History of Massachusetts" (1842), bemoaned that "Thoreau would be a splendid entomologist if he had not been spoiled by Emerson," a conclusion reached after years of collaborating with Thoreau. Harris also insightfully reflected that "there were people who criticised Thoreau as being an eccentric loafer or an impractical dreamer. It is not known who all these were. Apparently their sole claim to immortality lies in the fact that they criticised Thoreau." Thoreau would have disagreed with Harris, however, as to the value of Emerson's influence. Being infused with Transcendentalism, valuing most "that branch of science . . . which deals with the higher law," is exactly what in Thoreau's view proffered meaning on his science, is what excited him to enthuse that "the earth is all alive & covered with feelers of sensation" a few weeks before he recorded the richly poetic account of the thawing sand bank at Walden in his March 1854 journal.[21]

Harris further points out Thoreau's good fortune in friends: "Scarcely ever was a man more fortunate in the character of his friendships or more profoundly influenced by them. Perhaps, too, there scarcely ever was a man more fully appreciative of them." Despite Thoreau's self-proclaimed "immense appetite for solitude," Harris's conclusion is accurate. Thoreau enjoyed intensely devoted friendships over the course of his life with a handful of men.[22] Daniel Ricketson†, a wealthy abolitionist from New Bedford, contacted him after reading *Walden,* clearly desirous for the relationship that soon materialized. Until Thoreau died, the two corresponded and shared extended visits that often included mutual friends William Ellery Channing† and Amos Bronson Alcott† as well. Although Ricketson's desire for intimacy and time occasionally irritated Thoreau, Ricketson confided to his friend Thoreau that he had "more than any other to me discovered the true secret of living comfortably in the world" and that he regarded him as "the only 'millionaire' among my acquaintance." Thoreau similarly inspired Harrison Gray Otis Blake†, a teacher from Worcester, Massachusetts. During the last decade of his life, Thoreau engaged in unique epistolary candor with Blake, who later recognized that "probably the most genuine part of the little service I have rendered to my fellow men was the unintended one . . . of being the occasion of those letters."[23]

Two men who aspired to such intimacy with Thoreau, Isaac Hecker and Thomas Cholmondeley, were ultimately disappointed. After boarding with the Thoreaus for a few months in 1844, Hecker—a former tenant of Transcendentalist utopias Brook Farm and Fruitlands and later the founder of the Roman Catholic society of Paulist fathers—urged on Thoreau the idea of a two-man tramp across Europe, "to walk, work, and beg, if needs be, as far when there as we are inclined to do so." Thoreau declined the invitation, Hecker converted to Catholicism, and from the solitude of a Belgian cloister he later proselytized Thoreau: "I would like marvellously to free your soul by placing it in the light of Catholicity. . . . Why indeed my brother, should you beat out your brains against the prison bars of error or sink back into helpless inanity or utter despair. . . . Ah, my dear brother, could I induce you to bend your knees once in solitude & silence before God then new life would spring up into yr. heart."[24]

After meeting Thoreau in 1854, the British aristocrat Thomas Cholmondeley had shipped to him a forty-four-volume "princely gift" of Indian religious texts. Like Hecker, Cholmondeley also desired Thoreau to travel abroad with him—to the West Indies rather than to Europe. And although less severe than Hecker, Cholmondeley all the same counseled Thoreau on the error of his ways: "You ought to have society. . . . You want it greatly, and without this you will be liable to moulder away as you get older." Unlike Ricketson, Blake, and others who valued Thoreau's originality, Cholmondeley and Hecker preferred a more pliant Thoreau. Cholmondeley continued to correspond with him until Thoreau's death, but Hecker held a permanent grudge against the Concord naturalist. In 1854, he urged fellow Catholic and former Transcendentalist Orestes Brownson to review *Walden,* which Hecker admitted having only "read enough in it to see that under his seeming truthfulness & frankness he conceals an immense amount of pride, pretention & infidelity." Within his own circle at least, Hecker's animus against Thoreau was the dominant perception. In *The Catholic World,* which Hecker established in 1865, J. V. O'Connor published a strident tirade against Transcendentalism in general and Thoreau, the "hermit" of the movement, in particular: "He was the only man among the Transcendentalists that allowed their theories the fullest play in him, and the incompleteness and failure of his life cannot be concealed by all the verbiage and praise of his biographers. . . . He appears to have cherished some crude notions about the glory and bountifulness of Nature and her soothing and uplifting ministry, but these notions are, in the ultimate analysis, admissive of much limitation and qualification."[25]

With the Concord authors of his generation—Bronson Alcott, Ellery Channing, Nathaniel Hawthorne, and Ralph Waldo Emerson—Thoreau's relationships generally reflected and profited from their common vocation. Ever a loyal friend, Alcott regularly attended and praised Thoreau's lectures in various cities; he also trekked out to Walden nearly every Sunday during the winter of 1846 to hear Thoreau read from his works in progress. Although at times Thoreau took offense at the "coarseness & vulgarity" of poet William Ellery Channing, as his constant outdoor companion for many years, Channing no doubt witnessed the inception of many ideas that eventually made their way into Thoreau's published writings.[26] In his journal Thoreau claimed that "more than any man [he] disappoints my expectation," but over the years, he accommodated himself to Channing's "boorish" behavior and complimented Channing's poetry and lectures. For his part, Channing venerated Thoreau: "He is so noble and admirable a man, that I wonder he was not long since canonized, or raised up among men as an elder or a guide. . . . [He] has not only instructed us by his excellent writings, but has also led us forward, to do and to dare, by the example of a brave and generous life."[27]

In marked contrast, from their first acquaintance in 1843, Nathaniel Hawthorne rarely praised Thoreau without simultaneously belittling him. Mentions of Thoreau to influential literary friends typically came with caveats, as when Hawthorne explained to Henry Wadsworth Longfellow that

Thoreau would accompany him to a scheduled dinner in 1848: "You would find him well worth knowing; he is a man of thought and originality, with a certain iron-pokerish-ness, an uncompromising stiffness in his mental character, which is interesting, though it grows rather wearisome on close and frequent acquaintance." Hawthorne perhaps did not know that Thoreau had been Longfellow's student at Harvard. Nevertheless, Longfellow's remark years later that he was "familiar with his [Thoreau's] peculiarities" may indeed reflect the influence of Hawthorne's critique in addition to his own knowledge of Thoreau from the classroom. A short sojourn at Brook Farm in 1841 had solidified Hawthorne's lifelong disregard for the Transcendentalists, in addition to which his anti-abolitionist politics and campaign biography of proslavery President Franklin Pierce (1852) kept him at odds with the Thoreaus, Emersons, Alcotts, and other Concord abolitionists during the years he and Sophia Hawthorne resided there. Ironically, evaluations of Hawthorne emphasize the extent to which he guarded his privacy, such that few people knew him apart from his writings, a discretion he certainly did not permit Thoreau.[28]

Fellow Transcendentalist, neighbor, friend, mentor, Walden landlord, sometime employer, and progenitor of the spin on Thoreau's posthumous reputation, Waldo Emerson is unquestionably the Concord author whose twenty-five-year association with Thoreau was most significant. Comparison to Emerson plagued Thoreau his entire adult life. Whether as lecturer, writer, or thinker, Thoreau's voice, writing style, sentiments, and even his nose and handwriting were deemed derivative. Although the *New York Tribune* in 1844 called Thoreau one of "the deepest thinkers and most advanced minds in our country," earlier that year the *Tribune* had referred to him as a "young disciple and companion of Emerson." Best known of such identifications is James Russell Lowell's satirical portrait in "A Fable for Critics" (1848), where an unnamed Thoreau "Tread[s] in Emerson's tracks with legs painfully short; . . . How he jumps, how he strains, and gets red in the face, / To keep step with the mystagogue's natural pace!" This impression had not changed from Lowell's initial one when he had first encountered Thoreau ten years earlier: "It is exquisitely amusing to see how he imitates Emerson's tone & manner. With my eyes shut I shouldn't kn[ow] them apart."[29]

Similar observations dogged Thoreau throughout the 1840s. After meeting Thoreau at one of Bronson Alcott's Conversations in 1848, author

Ednah Dow Cheney described being "amused": "He is all overlaid by an imitation of Emerson; talks like him, puts out his arm like him, brushes his hair in the same way, and is even getting up a caricature nose like Emerson's." Yet Cheney also judged that Thoreau "has something in himself." Although that same year the *Salem Observer* judged Thoreau's lecture "Economy" to be "sufficiently *Emersonian* to have come from the great philosopher himself," fortunately for Thoreau's nascent public reputation, other reviewers diverged from such comparisons. Evaluating *A Week,* the reviewer for the *Holden's Dollar Magazine* maintained that "we think that Mr. Thoreau may be safely judged, in reference to his own merits, without comparing his name with Emerson's." The strength of Thoreau's abolitionist fervor in "Slavery in Massachusetts" (1854) also countered the common perception: "We have heard him spoken of, rather contemptuously, as a mere satellite and imitator of that erudite and transcendental philosopher [Emerson]; but we shall hereafter count such imputations as little better than profanity," averred the *National Anti-Slavery Standard.* To be sure, being considered one of the Concord authors did at times benefit Thoreau, as when a reviewer in the *Boston Transcript* predicted that *Walden* "will attract as much attention and be as widely read as if it were a new book by Hawthorne or Emerson."[30]

Thoreau's relationship with Emerson has spawned considerable scholarship, including several book-length studies.[31] Emerson promoted Thoreau's lecture career, encouraged Thoreau's literary aspirations, and published Thoreau's first poems and articles in the *Dial.* But by the late 1840s, both men had revealed their mutual disappointment in the other—when Thoreau failed to fulfill Emerson's idealized goals for his young protégé, and when Emerson similarly fell short of Thoreau's lofty notions of friendship. In 1848, Emerson recorded in his journal that "I spoke of friendship, but my friends & I are fishes in their habit. As for taking T[horeau]'s arm, I should as soon take the arm of an elm tree."[32] Showcasing Concord for author Rebecca Harding Davis a few months after Thoreau died, Emerson lamented that she hadn't met him and then went on to tell her, "Henry often reminded me of an animal in human form. He had the eye of a bird, the scent of a dog, the most acute, delicate intelligence—but no soul." Then, Davis reports, Emerson shook his head and continued, "No, Henry could not have had a human soul."[33]

By 1850, Thoreau's disappointment with Emerson had grown equally palpable: "While my friend was my friend he flattered me, and I never heard the truth from him, but when he became my enemy he shot it to me on a poisoned arrow. There is as much hatred as love in the world. Hate is a good critic." Two years later, Thoreau was resigned to their altered relations: "I am peacefully parting company with the best friend I ever had, by each pursuing his proper path. I perceive that it is possible that we may have a better *understanding* now than when we were more at one." Nevertheless, just a few sentences before this resolution, Thoreau explains his objection to Thomas Wentworth Higginson's recent lecture in Concord because, in the final analysis, "he reminded me of Emerson—& I could not afford to be reminded of Christ himself." Much of this bitterness can likely be attributed to Thoreau's residual disappointment and surprise at Emerson's lack of support for *A Week* on its publication in 1849. Not only had Emerson urged Thoreau to write and take on immense debt in publishing the book, but he backed away from any public endorsement and declined Theodore Parker's offer to review it for the *Massachusetts Quarterly Review*. Perhaps Thoreau also felt keenly that Ellery Channing had "temporarily displaced" him "as Emerson's hope for a Transcendental bard," as Linck Johnson asserts. Ultimately, Thoreau admitted his share of the blame in the downfall of this friendship: "I got no more partly because I gave so little."[34]

As with his and Emerson's relationship, scholars have also been attentive to Thoreau's conflicted attitude toward and contradictory statements about women. Some go so far as to label Thoreau a misogynist or to imagine that his perceived negativity toward women resulted from questions about his sexual orientation. But how did the women who knew him regard Henry Thoreau? Examining their comments and assessing the kind and number of his relationships with various women validates one Concord neighbor's judgment that Thoreau responded readily to others "where there were points of contact."[35] To be sure, multiple journal entries attest to Thoreau's acerbic disapproval of individual women and men as well as his frustration with humanity in general, and, occasionally, to women in particular. But like the charge of misanthropy in his time, the allegation of misogyny in ours overstates the case.

From the apparently platonic intimacy of his friendship with Lidian Emerson†, and, to a more limited extent, with her sister, Lucy Brown; to his admiration of women young and old who shared his love of nature, including Louisa May Alcott, Mary Russell Watson, Kate Brady, and Sarah

Alden Bradford Ripley†; to the sibling devotion of his sisters, Helen and Sophia Thoreau†; to his frequent efforts on behalf of the local female anti-slavery society, Thoreau enjoyed several mutually respectful relationships with women, notwithstanding his at times hostile generalizations about the female gender. In 1851, he complained in his journal after conversing with feminist Elizabeth Oakes Smith when she spoke in Concord that to talk to her "you had to substitute courtesy for sense & argument"; yet he admired the 1859 lecture given in town by reformer Caroline Healey Dall†, whose "Lives of Noted Women" had focused on Mary Wollstonecraft and Margaret Fuller. Such reactions and his own words suggest that Thoreau disapproved not of feminist subjects or women per se but, rather, to Smith herself. He explained to his sister, Sophia, that Dall's lecture "was good" and that he "liked her—because she did not look in the least like Mrs Smith!"[36] Further conversation with Smith had convinced him that "the championness of womans rights still asks you to be a ladies' man." Carrying "her lecture for her," Thoreau was disgusted by the odor left by her cologne in his pocket. His reaction calls to mind Mary Wollstonecraft's own complaints a half-century earlier that women of her time "constantly demand homage as women" and are given over to "a trifling turn" in both their behavior and interests.[37]

Thoreau's relationship with the best-known female Transcendentalist, Margaret Fuller, was friendly though never close. As editor of the Transcendentalist journal, the *Dial,* Fuller rejected more than one of Thoreau's submissions, with not so subtle, or constructive, critiques. About his essay "The Service," she explained that it "is rich in thoughts, and I should be *pained* not to meet it again. But then the thoughts seem to me so out of their natural order, that I cannot read it through without *pain.* I never once feel myself in a stream of thought, but seem to hear the grating of tools on the mosaic." Fuller enjoyed private jokes at Thoreau's expense, as she did with others who fell short of her high standards. In 1841, she inquired of Emerson whether Thoreau might have time to tutor her brother, Richard, for Harvard's entrance exams, since "even those who can live on board nails may sometimes wish to earn a little money." Visiting Concord in 1845, Fuller's friend Caroline Sturgis similarly mocked that "H. Thoreau imitates porcupines successfully." Wondering why Fuller had not sent a particular book to him, Sturgis mused that "he would only have given it to his squirrels to nibble." Yet Sturgis and Fuller both enjoyed his company well enough that Sturgis visited Thoreau twice at Walden in the winter of 1846, although she found him absent on both occasions. In 1844, Fuller woke up "at the crack of dawn" one morning while visiting the Hawthornes to enjoy a "'very pleasant' two-hour boat ride on the Concord River" with Thoreau.[38]

Thoreau both proposed and declined offers of marriage. In 1840, he was rejected by Ellen Sewall, the eighteen-year-old niece of family friend Prudence Ward, who had also turned down the hand of Henry's brother, John, obeying her father's insistent counsel in both cases. Seven years later, Thoreau rebuffed the epistolary proposal to marry Sophia Foord, a former governess of the Alcott girls whom he'd known during the months they had both lived with the Emerson family. Although an embarrassed Thoreau hurried to refuse Foord with "as distinct a *no* as I have learned to pronounce," he remained friendly throughout their lives with Sewall and her eventual husband, Joseph Osgood.[39]

When the extraordinary scholar Sarah Alden Bradford Ripley moved to Concord in 1846 after her husband retired from the ministry, she and Thoreau shared their mutual interest in science, including studying lichens and discussing Charles Darwin's *Origin of Species,* which appeared in Concord on New Year's Day in 1860. Ripley's intellectual friend and Waldo Emerson's aunt, Mary Moody Emerson, also admired Thoreau and borrowed his journals and lecture drafts to read, one of which she remembered well enough to cite when writing to her nephew.[40] Thoreau responded in kind to Mary Emerson. Not only did he rein in his usual sarcasm toward religion when studying and talking with her, he extolled Emerson as "the wittiest & most vivacious woman that I know— . . . singular among women."[41]

Encountering Thoreau over several years, Sophia Hawthorne† modified her initial indifference such that by the time he died she regarded him with real affection. Similarly, intimate Emerson family friend Elizabeth Hoar softened toward Thoreau considerably, a change that Elizabeth Maxfield-Miller credits to his extended stays in the Emerson household. Hoar's thoughtful gift and note in May 1843 as Thoreau left Concord to live in New York with William Emerson's family evidences her regard:

> We have become better acquainted within the past two years than in our whole life as schoolmates and neighbors before; and I am unwilling to let you go away without telling you that I, among your other friends, shall miss you much, and

follow you with remembrance and all best wishes and confidence. Will you take this little inkstand and try if it will carry ink safely from Concord to Staten Island? and the pen, which if you can write with steel, may be made sometimes the interpreter of friendly thoughts to those whom you leave beyond the reach of your voice,—or record the inspirations of Nature, who, I doubt not, will be as faithful to you who trust her in the sea-girt of Staten Island as in the Concord woods and meadows.

At this same leave-taking, Prudence Ward bestowed to Thoreau the parting gift of a small microscope.[42]

Thoreau's correspondence with Sophia Thoreau and frequent journal mentions of their outings together at times suggests an almost Wordsworthian closeness between brother and sister. Indeed, one neighbor characterized them as "twins" and claimed that Henry "opened his thought to" Sophia. In the waning months of her brother's life, Sophia took on the role of amanuensis when Thoreau could no longer write. As his literary executor, she exercised a savvy editorial sense as well as a proprietary defensiveness about Henry's writings. Indeed, in 1865, Thomas Wentworth Higginson† may well have lost the opportunity to edit Thoreau's journals as a result of miscalculating Sophia's astuteness of the literary marketplace. When he explained that publisher James T. Fields† had expressed an interest in his editing Thoreau's journals, Higginson warned that she should not expect the venture to be "pecuniarily profitable." In her politely terse response, Sophia not only refused to part with the "sacred" manuscripts but disagreed with Higginson's estimate of their worth: "Judging from the sale of my brother's late works, I feel confident that a selection might be made which would prove successful in every respect." Nearly a decade passed before Sophia deposited Henry's voluminous journal notebooks in the Concord library for safekeeping; at her death in 1876, she bequeathed them to H. G. O. Blake.[43]

Although their contemporaries noted Sophia's and her brother's shared commitment to social reform, it was a later century that valorized Henry Thoreau as an anarchist, a nonviolent civil disobedient, and an environmentalist. In the nineteenth century his reputation as a reformer resulted from his critique of contemporary society in *Walden* and from his abolitionist speeches and writings as well as his family's activism. The political writing most synonymous today with Thoreau's name, "Civil Disobedience," received scant attention when published with the title "Resistance to Civil Government" in 1849, except from a few readers such as British feminist Sophia Dobson Collett, who in favorably reviewing *A Week* urged fellow Britons to read this political essay as well.[44] In response to Thoreau's provocative questions on the limits of government, political morality versus expediency, and an individual's duty to the higher law of conscience, antebellum reviewers were largely silent.

Thoreau and his family were allies of Boston's most radical abolitionists, including *Liberator* editor William Lloyd Garrison, who published Thoreau's provocative speech, "Slavery in Massachusetts," on 21 July 1854. As a result of these ardent sentiments, delivered at its crowded antislavery rally on July Fourth, the Massachusetts Anti-Slavery Society formally "welcome[d] Henry D. Thoreau to the public advocacy of our cause." Five years later, Thoreau heightened his standing as an antislavery firebrand with "The Character and Actions of Captain John Brown," a speech he delivered in Concord, Worcester, and Boston and in which he passionately defended the actions and character of the Harpers Ferry militant. A *Liberator* columnist wryly noted that John Brown "seemed to have awakened 'the hermit of Concord' from his usual state of philosophic indifference." Even those who knew Thoreau found the speech uncharacteristically outspoken. Despite his family's decades of activism in local antislavery efforts and Thoreau's own prior speeches and writings, Concord abolitionist Minot Pratt expressed surprise that Thoreau's "sympathies were so strong in favor of the poor slave." Thomas Wentworth Higginson, one of Brown's financial conspirators, perhaps phrased it most aptly: "Thoreau, after all his seeming theories of self-absorption, ranged himself on the side of John Brown as placidly as if he were going for huckleberries."[45] Not everyone, however, celebrated Thoreau's alliance with the radicals. When anti-abolitionists in Concord hanged Brown in effigy on the day of his execution in Virginia, those who participated in Concord's memorial service for Brown, including Thoreau, were mocked in a last will and testament left beside the image.[46]

Thoreau's career as a public speaker, including "Captain John Brown" and other antislavery lectures, are at the center of Bradley Dean and Ronald Hoag's exhaustive study of the seventy-plus addresses Thoreau gave from 1838 to 1860.[47] The lecture podium provided Thoreau with trial runs of his writings in progress, particularly as he refined the drafts of *Walden* over the course of nearly a decade. The excursions to Maine and Canada also appealed to a general audience on the lecture circuit. Measured by the usual standards, however—such as number of talks given or pecuniary rewards—Dean and Hoag conclude that Thoreau enjoyed only minimal success in this profession. Much of the negative commentary centered on his uneven delivery and "monotonous style" rather than on the lecture's substance: "We wish Mr. Thoreau had communicated some of the enthusiasm of his heart to his words, for then we think his lecture would have interested many more than it did. We feel compelled to say that we think that he is a far better writer than reader or lecturer; and it is to us rather a mystery how a man with so much real fire, so much wholesome love of the beautiful in nature, can be so tame, so dull, even, in expressing the thoughts that fill his soul and pervade every part of his being."[48]

In the early years of his public speaking career, friends and family turned out to hear Thoreau; on one occasion, Ellen Emerson made it clear that his lectures appealed even to the youngsters in his audience: "Last night Mr Thoreau lectured a grand lecture on Autumnal Tints. Father and Mother, Mr Sanborn and Eddy were equally delighted. It was funny and Father said there were constant spontaneous bursts of laughter and Mr Thoreau was applauded."[49] In the 1840s, Lidian Emerson, Sophia Hawthorne, and Abigail Alcott† all promoted Thoreau's lectures, although some of his topics weren't to one of his relative's liking. Maria Thoreau† complained that "these Transcendentals . . . so transmography their words and pervert common sense that I have no patience with them." Maria did relish her nephew's lectures on more grounded subjects, however: "Henry is writing lectures on his tour to Cape Cod. I think they will be very entertaining, and much liked." In contrast, her friend Prudence Ward took pleasure in the full complement of Thoreau's subjects, including the Transcendentalism of his Walden-related talks:

> Henry repeated his lecture to a very full audience a week since—It was an uncommonly excellent lecture—Tho' of course few would adopt his notions—I mean as they are shown forth in his life. . . . There were very beautiful illustrations drawn from classical lore—Maria happened not to be well enough to go—by the way she could scarcely keep awake during Mr. Emerson's lecture—& said she would'nt go fifteen rods to hear him again—In matters of taste &c—my friend Maria, & I must agree to differ.

Ward also offers her assessment of Thoreau's Walden home: "Henry T has built him a house of one room a little distance from Walden Pond & in view of the public road. There he lives—cooks, eats, studies & sleeps & is quite happy. He has many visitors, whom he receives with pleasure & does his best to entertain. We talk of passing the day with him soon."[50]

Contrary to the mixed reviews of his performances as a public speaker as well as his own frustrations with this vocation are those who highlight Thoreau as "a charming talker," an "extraordinary" and "admirable conversationalist, and a good story-teller." The impersonal "cheapening" Thoreau deemed necessary "to interest my audiences" was not required in one-on-one conversation. In *Walden,* Thoreau divulged that he "dearly love[d] to talk." His interlocutors mirrored his pleasure: "I loved to hear him talk. . . . He kept the talk on a high plane," recollected Concord neighbor Maria Pratt.[51] In contrast to Edward Emerson†, who felt that Thoreau could be "combative in conversation," Eben Loomis emphasized his openmindedness: "I always, found Henry very hospitable to a new idea. If I happened to suggest some new thought, he would think it over, not saying much at the time, but afterward, perhaps the next day, or week, he would refer to it, having made up his mind whether to accept or reject it. It was delightful to hear him talk; his opinions were well formed, clear and gave no uncertain sound." Thoreau's own sense that he compromised what he most valued about himself when lecturing was obviously not the case when he talked with individuals one-on-one.[52]

For all his self-proclaimed desire for solitude, Thoreau consistently sought out opportunities to pay the social courtesies expected of his society. When away from Concord, Thoreau routinely called on friends of his family; several reminiscences make clear his pleasure in these visits with no indication that he felt obligated to perform them. Abolitionist and women's rights activist Sallie Holley describes that the day after she and a friend attended his lectures on "Autumnal Tints" and "Chesuncook" in Worcester in 1859, Thoreau "paid us the compliment of a nice long morning call . . . and remembered our being once at his mother's to tea, and Miss Putnam's looking over his herbarium with his sister." Franklin Sanborn† recalls Thoreau bringing a copy of *A Week* to college student Edwin Morton, who had recently reviewed it and *Walden* in the *Harvard Magazine*. A thank-you note from Thoreau's former student Richard Fuller acknowledges a similar gift, this one an inscribed copy of *Walden*. Although pleased with this "kind remembrance," Fuller also admonished that Thoreau "should leave it to his friends to purchase his book." On first meeting him, Thomas Wentworth Higginson relayed to his wife that Thoreau was "more human and polite than I supposed" and had taken care to let Higginson know that "he had heard Mr. Emerson speak of me."[53] Such considerations reveal a thoughtful and sociable individual whose sensitivity to others often exceeded nineteenth-century conventions, a decided contrast with Emerson's image of the "terrible Thoreau."

In addition to Sallie Holley, other abolitionists who admired Thoreau's antislavery writings differed in their appraisals of *Walden*. In 1854, Quaker poet John Greenleaf Whittier denounced the book as "very wicked and heathenish," although as an elderly man he called the "wise, wonderful Thoreau" a "rare genius." The editor of the *National Anti-Slavery Standard*, Lydia Maria Child, deemed both *A Week* and *Walden* "refreshing" and extolled the "simple grandeur of Mr. Thoreau's position."[54]

Other contemporary authors occasionally made known their dismissive views of Thoreau and/or Transcendentalism. Given their mutual exaltation of the individual's flouting of convention and affinity for nature, the somewhat uneven commentary of poet Walt Whitman† on Thoreau, based on their one brief meeting in 1856, seems surprising. Whitman appreciated Thoreau's literary talent and certainly valued Thoreau's regard for *Leaves of Grass*, but he could not "'reconcile' himself to" what he regarded as Thoreau's disdain for "the common man." In his ridicule of the Transcendentalists as residents of "Frogpondium," Edgar Allan Poe omitted Thoreau from "the Humanity *clique*," even though Emerson, Fuller, Lowell, and the decidedly un-Transcendental Hawthorne made the list. Some scholars argue that Herman Melville derides both the "pantheistic mystic" Thoreau and his "transcendental optimism" in stories such as "Apple Tree Table" and "Cock-A-Doodle-Do!" as well as in the novel *The Confidence Man*. Yet the target of Melville's critical invective is rarely so clear. Both Melville and Thoreau offer fervent critiques of their antebellum society; indeed, Michael Paul Rogin proposes that the title character of "Bartleby, the Scrivener" reflects Melville's creation of a Thoreauvian-inspired civil disobedient.[55]

Both Thoreau and his writings were frequently pronounced emblematic of the archetypal American experience. Friend and Concord neighbor Bronson Alcott, especially, attends to this aspect. To him, *A Week on the*

Concord and Merrimack Rivers was "purely American, fragrant with the lives of New England woods and streams, and could have been written nowhere else. It preserves to us whatever of the wild and mystic remains to us along our brooksides and rivers, and is written in a style as picturesque and flowing as the streams he sails on." Alcott renders Thoreau "a native New Englander,—as much so as the oak, or granite ledge." He predicted, inaccurately as it turned out, that Thoreau's work was "likely to become a popular book with our people here." To Nathaniel Hawthorne, however, Thoreau's lack of a conventional profession resulted from his native Americanness rather than from being "a native New Englander." Hawthorne introduced Thoreau to editor Epes Sargent as "a wild, irregular, Indian-like sort of fellow, who can find no occupation in life that suits him." He recurs again to this comparison with British editor Richard M. Milnes: "There is more of the Indian in him, I think, than of any other kind of man." Oliver Wendell Holmes likewise cast Thoreau as "half college-graduate and half Algonquin, the Robinson Crusoe of Walden Pond."[56]

Gary Scharnhorst claims that Thoreau "apparently gave little thought to how he would be regarded by posterity." Yet fortuitously, as Wendell Glick points out, as a result of spending his last months readying several manuscripts for immediate publication in the *Atlantic Monthly,* "Thoreau was perhaps the best defender of his own posthumous reputation until the centenary of his birth in 1917." Certainly during the final decade of his life, Thoreau had ample evidence of his legacy in the form of admirers who wrote to express gratitude for *Walden* and/or *A Week,* to seek treatment from "Dr. Thoreau," and to share gifts of mayflowers and blood-root for his garden.[57] As early as 1850, George Bailey of Portland, Maine, had inquired when *Walden* would be published and then peppered Thoreau with questions about *A Week:* "What were the names of the 'aged shepherd' and 'youthful pastor,'" "what that of the 'Concord poet,'" "of the Justice of the Peace and Deacon," "what the name of 'one who was born on its head waters?'" In 1856, Thoreau had assured Calvin H. Greene, a reader in Michigan who longed to meet him, that "you have the best of me in my books. . . . I am not worth seeing personally—the stuttering, blundering, clod-hopper that I am." Two months before he died, Thoreau gratefully acknowledged the admiration of New Yorker Myron Benton: "I am encouraged to know, that, so far as you are concerned, I have not written my books in vain."[58]

Stephen Fink further notes the significant fact that at the end of his life,

Thoreau enjoyed "the enviable position of being asked to contribute to a distinguished magazine owned by his successful publisher," James T. Fields, who had solicited "The Forester" from Bronson Alcott precisely to jumpstart Thoreau's posthumous reputation. In this warm tribute, published in the *Atlantic Monthly* a month before his death, Thoreau could read one early example of the multifaceted keystone on which friends would project his memory—"a son of Nature" whose "verses are suffused with an elegiac tenderness" and are "sure of a reading in the future."[59] The three articles published immediately after Thoreau's death—"Walking," "Autumnal Tints," and "Wild Apples"—may have received mixed reviews. But nevertheless, they and the reprints of *Walden* and *A Week* published that year provoked immediate critical attention. When *The Maine Woods* came out in 1864, Thoreau remained in the public eye.

Without doubt the most entrenched image of Thoreau came, on his death, from the fellow author and Transcendentalist with whom he had constantly been compared—Waldo Emerson. As in his obituary of Thoreau that ran on 8 May 1862 in the *Boston Daily Advertiser,* so in the formal eulogy delivered at Thoreau's funeral, Emerson conveyed not only his "bitter disappointment" at Thoreau's passing but established an enduring image of Thoreau's life as a "broken task."[60] Their friendship was strained considerably by the time Thoreau died, but Emerson nevertheless took charge of arranging his old friend's funeral service at Concord's First Church, "a thing Henry would not have liked," according to Louisa May Alcott, who understood her "wood god's" disdain for orthodox religion. Alcott adored Emerson, but she further disapproved of his eulogy—"good in itself but not appropriate to the time or place." Rather than celebrate his friend's life, Emerson used the occasion to concretize his own view of Thoreau as a "hermit and stoic," whose "virtues of course sometimes ran into extremes," and who maintained his "haughty independence to the end."[61] Near the conclusion of his remarks, however, as William Rossi and Robert Sattelmeyer have argued, Emerson "fix[ed], for generations down to the present day, the image of that life as one of 'renunciation and withdrawal'":

> Had his genius been only contemplative, he had been fitted to his life, but with his energy and practical ability he seemed born for great enterprise and for command: and I so much regret the loss of his rare powers of action, that I cannot help counting it as a fault in him that he had no ambition. Wanting this, in-

stead of engineering for all America, he was the captain of a huckleberry party. Pounding beans is good to the end of pounding empires one of these days, but if, at the end of years, it is still only beans!—[62]

Joel Myerson speculates that the funeral address reveals far more about Emerson than it does about Thoreau. Just as his memory soon displaced Thoreau with a one-dimensional figure, so was the subject of Emerson's "Thoreau" "essentially a character of his devising," as Robert Sattelmeyer has aptly contended.[63]

When the eulogy was published as "Thoreau" in the *Atlantic Monthly* in August 1862, many readers concurred with Louisa May Alcott's dismay at Emerson's flawed portrait. Sophia Thoreau confided to Daniel Ricketson that "reading it for consolation as a stricken mourner, I felt somewhat disappointed." Thoreau's Harvard classmate John Weiss could not "subscribe to the regret that is expressed in the inimitable biographical sketch." Of Emerson's denigration of Thoreau's huckleberry-partying prowess, Weiss rebuts, "But what if the berries that filled his pail were of a kind never picked before, from a stock not previously discovered in our pastures, staining his hands and pages with the blood that circulates behind the earth, that puts forth, indeed, the earth itself as a berry on the tree Igdrasil."[64] With Emerson safely in his grave by the late nineteenth century, others continued to disparage his originating sketch. "Emerson regretted Henry's want of ambition, we are told. He might have spared himself. . . . He was following an ambition of his own," declared the coeditor of Thoreau's journals, Bradford Torrey. Like Weiss, Torrey, and others, Waldo Emerson's own son, Edward, diverged sharply from his father in assessing Henry Thoreau, albeit he waited long after Waldo Emerson died to publish a corrective. In his preface to *Henry Thoreau as Remembered by a Young Friend* (1917), Edward speaks specifically to his father's contention that Thoreau lacked ambition: "This man, in his lifetime little known, except outwardly, even in his own town, whose books were returned to him as unsalable, is better known and prized more nearly at his worth each year, and to-day is giving freedom and joy in life to fellowmen in the far parts of this country, and beyond the ocean. Let us not misprize him, and regret that he did not make pencils and money." Years earlier, Waldo Emerson had dismissed such sentiments as the regret of Thoreau's admirers who "did not want me to place any bounds to his genius." His own journal reveals, however, that as a result of poring over Thoreau's voluminous journal notebooks, which he'd borrowed after Thoreau died from Sophia, Emerson had himself begun to reevaluate the extraordinary artistry and scope of Thoreau's life work.[65] Yet he never altered the public expression of what Thoreau had become in his mind's crafting. Rather than revise "Thoreau," Emerson instead reprinted it as the introduction to his edition of Thoreau's *Excursions* in 1863; over the next forty years, it appeared in several additional volumes and became a lasting summation of his friend's life.

Assisting Emerson with his edition of Thoreau's letters in 1865, Sophia Thoreau found herself in the awkward position of voicing her concerns about Emerson's selection criteria to publisher James T. Fields. She did "not like to express any dissatisfaction," yet she "despair[ed] of justice being done to Henry's character by any one." Sophia confided to Daniel Ricketson that she was particularly

> disappointed to find that some passages betraying natural affection had been omitted. I consulted Mrs. Emerson, who said that her husband was a Greek, and that he treated his own writings in the same manner. I expressed my desire that the passages should not be left out—it did not seem quite honest to Henry not to print them. I presume that the sentences to which I refer seemed to Mr. Emerson trivial. Mr. Fields thought it best to use them, and they were retained. . . .
>
> At the close of a beautiful letter to Mrs. Emerson, Henry wrote, "Shake a day-day to Edith, and say 'good-night' to Ellen for me." This ending was omitted, so the world might never have known that he loved the babies. I did not see any of the proofs after Mr. Emerson's return. He told me that he had *bragged* that the coming volume would be a most perfect piece of stoicism, and he feared that I had marred his classic statue.

Sophia's concerns proved apt. When *Letters to Various Persons* came out that year, reviewers echoed her sentiments. "We would have liked to see in this volume more letters of a domestic nature, to the members of his own family, if such exist and could have been published without impropriety," lamented a notice in the *New England Farmer*. The *Atlantic Monthly* reviewer agreed, judging *Letters* one of the best literary products yet from Thoreau's pen, despite "the entire omission of many important aspects of human life."[66]

In addition to these omissions, an ostensible review of *Letters* gave rise to the posthumous appraisal most damning to Thoreau's nineteenth-century standing. In "Letters to Various Persons," a review of *Letters* published in the October 1865 *North American Review* (and reprinted in 1871 in *My Study Windows*), influential editor James Russell Lowell blasted Thoreau after the manner of his earlier tirades directed at Edgar Allan Poe. First he assails Transcendentalism; then he targets Thoreau—"a man with so high a conceit of himself that he accepted without questioning, and insisted on our accepting, his defects and weaknesses of character as virtues and powers peculiar to himself," a man who "valued everything in proportion as he fancied it to be exclusively his own," who "only saw the things he looked for," who "thought everything a discovery of his own," who "had no humor," who "had not a healthy mind," whose "whole life was a search for the doctor." Many, including Thomas Wentworth Higginson in the *Literary World,* defended Thoreau against such a severely personal attack, but Lowell's eminence assured that this blow, delivered at the outset of Thoreau's public reckoning, would endure.[67]

Those who knew Thoreau, including Emerson, surmised that Lowell's antipathy resulted at least partially from residual bitterness over Thoreau's angry withdrawal of his essay "Chesuncook" from the *Atlantic Monthly* in the midst of its serial publication in 1858, when as editor, Lowell excised text he deemed irreverent without seeking Thoreau's approval. This editorial intrusion caused an incredulous Thoreau to demand that Lowell reprint the article with the sentence restored: "I do not ask anybody to adopt my opinions, but I do expect that when they ask for them to print, they will print them, or obtain my consent to their alteration or omission." Lowell evidently never responded to this or a second letter, sent weeks later, in which Thoreau asked to be paid the $198 payment due for the three installments of "Chesuncook" that had been published.[68]

Interestingly, "Letters to Various Persons" occupies the midpoint of Lowell's commentaries on Thoreau. In 1848, he had lampooned Thoreau in "A Fable for Critics," but a year later his evaluation of *A Week* had delighted Maria Thoreau, who found it "so just, and pleasant and some parts of it so laughable that I enjoyed reading it very much." Lowell objected to the book's repeated digressions and to being "preached at," but he nonetheless recommended *A Week,* even at the expense of other authors: "We know nothing more thoroughly charming than his description of twilight at the river's bottom. . . . Melville's pictures of life in Typee have no attraction beside it." In 1870, five years after his scathing "Letters to Various

Persons," Lowell circled favorably back toward Thoreau, "'the only poet who has fitly sung' about winter." Finally, in 1885, with Thoreau's critical stock on the rise, Lowell distinguished Concord, the illustrious home to Hawthorne and Emerson, and to Thoreau, whose writing about "Nature is as friendly, as inspiring here as in Wordsworth's country."[69] Plainly, Lowell could suppress his personal aversion for Thoreau when acting as the self-appointed arbiter of American literary taste.

The first book-length studies of Thoreau's life came from devotees who conferred a sympathetic treatment of a more multidimensional figure than those hitherto afforded by Lowell or Emerson. In 1873, William Ellery Channing compiled *Thoreau: The Poet-Naturalist,* a hodgepodge of material expanded from eight pieces that had previously appeared in 1863 and 1864 in the *Boston Commonwealth.* Interspersed with Channing's narrative were the "Memorial Verses" he read at Thoreau's funeral, substantial extracts from Thoreau's journals, and imagined dialogues from the two men's extensive walks. While many found *Poet-Naturalist* "very disappointing," other reviewers applauded its recovery of Thoreau's "sympathy," "vividness," and "completeness."[70]

A decade later, Thoreau's Concord neighbor and friend Franklin Sanborn published his *Henry D. Thoreau* to similar responses: "It is Thoreau's good fortune to have biographers who improve upon each other," declared Samuel A. Jones† in *Lippincott's.* Only the third book to appear in Houghton Mifflin's new *American Men of Letters* series, edited by Charles Dudley Warner, it was also the first of Sanborn's three lives of Thoreau. Here Sanborn brought out for the first time excerpts from Thoreau's college essays and provided a broad, largely uncritical overview of Thoreau's friendships, Transcendentalism and the Walden years, and social activism, taking particular pride in Thoreau's admiration for John Brown, to whom Sanborn had first introduced Thoreau. Sanborn would later claim that "Thoreau hardly needs a biographer," but Leo Marx points out that this study establishes Thoreau "where he belongs, in the midst of a remarkable literary ferment." Sanborn was especially bent on humanizing Thoreau, on freeing him from the immobile "classic statue" preferred by Emerson, an objective in which he succeeded, in the view of many reviewers, including author and editor George William Curtis: "Mr. Sanborn speaks of pranks and jokes in which Thoreau took part during his college life, and of merry story-telling to children. This is a new and charming aspect of him."[71]

Two British authors also brought out biographical studies of Thoreau in the nineteenth century—in 1877, *Thoreau: His Life and Aims,* by H. A. Page (published pseudonymously as Alexander H. Japp), and, in 1890, *The Life of Henry Thoreau,* by Henry Stephens Salt†. The author of biographies on Thomas de Quincey and Robert Louis Stevenson, Page undertook his *Thoreau* expressly to overturn what he felt was the common misperception of Thoreau as Emerson's "morbid and stoical" figure. It was Salt, however, as a committed social activist, whose study provided British readers with a more comprehensive view of Thoreau's life, attending especially to "Civil Disobedience."[72]

At the pen of another Briton at this time, popular British author Robert Louis Stevenson, came an intensely negative appraisal. In "Henry D. Thoreau: His Character and His Opinions" (1880), Stevenson offered a curiously personal critique given that he and Thoreau had never met. He was "not easy, not ample, not urbane, not even kind," and, most famously, Thoreau was "a skulker," Stevenson insisted. Spirited defenses in the American press against this "most ungracious fling" not only kept Thoreau's name in the headlines, but in a preface to a reprint of this article two years later in his *Familiar Studies of Men and Books Criticisms,* Stevenson stood corrected on points of Thoreau's biography, supplemental details that to him humanized Thoreau.[73]

In sync with his own penchant for nonconformity, Thoreau's critical reputation largely commenced at the hands of those who admired him precisely *because* he was not canonical—because he was excluded from the Emerson-Hawthorne-Longfellow-Lowell-Holmes-Whittier American literary hall of fame. First-person travel guide, trail mate, and self-help guru before such a vocation existed, "Thoreau looms up not as a series of texts between covers but as a voice, a companion, sharing his love of nature with the reader through all his volumes," as Lawrence Buell observes. Nineteenth-century readers already valued this voice. Thoreau "was a man who *felt* the woods . . . and it was his forte to reproduce that feeling," declared the *Boston Post* just months after he died. In 1865, a reviewer referred to Thoreau's "faculty of *seeing*—seeing what the millions never see."[74]

Many such reflections continued to brand Thoreau's writings as authentically American. In 1864, Thomas Wentworth Higginson dubbed *The Maine Woods* "a purely American product" in the *Atlantic Monthly;* the next year, a mixed review of *Cape Cod* in the *New York Evening Post* assessed that "Thoreau is without his prototype. He is our most original man, the growth of this soil—in a word, our most American writer. He is one of the few American men who have written a book that is vital, and which does not echo European thought." "Few books possess a more genuine American scope and flavor" read Thoreau's mention in *A Complete Manual of English Literature,* published in 1868. A decade later, editor George William Curtis reckoned Thoreau an author "whose name is very sure to survive among those of the most original Americans." By the turn of the century, Daniel Mason and Barrett Wendell had raised the bar: Thoreau "was a citizen of the New World, a worthy avatar of the American genius"; "the Nature he delighted in was characteristically American."[75]

In his extended study of Nathaniel Hawthorne in 1879, quintessential American Realist Henry James offers a begrudging approval of Thoreau, which, given his lack of regard for American Romantic authors generally, comes as a surprise:

> Whatever question there may be of his talent, there can be none, I think, of his genius. It was a slim and crooked one, but it was eminently personal. He was imperfect, unfinished, inartistic; he was worse than provincial—he was parochial; it is only at his best that he is readable. But at his best he has an extreme natural charm, and he must always be mentioned after those Americans—Emerson, Hawthorne, Longfellow, Lowell, Motley—who have written originally. He was Emerson's independent moral man made flesh—living for ages, and not for Saturday and Sunday; for the Universe, and not for Concord. In fact, however, Thoreau lived for Concord very effectually; and by his remarkable genius for the observation of the phenomena of woods and streams, of plants and trees, and beasts and fishes, and for flinging a kind of spiritual interest over these things, he did more than he perhaps intended towards consolidating the fame of his accidental human sojourn.[76]

What James calls Thoreau's "remarkable genius" in treating nature was hallowed ground for a generation of authors who followed. Thoreau was the consummate, originating "nature writer" whose works legitimated the natural world as a respectable subject of inquiry for serious authorship and literary endeavor, with authors as esteemed as Irish poet William Butler Yeats crediting the Walden site as inspiration for the idyllic cabin he envisions in his poem "The Lake Isle of Innisfree." A second generation of Transcendentalists, such as Thomas Wentworth Higginson in *Out-door Papers* (1863), acknowledged Thoreau's inspiration, but other writers contended with the critical ambivalence and ridicule to which Thoreau, Transcendentalism, and nature writing were occasionally subjected in postbellum America. For instance, essayist and conservationist John Burroughs greatly admired Waldo Emerson and Walt Whitman but alternated between caustic criticism and effusive praise of Thoreau. Lawrence Buell speculates that to Burroughs, Thoreau was "the imposing precursor whose shadow he must disown or destroy to establish his own legitimacy." Burroughs himself explained that Thoreau's concerns were "mainly ethical" as compared to his own "entirely artistic" goals. Decidedly more affirming is the influence of both Emerson's and Thoreau's writings on naturalist John Muir, one of the founders of the Sierra Club. To Muir, both authors provided a "philosophical interpretation of the value of mountains and natural landscapes" that inspired his preservation efforts as well as his own writing. Friends claimed that Muir inspired them to read Thoreau and noted the qualities they shared, including "mechanical ability," "fondness for the handling of tools," and "happiness in solitude with nature," in addition to a "lack of sympathy with crowds of people" and "intense love of animals." Although he had met Emerson in 1871, Muir did not visit the sites of Concord until 1893, when he further identified with Thoreau after a pilgrimage to Walden Pond: "No wonder Thoreau lived here two years. I could have enjoyed living here two hundred years or two thousand. . . . How people should regard Thoreau as a hermit on account of his little delightful stay here I cannot guess."[77]

Gary Scharnhorst's *Henry David Thoreau: An Annotated Bibliography of Comment and Criticism before 1900* (1992) is an essential resource for overturning the view dominant through most of the twentieth century that Thoreau's critical reputation remained flat until the end of the 1800s. Private writings lend additional credence to Scharnhorst's conclusion in his companion book, *Henry David Thoreau: A Case Study in Canonization* (1993), that "Thoreau's death . . . spurred a modest if short-lived revival of interest in his work." Even by April 1864, Thoreau's autographs had become "great commodities at fairs," according to Mary Peabody Mann. Further, Concord teenager Annie Keyes Bartlett describes a "large picnic" scene at Walden Pond in July 1865 where a group of fans "had come to celebrate Mr. Thoreaux birthday." "The Thoreauvian pilgrimage" to Walden Pond had commenced.[78] At the turn of the twentieth century, one reviewer judged that "in one respect at least, Thoreau has been a singularly fortunate man. He won for himself during his lifetime a devoted friendship which after his death made it a labor of love to see that his writings were adequately presented to a public that had not received them entirely with gratitude." By 1896, those who praised and those who disparaged Henry Thoreau fell discretely enough into two camps that George Willis Cooke could make a compelling case for "Two Thoreaus": "Whatever of genius there was in him they are quick to recognize; but his faults they ignore or prefer to overlook. The other class . . . are inclined to see what was odd in Thoreau; they emphasize his excesses, and do not fully credit the genius which he undoubtedly possessed." Cooke advocates that both points of view "must be understood . . . in order fully to appreciate him."[79]

Thoreau inspired an enormous outpouring of kindness from residents who knew for more than a year before he died that his health was failing. From friends sending flowers and herbs to a neighbor lending his horse and carriage for drives, small gestures indicate the regard with which Concord had come to hold Thoreau by 1860. During the months of his final illness, Sophia Thoreau observed the community's kindness in "minister[ing] to his comfort. Total strangers sent grateful messages, remembering the good he had done them." Such social courtesies are not unusual of course when someone in a close-knit community is dying. Nonetheless, they remind us that the annoyance felt by some in response to the young Thoreau's unconventional behavior had given way over twenty-five years to an affectionate regard. Interviewed late in the nineteenth century, Edward Hoar explained that this outpouring caused Thoreau "to feel very differently toward people, and [he] said if he had known he wouldn't have been so offish. He had got into his head before that *people* didn't mean what they said." His journal evidences Thoreau's own change of mind: "For nearly twoscore years I have known, at a distance, these long-suffering men, whom I never spoke to, who never spoke to me, and now feel a certain tenderness for them, as if this long probation were but the prelude to an eternal friendship."[80]

When he died at age forty-four on 6 May 1862, Henry Thoreau did not yet enjoy wide renown as an author. Nevertheless his death inspired notices from the major news outlets in New York, Boston, and Philadelphia as well as from periodicals directed to more targeted audiences, including scientific journals. Regardless of his stated readiness to move on—"never saw a man dying with so much pleasure & peace," Sam Staples reported to Waldo Emerson[81]—in 1862, Thoreau was just on the verge of realizing the literary success for which he had striven most of his life. Not only did James T. Fields publish that year several new articles and second editions of *Walden* and *A Week,* and two years later bring out *The Maine Woods,* but Thoreau's most scientific work, "The Succession of Forest Trees" (1860), had also begun generating attention from a new audience. His death inspired family and friends to recall Thoreau's personal warmth and professional generosity. Sophia Thoreau spoke for the family in lamenting that "the light, and glory, of our household, [is] forever gone," while Louisa May Alcott wryly noted the throng from Boston who showed up for his funeral: "Though he was'nt made much of while living, he was honored at his death." With few exceptions, those who loved and admired him knew that Thoreau had satisfied his own vivid prescription, as laid out in *Walden:* When he came to die, Henry Thoreau did not discover that he had not lived.[82]

The selections presented in *Thoreau in His Own Time* offer a wide range of nineteenth-century commentary that humanizes and complicates traditional understandings of Henry Thoreau, particularly as individuals' reflections evolved over time—as with the journal and epistolary comments of the Emersons, the Alcotts, Hawthorne, and others. Selections from the correspondence of Caroline Wells Healey Dall, Maria Thoreau, Sophia Hawthorne, Sarah Alden Bradford Ripley, and Amanda Mather amplify our understanding of how nineteenth-century women viewed Thoreau. Similarly, Louise Chandler Moulton's 1874 review of William Ellery Channing's *Thoreau: The Poet-Naturalist* provides this popular woman author's assessment of Thoreau during the heyday of American Realism. Items readily available in several other venues, however, such as Ralph Waldo Emerson's "Thoreau" and James Russell Lowell's "Letters to Various Persons" are not reprinted here.

Obvious errors of spelling, punctuation, and capitalization in published items have been silently corrected. Similarly, slight errors in manuscript and other unpublished items have been normalized in cases where the sense was not clear. Square brackets supply information as needed to identify individuals and to indicate conjectural dates and readings. Throughout this introduction, a dagger (†) indicates an author whose writing appears as a selection in this volume. The texts reprinted here are generally from their first published version. The texts from modern, scholarly editions show only the author's final level of inscription. Complete bibliographic information for each text is given in the unnumbered source note at the end of the selection. The bibliography at the end of the volume includes all of the texts cited in the introduction and in the biographical headnotes that precede each selection.

My sincere thanks to series editor Joel Myerson for asking me to take on this project and for his sensible advice and generosity throughout the process. I'm grateful to editors Holly Carver and Charlotte Wright for their guidance and exemplary judgment, and to copyeditor David Coen for his expertise. For internal grants that funded release time from teaching and travel to archives, I thank Ken Womack, Brian Black, Lori Bechtel, and L. A. Wilson at Pennsylvania State University, Altoona, and the university's Institute for the Arts and Humanities. For valuable insights on the contents and multiple readings of the introduction, a resounding thank you to Noelle Baker. For their readings of and comments on the introduction as well, my thanks to Joel Myerson and Bob Sattelmeyer. For sharing research materials, suggesting sources, and reviewing the chronology, I am grateful to Bob Burkholder, Bob Hudspeth, Megan Marshall, Joel Myerson, Gary Scharnhorst, Daniel Shealy, Laura Dassow Walls, Leslie Wilson, and Beth Witherell. For research and editorial assistance, I am indebted to Jennifer Cowfer, who undertook the Herculean task of reading through sixty years' worth of *Thoreau Society Bulletins* and *Concord Saunterers* on the lookout for recollections of Henry. To Jennifer and to Christina Seymour, my thanks for astute comments on the prefatory headnotes, the selections, and the introduction. For providing copies of manuscript materials at their institutions, thank you to Rachel Howarth, Susan Halpert, and Micah Hoggatt at the Houghton Library; to Jeffrey Cramer at the Thoreau Institute; to Scott Sanders at Antioch College; to Susan Hodson and Natalie Russell at the Huntington Library; to Stephen O'Neill at the Pilgrim Hall Museum in Plymouth; to Sean Casey and Kimberly Reynolds at Boston Public Library; and, as always, for recommending, locating, and providing copies of little known resources at a moment's notice, my sincere thanks to Leslie Wilson and Conni Manoli at the Concord Free Public Library. My gratitude to Joe and Laurel for their love, their patience, and their abiding interest in Henry and Concord. Finally, since much of the work on this book was completed during a rewarding Fulbright leave in Jena, Germany, it is dedicated with the greatest respect to my students at Friedrich Schiller University, whose response to Thoreau and his time was inspiring.

Notes

1. Henry David Thoreau, *The Correspondence of Henry David Thoreau,* ed. Walter Harding and Carl Bode (New York: New York University Press, 1958), 186.

2. Henry D. Thoreau, *Walden,* ed. J. Lyndon Shanley (Princeton: Princeton University Press, 1971), 326, 323, 23, 91, 321, 333; Thoreau, "Walking," *Excursions,* ed. Joseph J. Moldenhauer (Princeton: Princeton University Press, 2007), 202.

3. Harding qtd. in Michael Meyer, *Several More Lives to Live: Thoreau's Political Reputation in America* (Westport, Conn.: Greenwood, 1977), 9. For the scope of Thoreau's twentieth-century status as a "folk hero," see the chapter "The Thoreauvian Pilgrimage" in Lawrence Buell's *The Environmental Imagination: Thoreau, Nature Writing, and the Formation of American Culture* (Cambridge, MA: Belknap Press of Harvard University Press, 1995), 311–38.

4. Sattelmeyer, "General Introduction" to Thoreau, *Journal,* ed. John C. Broderick et al., 8 vols. to date (Princeton: Princeton University Press, 1981–), 1:587; Isaac Hecker qtd. in Walter Harding, *The Days of Henry Thoreau,* rev. ed. (Princeton: Princeton University Press, 1982), 168; qtd. in Gary Scharnhorst, *Henry David Thoreau: An Annotated Bibliography of Comment and Criticism Before 1900* (New York: Garland, 1992), 29; "The Magazines," *New Hampshire Patriot and State Gazette,* 15 July 1862; "New Publications," *Salem Register,* 10 August 1854; "Books Notices," *Portland Transcript,* 19 August 1854; "Recent Publications," *Western Christian Advocate,* 6 September 1882; H. N. Powers, "Thoreau," *Dial* 3 (August 1882): 70; [Amos Bronson Alcott], "The Forester," *Atlantic Monthly* 9 (April 1862): 445.

5. *Christian Register* qtd. in Alan Seaburg, "A Thoreau Document," *Thoreau Society Bulletin* 109 (Fall 1969): 5; E. Harlow Russell qtd. in Thomas Blanding and Edmund A. Schofield, "E. Harlow Russell's Reminiscences of Thoreau," *Concord Saunterer* 17 (August 1984): 6.

6. *Correspondence,* 386; Moller, *Thoreau in the Human Community* (Amherst: University of Massachusetts Press, 1980), 89; Joel Myerson, "Emerson's 'Thoreau': A New Edition from Manuscript," *Studies in the American Renaissance 1979,* ed. Joel Myerson (Boston: Twayne, 1979), 52; Walter Harding and Michael Meyer, *The New Thoreau Handbook* (New York: New York University Press, 1980), 204; Robert A. Gross, "'That Terrible Thoreau': Concord and Its Hermit," in *A Historical Guide to Henry David Thoreau,* ed. William E. Cain (New York: Oxford University Press, 2000), 181; Raymond Adams, "Thoreau and His Neighbors," *Thoreau Society Bulletin* 44 (Summer 1953): 1.

7. *Walden,* 10; "Reminiscences of the Thoreaus," *Thoreau Society Bulletin* 167 (Spring 1984): 5; Moller, *Thoreau in the Human Community,* 90.

8. Bradley P. Dean, ed., "A Rare Reminiscence of Thoreau as a Child," *Thoreau Society Bulletin* 245 (Fall 2003): 1–2.

9. Keyes, diary entries for 2 August 1839 and 27 January and 15 September 1841, Vault A45, Keyes, Unit 2, by permission of Special Collections, Concord Free Public Library, Concord, MA.

10. [Henry Williams], "Henry D. Thoreau," in *Memorials of the Class of 1837 of Har-*

vard University (Boston: George H. Ellis, 1887), 39; David Green Haskins, "The Maternal Ancestors of Ralph Waldo Emerson," *Literary World* 17 (4 September 1886): 298; Amos Perry qtd. in Kenneth Walter Cameron, "Thoreau at Harvard: Diligent, Bright and Cheerful," *ESQ* 42 (1st quarter 1966): 1.

11. Qtd. in *Remembrances of Concord and the Thoreaus: Letters of Horace Hosmer to Dr. S. A. Jones,* ed. George Hendrick (Urbana: University of Illinois Press, 1977), 131; Ward to Caroline Sewall, 25 September [1837], HM 64963–64966, Thoreau-Sewall Papers, by permission of the Huntington Library, San Marino, CA.

12. Qtd. in Edward Waldo Emerson, *Henry Thoreau as Remembered by a Young Friend* (Boston: Houghton, Mifflin, 1917), 128–129.

13. John Pratt qtd. in Sarah Hosmer Lunt, "Memories of Concord," unpublished typescript, series 2, Sarah Hosmer Lunt Papers, folder 3, p. 18, by permission of Special Collections, Concord Free Public Library, Concord, MA; Downs, "Mr. Hawthorne, Mr. Thoreau, Miss Alcott, Mr. Emerson, and Me," ed. Walter Harding, *American Heritage* 30 (December 1978): 100–1.

14. Simmons, *From Seven to Seventy: Memories of a Painter and a Yankee* (New York: Harper Brothers, 1922), 5–6.

15. Edward Waldo Emerson, 128; Alcott qtd. in Madeleine B. Stern, "Introduction" to *The Selected Letters of Louisa May Alcott,* ed. Joel Myerson, Daniel Shealy, and Madeleine B. Stern (Boston: Little, Brown, 1987), xix.

16. Qtd. in Oehlschlaeger and Hendrick, *Toward the Making of Thoreau's Reputation: Selected Correspondence of S. A. Jones, A. W. Hosmer, H. S. Salt, H. G. O. Blake, and D. Ricketson* (Urbana: University of Illinois Press, 1979), 247.

17. Downs, 99; Abigail Hosmer qtd. in Adams, 4; Ellen Tucker Emerson, *Life of Lidian Jackson Emerson,* ed. Delores Bird Carpenter (East Lansing: Michigan State University Press, 1992), 85; Thoreau, "To Edith," *Collected Essays and Poems,* ed. Elizabeth Hall Witherell (New York: Library of America, 2001), 570–71.

18. Ellen Tucker Emerson, *The Letters of Ellen Tucker Emerson,* ed. Edith E. W. Gregg (Kent, OH: Kent State University Press, 1982), 1:138; Moller, 90–91; Thoreau, *PEJ,* 8:208, 34.

19. John Burroughs, "Thoreau's Wildness," *Critic* 1 (26 March 1881): 74; [Fanny Hardy Eckstorm], "Thoreau's 'Maine Woods,'" *Atlantic Monthly* 52 (August 1908): 243; George Bartlett, *The Concord Guide Book* (Boston: D. Lothrop, 1880), 64; Joshua Bellin, "Native American Rights," in *The Oxford Handbook of Transcendentalism* (New York: Oxford University Press, 2010), 198, 203–5; [George William Curtis], "Editor's Easy Chair," *Harper's Monthly* 25 (July 1862): 271, and *Harper's Monthly* 38 (February 1869): 415.

20. Frederick H. L. Willis, *Alcott Memoirs* (Boston: Richard G. Badger, 1915), 92; Lunt, 16; [Weiss], "Thoreau," *Christian Examiner* 79 (July 1865): 99; Wasson, "Modern Speculative Radicalism," *The Radical* (July 1867): 5.

21. Conway, *Autobiography Memories and Experiences* (Boston: Houghton Mifflin, 1904), 1:148, 285; Havelock Ellis, "Thoreau," in *Thoreau: A Century of Criticism,* ed. Walter Harding (Dallas: Southern Methodist University Press, 1954), 93; *Annual of Scientific Discovery . . . ,* ed. David A. Wells (Boston: Gould and Lincoln, 1863), 335; [Jackson],

Proceedings of the Boston Society of Natural History 9 (1865), 71; Harris qtd. in J. S. Wade, "The Friendship of Two Old-Time Naturalists," *Scientific Monthly* 23 (August 1926): 152, 155; Thoreau, *PEJ*, 5:469, 7:285, 8:25–26.

22. Harris qtd. in Wade, 155; Thoreau, *Correspondence*, 493.

23. Thoreau, *Correspondence*, 382; Blake to H. S. Salt, 25–26 November 1889, Walter Harding Collection, Henley Library, Thoreau Institute, by permission of the Thoreau Institute, Lincoln, MA.

24. *Correspondence*, 154; qtd. in Harding, *The Days of Henry Thoreau*, 166.

25. *Correspondence*, 397, 528, 452; Hecker qtd. in *The Brownson-Hecker Correspondence*, ed. Joseph F. Gower and Richard M. Leliaert (Notre Dame, IN: University of Notre Dame Press, 1979), 170; O'Connor, *Catholic World* 27 (June 1878): 296.

26. Thoreau, *PEJ*, 4:440.

27. Thoreau, *PEJ* 6:151, 1:459, 4:303; Channing qtd. in *Daniel Ricketson and His Friends: Letters Poems Sketches Etc.*, ed. Anna and Walton Ricketson (Boston: Houghton, Mifflin, 1902), 207.

28. Hawthorne, *The Letters*, ed. Thomas Woodson et al. (Columbus: Ohio State University Press, 1985), 2:248; Robert Sattelmeyer, *Thoreau's Reading: A Study in Intellectual History with Bibliographical Catalogue* (Princeton: Princeton University Press, 1988), 14; Longfellow qtd. in Ellen E. Dickinson, "A Morning with Mr. Longfellow," *New York Evangelist*, 7 April 1881.

29. *New York Tribune* qtd. in Scharnhorst, *Annotated Bibliography*, 4, 3; Lowell, *The Poetical Works of James Russell Lowell* (Boston: Houghton Mifflin, 1978), 128; Joel Myerson, "Eight Lowell Letters from Concord in 1838," *Illinois Quarterly* 38 (1975): 28.

30. Cheney qtd. in F. B. Sanborn, *Recollections of Seventy Years*, 2 vols. (Boston: Gorham, 1909), 2:469; *Salem Observer* qtd. in Bradley P. Dean and Ronald Wesley Hoag, "Thoreau's Lectures Before *Walden*: An Annotated Calendar," in *Studies in the American Renaissance 1995*, ed. Joel Myerson (Charlottesville: University of Virginia Press, 1995), 158; "Topics of the Month," *Holden's Dollar Magazine* 4 (July 1849): 448; "Words That Burn," *National Anti-Slavery Standard*, 12 August 1854; qtd. in Scharnhorst, *Annotated Bibliography*, 23.

31. See, for example, Harmon Smith, *My Friend, My Friend: The Story of Thoreau's Relationship with Emerson* (Amherst: University of Massachusetts Press, 2001); John T. Lysaker and William Rossi, eds., *Emerson and Thoreau: Figures of Friendship* (Bloomington: Indiana University Press, 2010); Robert Sattelmeyer, "'When He Became My Enemy': Emerson and Thoreau 1848–49," *New England Quarterly* 62 (June 1989): 187–204; and Robert Sattelmeyer, "Thoreau and Emerson," in *The Cambridge Companion to Henry David Thoreau*, ed. Joel Myerson (Cambridge: Cambridge University Press, 1995).

32. Ralph Waldo Emerson, *Journals and Miscellaneous Notebooks*, ed. William H. Gilman et al. (Cambridge, MA: Belknap Press of Harvard University Press, 1960–1982), 10:343 (hereinafter cited as *JMN*). I am grateful to Joel Myerson for providing the contents of his textual note explaining the nuances of the often cited elm tree remark, which will appear in Ralph Waldo Emerson, *Uncollected Prose Writings: Addresses, Essays, and Reviews*, vol. 10, ed. Ronald A. Bosco and Joel Myerson (Cambridge, MA: Harvard Uni-

versity Press, forthcoming): "Emerson's journal for 1843 attributes 'I love H., but do not like him' to Elizabeth Hoar (*JMN*, 8:375); the distinction between loving and liking may have originated in Thoreau's comment 'to a lady' about his feelings for his own father . . .: see [textual note] III, 62. Edward Waldo Emerson says that 'this was Mr. Emerson's own remark' (*W[ritings]*, X, 611), though apparently only the last clause: see *JMN*, 10:343. In Emerson's manuscript, 'nobody ever took his arm, any more than the arm of an elm tree' was originally in the voice of the essayist, not a third person (see *Alterations in the MS*, paragraph 7)."

33. Waldo Emerson qtd. in Davis, *Bits of Gossip* (Boston: Houghton, Mifflin, 1904), 44.

34. Thoreau, *PEJ*, 3:26, 4:274; Linck Johnson, Historical Introduction to *A Week on the Concord and Merrimack Rivers*, ed. Carl F. Hovde (Princeton: Princeton University Press, 1980), 434, 477–79, 451; Thoreau, *PEJ*, 4:314.

35. See, for example, Mary Elkins Moller, "Thoreau, Womankind, and Sexuality," *ESQ* (third quarter 1976); and Walter Harding, "Thoreau's Sexuality," *Journal of Homosexuality* 21.3 (1991): 23–45; qtd. in Edward Emerson, 141.

36. Thoreau, *PEJ*, 4:233; Thoreau qtd. in *Daughter of Boston: The Extraordinary Diary of a Nineteenth-Century Woman, Caroline Healey Dall,* ed. Helen R. Deese (Boston: Beacon Press, 2005), 290.

37. Thoreau, *PEJ*, 4:233; Wollstonecraft, *A Vindication of the Rights of Woman,* ed. Deirdre Lynch (New York: Norton, 2009), 59, 65.

38. *The Letters of Margaret Fuller,* vol. 2, ed. Robert N. Hudspeth (Ithaca: Cornell University Press, 1983), 185, 231–32; Sturgis qtd. in Francis B. Dedmond, "Letters of Caroline Sturgis to Margaret Fuller," *Studies in the American Renaissance 1988,* ed. Joel Myerson (Charlottesville: University of Virginia Press, 1988), 249; qtd. in Charles Capper, *Margaret Fuller: An American Romantic Life,* vol. 2 (New York: Oxford University Press, 2007), 160.

39. Harding, *The Days of Henry Thoreau,* 100, 103; Thoreau, *Correspondence,* 190–1.

40. Thoreau, *PEJ*, 5:444; Joan W. Goodwin, *The Remarkable Mrs. Ripley: The Life of Sarah Alden Bradford Ripley* (Boston: Northeastern University Press, 1998), 296–97; *The Selected Letters of Mary Moody Emerson,* ed. Nancy Craig Simmons (Athens: University of Georgia Press, 1993), 538.

41. Thoreau, *PEJ*, 4:183.

42. Hawthorne qtd. in Harding, *The Days of Henry Thoreau,* 236; Maxfield-Miller, "Emerson and Elizabeth of Concord," *Harvard Library Bulletin* 19 (July 1971): 304; Thoreau, *Correspondence,* 98; Harding, *The Days of Henry Thoreau,* 147.

43. Edward W. Emerson Papers, unpublished notes from interview with Elizabeth J. Weir, Vault A45, Emerson, Unit 3, series 1, box 1, folder 20; Higginson to Thoreau, 21 September 1865, Vault A45, Thoreau, Unit 3, Letter File 3a, H35, CAS D-2030i; both by permission of Special Collections, Concord Free Public Library, Concord, MA; "Sophia Thoreau, T. W. Higginson, and the Journal," *Thoreau Society Bulletin* 181 (Fall 1987): 2. For the history of Thoreau's journal manuscripts after Sophia's death, see Sattelmeyer, "General Introduction," 582–86.

44. "Thoreau and Sophia Dobson Collet," *Thoreau Society Bulletin* 179 (Spring 1987): 5.

45. Samuel May, Jr., "Annual Statement of the General Agent of the Massachusetts

Anti-Slavery Society," *Liberator,* 2 February 1855; C. K. W., "Fifth Fraternity Lecture," *Liberator,* 4 November 1859; Pratt qtd. in Sandra Harbert Petrulionis, *To Set This World Right: The Antislavery Movement in Henry Thoreau's Concord* (Ithaca: Cornell University Press, 2006), 136; Thomas Wentworth Higginson, *Part of a Man's Life* (1905; repr., Port Washington, NY: Kennikat Press, 1971), 16.

    46. Petrulionis, 140.

    47. See Bradley P. Dean and Ronald Wesley Hoag, "Thoreau's Lectures before *Walden*: An Annotated Calendar," 129–230; and Bradley P. Dean and Ronald Wesley Hoag, "Thoreau's Lectures after *Walden:* An Annotated Calendar," *Studies in the American Renaissance 1996,* ed. Joel Myerson (Charlottesville: University of Virginia Press, 1996), 241–362.

    48. Qtd. in Dean and Hoag, "Thoreau's Lectures after *Walden,*" 352, 302.

    49. *Letters of Ellen Tucker Emerson,* 1:174.

    50. Thoreau to Ward, 25 September 1847 and 17 December 1849; and Ward to Caroline Sewall, 26 February 1847, all in Thoreau-Sewall Papers, HM 64963–64966, and 64930–64938, by permission of the Huntington Library, San Marino, CA.

    51. Irving Allen, "Of the Thoreaus and of Other Notable People in Concord," *Boston Daily Advertiser,* 23 April 1894; [Moncure Conway], "Thoreau," *Fraser's Magazine for Town and Country* 73 (April 1866): 461; Daniel Ricketson, *Daniel Ricketson and His Friends,* 252; Henry David Thoreau, *Journal,* ed. Bradford Torrey and Francis H. Allen (1906; New York: Dover, 1962), 14 vols. bound as 2, 7:79–80; Thoreau, *Walden,* 81; Maria Pratt qtd. in Edward Emerson, *Henry Thoreau as Remembered,* 80.

    52. Edward Emerson, 29; Eben Loomis, "On Concord, Emerson, and Thoreau," MS 496A, series 2, box 12, folder 198, Loomis Wilder Papers, by permission of Manuscripts and Archives, Yale University, New Haven, CT.

    53. *A Life for Liberty: Anti-Slavery and Other Letters of Sallie Holley,* ed. John White Chadwick (New York: G. P. Putnam's Sons, 1899), 167; Sanborn, *Henry D. Thoreau* (Boston: Goodspeed, 1882), 196–97; Fuller to Thoreau, 31 August 1854, in *Correspondence,* vol. 2, ed. Robert N. Hudspeth (Princeton: Princeton University Press, forthcoming) transcription of letter cited by permission of *The Writings of Henry D. Thoreau*; Higginson qtd. in Mary Thacher Higginson, *Thomas Wentworth Higginson: The Story of His Life* (Boston: Houghton, Mifflin, 1914), 98.

    54. *The Letters of John Greenleaf Whittier,* vol. 2, ed. John B. Pickard (Cambridge, MA: Belknap Press of Harvard University Press, 1975), 267, 268 n. 1; [Child], "Review of A Week and Walden," in *Recognition of Henry David Thoreau: Selected Criticism Since 1848,* ed. Wendell Glick (Ann Arbor: University of Michigan Press, 1969), 10, 11.

    55. Whitman qtd. in Horace Traubel, *With Walt Whitman in Camden,* vol. 1 (New York: D. Appleton, 1908), 448; Poe qtd. in Richard Kopley, "Naysayers: Poe, Hawthorne, and Melville," in *The Oxford Handbook of Transcendentalism,* 599, 600; Joseph Rosenblum, "A Cock Fight Between Melville and Thoreau," *Studies in Short Fiction* 23 (spring 1986), 162, 165; Rogin, *Subversive Genealogy: The Politics and Art of Herman Melville* (1979; repr., Berkeley: University of California Press, 1985), 195–200.

    56. Bronson Alcott, *The Selected Journals of Bronson Alcott,* ed. Odell Shepard (Bos-

ton: Little, Brown, 1938), 213–14, 238; Hawthorne, *Letters,* 1:656, 3:279; Holmes, *Ralph Waldo Emerson* (Boston: Houghton, Mifflin, 1884), 72.

57. Scharnhorst, *Henry David Thoreau: A Case Study in Canonization* (Columbia, SC: Camden House, 1993), 14; Glick, "Preface" to *The Recognition of Henry David Thoreau,* viii; Thoreau, *Correspondence,* 394, 510.

58. Bailey qtd. in Joel Myerson, "Thoreau Receives a Fan Letter for *A Week,*" *Thoreau Society Bulletin* 208 (Summer 1994): 10; Thoreau, *Correspondence,* 407, 641.

59. Fink, "Thoreau and His Audience," in *The Cambridge Companion to Henry David Thoreau,* 89; [Alcott], "The Forester," 443, 444.

60. [Waldo] E[merson], "Henry D. Thoreau," *Boston Daily Advertiser,* 8 May 1862; Myerson, "Emerson's 'Thoreau,'" 55.

61. Alcott, *Selected Letters,* 74; Myerson, "Emerson's 'Thoreau,'" 55, 39, 52; Louisa May Alcott, "In Memoriam," *Springfield Republican,* 3 April 1878.

62. Rossi, "'In Dreams Awake': Loss, Transcendental Friendship, and Elegy," in *Emerson and Thoreau: Figures of Friendship,* ed. John T. Lysaker and William Rossi (Bloomington: Indiana University Press, 2010), 108; Myerson, "Emerson's 'Thoreau,'" 53.

63. Myerson, "Historical Introduction" to "Emerson's 'Thoreau,'" 17; Sattelmeyer, "Thoreau and Emerson," 37.

64. Sophia Thoreau qtd. in *Daniel Ricketson and His Friends,* 155; [Weiss], "Thoreau," 107. In Norse mythology, Yggdrasil, or the "World Tree," is a giant ash tree that connects the underworld with the land of the giants and the land of the gods.

65. Torrey, "Thoreau," in *The Recognition of Henry David Thoreau,* 149; Edward Emerson, *Henry Thoreau as Remembered,* 120; Waldo Emerson qtd. in *Emerson in His Own Time,* ed. Ronald A. Bosco and Joel Myerson (Iowa City: University of Iowa Press, 2003), 130; Emerson, *JMN,* 15:261–62.

66. Sophia Thoreau qtd. in *Daniel Ricketson and His Friends,* 165, 166; Richard E. Winslow III, "Thoreau Reviews in the *New England Farmer* (1863–1866)," *Thoreau Society Bulletin* 203 (Spring 1993): 5; [Thomas Wentworth Higginson], "Reviews and Literary Notices," *Atlantic Monthly* 16 (October 1865): 504.

67. Lowell, "Letters to Various Persons," *North American Review* 101 (October 1865): 601, 602, 604; Thomas Wentworth Higginson, "Short Studies of American Authors III," *Literary World* (24 May 1879): 169–70.

68. Thoreau, *Correspondence,* 515, 520–21. The offending sentence from "Chesuncook" reads: "It [the pine tree] is as immortal as I am, and perchance will go to as high a heaven, there to tower above me still" (*The Maine Woods,* ed. Joseph J. Moldenhauer [Princeton: Princeton University Press, 1972], 122.

69. Thoreau to Prudence Ward, 17 December 1849, Thoreau-Sewall Papers, by permission of the Huntington Library, San Marino, CA; Lowell, *Massachusetts Quarterly Review* 9 (December 1849): 47, 44–45; qtd. in Gary Scharnhorst, *Annotated Bibliography,* 145, 250.

70. "Notices of New Books," *New Englander* 125 (October 1873): 765; "Henry Thoreau, the Poet-Naturalist," *Eclectic Magazine* 19 (March 1874): 309; Edith Kellogg Dunton, "An Old and a New Estimate of Thoreau," *Dial* 33 (16 December 1902): 465.

71. Jones, "Thoreau and His Biographers," *Lippincott's* 48 (August 1891): 224; Franklin B. Sanborn, *Forum* 23 (April 1897): 218; Marx, "Introduction" to *Henry David Thoreau,* Frank B. Sanborn (New York: Chelsea House, 1980), xx; [Curtis], "Editor's Easy Chair," *Harper's Monthly* 65 (September 1882): 632.

72. Page, *Thoreau: His Life and Aims* (Boston: Osgood, 1877), ix; Salt, *The Life of Henry Thoreau* (London: Bentley and Son, 1890).

73. Stevenson, "Henry David Thoreau: His Character and His Opinions," *Cornhill Magazine* 41 (June 1880): 665, 666; H. W. B. qtd. in *New England Writers and the Press,* ed. Walter Cameron (Hartford, CT: Transcendental Books, 1980), 302; Stevenson, "Preface" to *Familiar Studies of Men and Books Criticisms* (New York: Charles Scribner's Sons, 1925), 12–14.

74. "Henry Thoreau Enters the American Canon," in *New Essays on Walden,* ed. Robert F. Sayre (Cambridge: Cambridge University Press, 1992), 32; qtd. in Scharnhorst, *Annotated Bibliography,* 70; "Contemporary Literature," *Universalist Quarterly and General Review* 22 (October 1865): 531.

75. *Atlantic Monthly* 14 (September 1864): 386; "Thoreau and His Writings," *The New England Writers and the Press,* 43; *A Complete Manual of English Literature* (New York: Shelden and Company, 1868), 532; [Curtis], "Editor's Easy Chair," *Harper's Monthly* 56 (March 1878): 624; Mason, "The Idealistic Basis of Thoreau's Genius," *Harvard Monthly* 25 (December 1897): 93; Wendell, *The Literary History of America* (New York: Charles Scribner's Sons, 1905), 334.

76. James, *Hawthorne* (New York: Harper and Brothers, 1879), 94.

77. Yeats qtd. in Robert F. Stowell, "Poetry about Thoreau: 19th Century," *Thoreau Society Bulletin* 112 (Summer 1970): 2–3; Buell, *Environmental Imagination,* 353; Burroughs qtd. in Johnson, Historical Introduction, 491; Terry Gifford, "Introduction" to *John Muir: His Life and Letters and Other Writings,* ed. Gifford (Seattle: Mountaineers, 1996), 7, 882, 131–34, 311.

78. Scharnhorst, *Henry David Thoreau: A Case Study in Canonization* (Columbia, SC: Camden House, 1993), 15; Mann to Horace Mann, Jr., 24 April 1864, Robert L. Straker Collection of Peabody Letters, Antiochana, by permission of Antioch College Library, Yellow Springs, OH; Bartlett to Edward Jarvis Bartlett, 17 July 1865, Vault A45, Bartlett, Unit 2, series 1, folder 1, by permission of Special Collections, Concord Free Public Library, Concord, MA; Lawrence Buell, *The Environmental Imagination,* 311.

79. Louis J. Block, "Thoreau's Letters," *Dial* 27 (16 October 1894): 228; Cooke, "The Two Thoreaus," *Independent* 48 (10 December 1896): 1671, 1672.

80. Thoreau qtd. in *Daniel Ricketson and His Friends,* 142; Hoar to Edward Sandford Burgess, 4 January [18]93, Vault A45, Burgess Unit 1, by permission of Special Collections, Concord Free Public Library, Concord, MA; Thoreau, *Journal* (1906), 9:151.

81. Staples qtd. in Emerson, *JMN,* 15:246.

82. Helen R. Deese, "Sophia Thoreau to Caroline Dall," *Thoreau Society Bulletin* 178 (Winter 1987): 7; Louisa May Alcott, *Selected Letters,* 77; Thoreau, *Walden,* 90.

Chronology

1817	12 July	Born in Concord, Massachusetts, to John and Cynthia Dunbar Thoreau
1818		Moves with family to Chelmsford, Massachusetts
1821		Moves with family to Boston
1823		Moves with family back to Concord
1828–1833		Attends Concord Academy
1833	30 August	Enters Harvard College
1835	December	Teaches school in Canton, Massachusetts, and studies German with Orestes Brownson for several weeks while on leave from Harvard College
1837	30 August	Graduates with a B.A. from Harvard College; speaks at commencement exercises on "The Commercial Spirit of Modern Times, Considered in Its Influence on the Moral Character of a Nation"
	September	Teaches for several days at Concord's Center School; resigns over disagreement with administrators regarding necessity of corporal punishment
	Fall	Attends meetings of the informal, newly-organized group of Transcendentalists known as the "Hedge Club," named for Unitarian minister and member Frederic Henry Hedge
	22 October	Begins keeping a journal, at Waldo Emerson's suggestion

	25 November	Obituary notice of longtime Concord resident Anna Jones published in *Yeoman's Gazette*
1838		Works with father in the family's pencil manufactory, labor that continues intermittently throughout his life
	11 April	Lectures on "Society" in Concord
	June	Opens small private school in his family's home in Concord
	September	Moves school from Thoreau home to the Concord Academy building; later joined by brother, John, in teaching and running school
	18 October	Elected Secretary of Concord Lyceum
	7 November	Elected a Curator of Concord Lyceum
1839	31 August	Leaves for two-week excursion with brother, John, on the Concord and Merrimack Rivers in the *Musketaquid,* a boat of their own construction
	6 November	Reelected Secretary and a Curator of Concord Lyceum
1840	July	"Sympathy" (poem) and "Aulus Persius Flaccus" published in first issue of the *Dial*
	November	Proposes marriage to Ellen Sewall, niece of family friend Prudence Ward
1841	January	"Stanzas" (poem) published in the *Dial*
	27 January	With brother, John, debates Bronson Alcott on "Is It Ever Proper to Offer Forcible Resistance?" at the Concord Lyceum
	March	Declines invitation to join the Transcendentalist community of Brook Farm, then being organized by George and Sophia Ripley in West Roxbury, Massachusetts
	April	Closes school due to John Thoreau Jr.'s ill health

	26 April	Moves in and lives with Emerson household through the spring of 1843
	July	"Sic Vita" (poem) published in the *Dial*
	October	"Friendship" (poem) published in the *Dial*
1842	11 January	Brother, John, dies of tetanus at age 26
	July	"Natural History of Massachusetts" and "Great God, I ask thee for no meaner pelf" (poem) published in the *Dial*
		With Richard Fuller, takes four-day hike to Wachusett Mountain
		Meets Nathaniel and Sophia Hawthorne, when the newlywed couple moves to Concord
	October	"The Black Knight," "The Inward Morning," "Free Love," "The Poet's Delay," "Rumors from an Aeolian Harp," "The Moon," "To a Maiden in the East," "The Summer Rain" (poems) published in the *Dial*
	18 November	Reelected a Curator of Concord Lyceum
1843	January	"The Laws of Menu" (selections) and "The Prometheus Bound" (translation) published in the *Dial*
		"A Walk to Wachusett" published in the *Boston Miscellany*
	8 February	Lectures on "The Life and Character of Sir Walter Raleigh" in Concord
	April	Edits the *Dial*
		"Anacreon" (translations), "Ethnical Scriptures: Sayings of Confucius" (selections), "To a Stray Fowl" "Orphics: I. Smoke II. Haze" (poems), and "Dark Ages" published in the *Dial*
	6 May	Until mid-December, lives with and tutors the three sons of William and Susan Haven Emerson in Staten Island, New York

	June	Declines invitation to join Fruitlands, a Transcendentalist community organized in Harvard, Massachusetts, by Bronson Alcott and Charles Lane
	October	"Ethnical Scriptures: Chinese Four Books" (selections) and "A Winter Walk" published in the *Dial*
		"The Landlord" published in the *United States Magazine, and Democratic Review*
	November	"Paradise (To Be) Regained" published in the *United States Magazine, and Democratic Review*
	29 November	Lectures on "Ancient Poets" in Concord
1844	January	"Homer. Ossian. Chaucer" (extracts from lecture), "Pindar" (translations), "The Preaching of Buddha" (selections), and "Ethnical Scriptures: Hermes Trismegistus" (selections) published in the *Dial*
	10 March	Lectures twice on "Conservatives and Reformers" in Boston
	April	"Herald of Freedom" and "Fragments of Pindar" (translation) published in the last issue of the *Dial*
	30 April	Accidentally sets fire to hundreds of wooded acres near Fair Haven Bay in Concord, while on an outing with Edward Hoar
	July	Takes trip to Mt. Monadnock, New Hampshire; Mt. Greylock, Massachusetts; and the Catskills, accompanied a portion of the way by Ellery Channing
	September	Assists father in the initial construction of new family home in Concord
1845	25 March	Lectures on "Concord River" in Concord

	28 March	"Wendell Phillips Before the Concord Lyceum" published anonymously in the *Liberator*
	4 July	Moves in and lives for two years, two months, and two days in a cabin of his own construction in woods owned by Waldo Emerson and bordering Walden Pond in Lincoln, Massachusetts
1846	4 February	Lectures on "The Writings and Style of Thomas Carlyle" in Concord, Massachusetts
	late July	Arrested and spends a night in Concord's Middlesex Jail for repeated failure to pay his poll tax
	1 August	Hosts Concord Female Anti-Slavery Society gathering at Walden Pond, where Waldo Emerson, William Henry Channing, and former slave Lewis Hayden, among others, give speeches
	31 August	Takes first trip to Maine woods with cousin George Thatcher, Penobscot guide Louis Neptune, and others
1847	19 January	Lectures on ["A History of Myself"] in Lincoln
	10 and 17 February	Lectures on "A History of Myself" in Concord
	March–April	"Thomas Carlyle and His Works" published in *Graham's Magazine*
	Summer	With Bronson Alcott, builds a small summer house for Ralph Waldo Emerson
	5 October	Moves in and lives with Emerson family until the following July while Ralph Waldo Emerson is abroad
	November	Declines proposal of marriage from Sophia Foord
1848	3 January	Lectures on "An Excursion to Ktaadn" in Concord

	26 January	Lectures on "The Relation of the Individual to the State" in Concord
	16 February	Lectures on "The Rights and Duties of the Individual in Relation to the State" in Concord
	Summer	First advertises himself as a professional property surveyor
	July–November	"Ktaadn, and the Maine Woods" published in the *Union Magazine*
	22 November	Lectures on "Student Life in New England, Its Economy" in Salem, Massachusetts
	20 December	Lectures on "Economy—Illustrated by the Life of a Student" in Gloucester, Massachusetts
1849		*A Week on the Concord and Merrimack Rivers* published
	3 January	Lectures on "White Beans and Walden Pond" in Concord
	28 February	Lectures on "Student Life, Its Aims and Employments" in Salem
	6 March	Lectures on "White Beans and Walden Pond" in Lincoln
	21 March	Lectures on "Economy" in Portland, Maine
	20 April	Lectures on "Economy" in Worcester, Massachusetts
	27 April	Lectures on "Life in the Woods" in Worcester
	May	"Resistance to Civil Government" published in *Aesthetic Papers*
	3 May	Lectures on "White Beans and Walden Pond" in Worcester
	14 June	Sister Helen dies from tuberculosis at age 36
	9 October	Leaves for first trip to Cape Cod, Massachusetts, accompanied by Ellery Channing

1850	23 and 30 January	Lectures on "An Excursion to Cape Cod" in Concord
	18 February	Lectures on "An Excursion to Cape Cod" in South Danvers, Massachusetts
	late June	Visits Cape Cod, Massachusetts
	24 July	At request of Waldo Emerson, travels to Fire Island, New York, to site of shipwreck in which Margaret Fuller and her family had died, to search for remains of her literary manuscripts
	August	Moves with family into home on Main Street in Concord
	25 September	Leaves for trip to Canada with Ellery Channing
	6 December	Lectures on "An Excursion to Cape Cod" in Newburyport, Massachusetts
	18 December	Elected a corresponding member of the Boston Society of Natural History
1851	1 January	Lectures on "An Excursion to Cape Cod" in Clinton, Massachusetts
	15 January	Lectures on "An Excursion to Cape Cod" in Portland, Maine
	22 January	Lectures on "Economy" in Medford, Massachusetts
	23 April	Lectures on "Walking, or the Wild" in Concord
	31 May	Lectures on "Walking, or the Wild" in Worcester
	30 September– 1 October	Assists the escape of Virginia slave Henry Williams, who stays overnight with the Thoreau family in Concord
	30 December	Lectures on "An Excursion to Canada" in Lincoln

1852	7 January	Lectures on "An Excursion to Canada" in Concord
	22 February	Lectures twice on "Life in the Woods" in Plymouth, Massachusetts
	17 March	Lectures on "An Excursion to Canada" in Concord
	22 March	Lectures on "Economy" in Boston
	6 April	Lectures on "Life in the Woods" in Boston
	23 May	Lectures on "Walking" and on "The Wild" in Plymouth
	July	"The Iron Horse" published in *Sartain's Union Magazine*
	August	"A Poet Buying a Farm" published in *Sartain's Union Magazine*
1853		"My Life Is Like a Stroll Upon the Beach" (poem) published in *Thalatta: A Book for the Sea-Side*
	January–March	"An Excursion to Canada" published in *Putnam's Monthly Magazine*
	13 September	Leaves for trip to Maine woods with cousin George Thatcher and Penobscot guide Joseph Attean
	14 December	Lectures on "An Excursion to Moosehead Lake" in Concord
	19 December	Declines membership in the American Association for the Advancement of Science
1854	Summer	Crayon portrait sketched by artist Samuel Rowse
	4 July	Lectures on "Slavery in Massachusetts" at an antislavery rally in Framingham, Massachusetts
	21 July	"Slavery in Massachusetts" published in *Liberator*

	29 July	"A Massachusetts Hermit" published in *New York Daily Tribune*
	2 August	"Slavery in Massachusetts" published in *New York Daily Tribune*
	9 August	*Walden; or, Life in the Woods* published
	12 August	Excerpts from "Slavery in Massachusetts" published in *National Anti-Slavery Standard*
	8 October	Lectures on "Moonlight" in Plymouth
	21 November	Lectures on "The Wild" in Philadelphia
	6 December	Lectures on "What Shall It Profit" in Providence, Rhode Island
	26 December	Lectures on "What Shall It Profit" in New Bedford, Massachusetts
	28 December	Lectures on "What Shall It Profit" in Nantucket, Massachusetts
1855		Characterized as "a humorist in the old English sense of the word" in Evert A. and George L. Duyckinck's *Cyclopaedia of American Literature*
	4 January	Lectures on "What Shall It Profit" in Worcester
	14 February	Lectures on "What Shall It Profit" in Concord
	June–August	"Cape Cod" published in *Putnam's Monthly Magazine*
	4 July	Leaves for trip to Cape Cod with Ellery Channing
1856	June	Daguerreotypes taken by Benjamin D. Maxham in Worcester
	26 October	Lectures on "Moosehunting" in Perth Amboy, New Jersey
	2 November	Lectures on "Walking, or the Wild" in Perth Amboy

	10 November	Visits Walt Whitman in Brooklyn, New York, accompanied by Bronson Alcott and Sarah Tyndale
	16 November	Lectures on "What Shall It Profit" in Perth Amboy
	18 December	Lectures on "Walking, or the Wild" in Amherst, New Hampshire
1857	3 February	Lectures on "Walking, or the Wild" in Fitchburg, Massachusetts
	13 February	Lectures on "Walking, or the Wild" in Worcester
	11 March	Meets and listens to abolitionist John Brown, who speaks in Concord
	mid-June	Takes last trip to Cape Cod
	20 July	Leaves for last trip to Maine woods with Concord neighbor Edward Hoar and Penobscot guide Joe Polis
1858	13 January	Lectures on ["An Excursion to the Maine Woods"] in Lynn, Massachusetts
	25 February	Lectures on "An Excursion to the Maine Woods" in Concord
	June–August	"Chesuncook" published in *Atlantic Monthly*
	July	Takes trip to White Mountains of New Hampshire with Edward Hoar, Theophilus Brown, and H. G. O. Blake
1859	3 February	John Thoreau Sr. dies at age 71
	22 February	Lectures on "Autumnal Tints" in Worcester
	23 February	Lectures on ["An Excursion to the Maine Woods"] in Worcester
	2 and 9 March	Lectures on "Autumnal Tints" in Concord
	3 March	Appointed to Committee for Examination on Natural History at Harvard College

26 April	Lectures on "Autumnal Tints" in Lynn, Massachusetts
8 May	Attends John Brown's lecture in Concord
9 October	Lectures on "Life Misspent" in Boston
30 October	Lectures on "The Character and Actions of Capt. John Brown" in Concord
1 November	Lectures on "The Character and Actions of Capt. John Brown" in Boston
3 November	Lectures on "The Character and Actions of Capt. John Brown" in Worcester
2 December	Helps organize Concord's memorial service for John Brown and reads "Martyrdom of John Brown" at this event
3 December	Aids the escape to Canada of Harpers Ferry raider Francis Jackson Meriam
1860		"A Plea for Captain John Brown" and "Martyrdom of John Brown" published in *Echoes of Harper's Ferry*, edited by James Redpath
	January	Excerpts from "A Plea for Captain John Brown" published in James Redpath's *The Public Life of John Brown*, which is dedicated to "Wendell Phillips, Ralph Waldo Emerson, and Henry D. Thoreau, Defenders of the Faithful"
	8 February	Lectures on "Wild Apples" in Concord
	14 February	Lectures on "Wild Apples" in Bedford, Massachusetts
	4 July	"The Last Days of John Brown" read by Richard Hinton at graveside ceremony for John Brown in North Elba, New York
	27 July	"The Last Days of John Brown" published in *Liberator*
	9 September	Lectures on ["Walking"] and "Life Misspent" in Lowell, Massachusetts

	20 September	Lectures on "The Succession of Forest Trees" in Concord
	6 October	"The Succession of Forest Trees" published in *New York Weekly Tribune*
	11 December	Lectures on "Autumnal Tints" in Waterbury, Connecticut
1861	11 May–9 July	Takes trip to Minnesota with Horace Mann Jr. in attempt to regain failing health
	August	Ambrotype made by E. S. Dunshee in New Bedford, Massachusetts
1862	6 May	Dies at home in Concord
	9 May	Funeral held at Concord's First Unitarian Church; eulogized by Ralph Waldo Emerson; interred at Concord's New Burying Ground
	June	"Walking" published in *Atlantic Monthly*
	August	Waldo Emerson's "Thoreau" published in *Atlantic Monthly*
	October	"Autumnal Tints" published in *Atlantic Monthly*
	November	"Wild Apples" published in *Atlantic Monthly*
1863	19 June	"Inspiration" (poem) published in *Boston Commonwealth*
	3 July	"The Funeral Bell" (poem) published in *Boston Commonwealth*
	24 July	"Traveling" and "Greece" (poems) published in *Boston Commonwealth*
	28 August	"The Departure" (poem) published in *Boston Commonwealth*
	October	"Life Without Principle" published in *Atlantic Monthly*
		Excursions, edited by Ralph Waldo Emerson and Sophia E. Thoreau, published

	9 October	"The Fall of the Leaf" (poem) published in *Boston Commonwealth*
	30 October	"Independence" (poem) published in *Boston Commonwealth*
	November	"Night and Moonlight" published in *Atlantic Monthly*
	6 November	"The Soul's Season" (poem) published in *Boston Commonwealth*
1864	May	*The Maine Woods,* edited by Ellery Channing and Sophia E. Thoreau, published
	October	"The Wellfleet Oysterman" published in *Atlantic Monthly*
	November	"Looming in the Sun" published in *Boatswain's Whistle*
	December	"The Highland Light" published in *Atlantic Monthly*
1865	March	*Cape Cod,* edited by Ellery Channing and Sophia E. Thoreau, published
	October	*Letters to Various Persons,* edited by Ralph Waldo Emerson, published
1866	August	*A Yankee in Canada, with Anti-Slavery Papers,* edited by Ellery Channing and Sophia E. Thoreau, published
1873	September	William Ellery Channing's *Thoreau: The Poet-Naturalist* published
1876		Journal manuscripts inherited by Harrison Gray Otis Blake when Sophia Thoreau dies
1877		H. A. Page's [Alexander H. Japp's] *Thoreau: His Life and Aims* published
1878	April	"April Days" (journal extracts) published in *Atlantic Monthly*
	May	"May Days" (journal extracts) published in *Atlantic Monthly*

	June	"Days in June" (journal extracts) published in *Atlantic Monthly*
	September	"Days and Nights in Concord" published in *Scribner's Monthly*
1879	7 August	"Thoreau's Thoughts" (journal extracts) published in *Boston Daily Advertiser*
	23 August	"Concord's Academia" (journal extracts) published in *Springfield Republican*
1880	14 August	"Thoreau, The Poet-Philosopher" (journal extracts) published in *Springfield Republican*
	15 August	"New Bits from Thoreau's Journals" published in *New York Daily Tribune*
1881		*Early Spring in Massachusetts*, edited by H. G. O. Blake, published
	26 March	"Thoreau's Unpublished Poetry," edited by Franklin B. Sanborn, published in *Critic*
	4 August	"Thoreau's Relation to His Time. As Interpreted by His Editor Mr. Blake" (journal extracts) published in *Springfield Republican*
1882		Franklin B. Sanborn's *Henry D. Thoreau* published
1883	12 August	"From Thoreau's Journals.—Passages Read by H. G. O. Blake before the Concord School of Philosophy" (journal extracts) published in *Springfield Republican*
1884	May	*Summer*, edited by H. G. O. Blake, published
1885	January	"Winter Days" (journal extracts) published in *Atlantic Monthly*
	25 July	"Thoreau, Unpublished Notes Read to the Concord School" (journal extracts) published in *Boston Daily Advertiser*

	26 July	"Thoreau's Wild Wood Philosophy" (journal extracts) published in *New York Daily Tribune*
1887	October	*Winter,* edited by H. G. O. Blake, published
1888	May	"Ding Dong" (poem) published in *Lippincott's Magazine*
1890		*Thoreau's Thoughts* (journal extracts), edited by H. G. O. Blake, published
		Anti-Slavery and Reform Papers published in London with "Introductory Note" by Henry S. Salt
	October	Henry S. Salt's *The Life of Henry David Thoreau* published
1892	May–June	"The Emerson-Thoreau Correspondence," edited by Franklin B. Sanborn, published in *Atlantic Monthly*
	September	*Autumn,* edited by H. G. O. Blake, published
1893	December	*Miscellanies,* with biographical sketch by Ralph Waldo Emerson, published
		"Thoreau and His English Friend Thomas Cholmondeley," edited by Franklin B. Sanborn, published in *Atlantic Monthly*
1893–1894		Eleven volumes of collected works, including *Familiar Letters of Henry David Thoreau,* edited by Franklin B. Sanborn, published in Riverside Edition by Houghton, Mifflin
1895	March	"Thoreau's Poems of Nature" published in *Scribner's Magazine*
	November	*Poems of Nature,* edited by Henry S. Salt and Franklin B. Sanborn, published
1898	April	Journal manuscripts inherited by Elias Harlow Russell, a Worcester, Massachusetts educator, when H. G. O. Blake dies

1899		*Some Unpublished Letters of Henry D. and Sophia E. Thoreau: A Chapter in the History of a Still-born Book,* edited by Samuel Arthur Jones, published
1901	December	Franklin B. Sanborn's *The Personality of Thoreau* published
1902		*The Service,* edited by Franklin B. Sanborn, published
		A Bit of Unpublished Correspondence between Henry D. Thoreau and Isaac T. Hecker, edited by Elias Harlow Russell, published
1903		Publication rights to journals sold by Elias Harlow Russell to Houghton, Mifflin
1905	January–May	"Thoreau's Journals" published in *Atlantic Monthly*
		The First and Last Journeys of Thoreau, edited by Franklin B. Sanborn, published
		Sir Walter Raleigh, edited by Henry Aiken Metcalf, published
1906		Twenty volumes of collected works, including fourteen volumes of the *Journal,* edited by Bradford Torrey and Francis H. Allen, published as Manuscript Edition and Walden Edition by Houghton, Mifflin
1907		*Unpublished Poems by Bryant and Thoreau* published
1909		Manuscript journal notebooks sold by Stephen H. Wakeman to J. Pierpont Morgan
1910		*Notes on New England Birds,* edited by Francis H. Allen, published
1916		*The Seasons* published
1917	May	Franklin B. Sanborn's *The Life of Henry David Thoreau* published

	July	Edward Waldo Emerson's *Henry Thoreau as Remembered by a Young Friend* published
1921	January	*Night and Moonlight* published
1927		*The Moon* published
1929		Five volumes of collected works published in Concord Edition by Houghton, Mifflin
1931		*The Transmigration of the Seven Brahmans,* edited by Arthur Christy, published
1939		Henry Seidel Canby's *Thoreau* published
1943	July	*Collected Poems of Henry Thoreau,* edited by Carl Bode, published
1956		"Four Uncollected Thoreau Poems with Notes on the Canon," edited by Kenneth Walter Cameron, published in *Emerson Society Quarterly*
1958	May	*Consciousness in Concord: The Text of Thoreau's Hitherto "Lost Journal" (1840–1841),* edited by Perry Miller, published
		The Correspondence of Henry David Thoreau, edited by Walter Harding and Carl Bode, published
1960		"A New Thoreau Poem To Edith," edited by Kenneth Walter Cameron, published in *Emerson Society Quarterly*
1965		Walter Harding's *The Days of Henry Thoreau* published
1970		*Huckleberries,* edited by Leo Stoller, published
1971		*The Writings of Henry D. Thoreau* commences publication of all collected works, under auspices of Modern Language Association's Committee on Scholarly Editions, and published by Princeton University Press

1973	Summer	"On Reform and Reformers," edited by Wendell Glick, published in *University*
1974	November	*The Indians of Thoreau: Selections from the Indian Notebooks,* edited by Richard F. Fleck, published
1986		Robert D. Richardson's *Henry Thoreau: A Life of the Mind* published
1993		*Faith in a Seed: The Dispersion of Seeds and Other Late Natural History Writings,* edited by Bradley P. Dean, published
2000		*Wild Fruits,* edited by Bradley P. Dean, published

Thoreau in His Own Time

[Epistolary Comments on Thoreau in the 1840s]

Lidian Jackson Emerson

LIDIAN JACKSON EMERSON (1802–1892) was born and grew up in Plymouth, Massachusetts. In 1835, she married Ralph Waldo Emerson and moved with him to Concord, Massachusetts. After meeting the Emersons in 1837, Henry Thoreau became an intimate of the family, living for two extended periods in their home while Waldo lectured abroad—in 1841–43 and 1847–48—during which periods Thoreau took on various editorial, handyman, gardener, and parenting responsibilities. Both his journals and correspondence reflect that his friendship with Lidian Emerson was one of the closest personal relationships of Henry Thoreau's life. From her initially positive response to Thoreau, over the years Lidian grew to depend on his company and his resourcefulness. She also promoted his writing career and enjoyed his lectures (Carpenter, "Introduction," xlv).

While living in New York with William and Susan Emerson's family, Thoreau sent letters to Lidian that reflect his homesickness for Concord and for her, whom he refers to "as some elder sister . . . a sort of lunar influence." He confides that "the thought of you will constantly elevate my life" (*Correspondence*, 103, 119). Together again in the Emerson household during Waldo Emerson's absence in 1847–48, Thoreau and Lidian both wrote letters to Waldo depicting a warm household, with Thoreau taking a lively interest in domestic activities—from making a toy watch for Ellen Emerson to "neat little cowhide shoes" for Lidian's chickens; to leading huckleberry parties; to planting the garden; to shoveling snow, parching corn, and cracking nuts (Ellen Tucker Emerson, *Life*, 85, 68, 107, 115; Lidian Jackson Emerson, *Selected Letters*, 126, 124). In November 1847, Thoreau informed Waldo that in his absence, "Lidian and I make very good housekeepers. She is a very dear sister to me." In an extended journal entry in 1849, entitled "A Sister," Thoreau defines this figure as one "Whose heart answers to your heart. Whose presence can fill all space. One who is a spirit. Who attends to your truth. . . . The stream of whose being unites with your own without a ripple or a murmur." He goes on to address this unnamed sister directly: "I still think of you as my sister. I presume to know you. Others are of my kindred by blood or of my acquaintance but you are mine. you are of me & I of you I can not tell where I leave off and you begin.—" Thoreau then contrasts a "sister" with a "friend": "My sister. . . . my inspirer. The feminine of me. . . . Whether art thou my mother or my sister—whether am I thy son or thy brother. On the remembrance of whom I repose— — So *old* a sister art thou—so newly has thou recreated me" (Thoreau, *Correspondence*, 189; *PEJ* 3:17, 18).

To Lucy Jackson Brown, [11 January 1842]

I begin my letter with the strange sad news that John Thoreau has this afternoon left this world. He died of lockjaw occasioned by a slight cut on his thumb. Henry mentioned on Sunday morning that he had been at home helping the family who were all ailing; and that John was disabled from his usual work by having cut his finger. In the evening Mr [Nathan] Brooks came for him to go home again, and said they were alarmed by symptoms of the lockjaw in John. Monday John was given over by the physicians—and to-day he died—retaining his sense and some power of speech to the last. He said from the first he knew he should die—but was perfectly quiet and trustful—saying that God had always been good to him and he could trust Him now. His words and behaviour throughout were what Mr. Emerson calls manly—even *great*. Henry has been here this evening and seen Mr Emerson but no one else. He says John took leave of all the family on Monday with perfect calmness and more than resignation. It is a beautiful fate that has been granted him and I think he was worthy of it. At first it seemed not beautiful but terrible. Since I have heard particulars and recollected all the good I have heard of him I feel as if a pure spirit has been translated. Henry has just been here—(it is now Wednesday noon) I love him for the feeling he showed and the effort he made to be cheerful. He did not give way in the least but his whole demeanour was that of one struggling with sickness of heart. He came to take his clothes—and says he does not know when he shall return to us. . . .

To Ralph Waldo Emerson, 15 January 1843

Henry [Thoreau] is about as well as when you were here—and a great comfort to Edith with whom he dances and for whom he plays the flute. Richard Fuller sent him a music box as a N. Years' gift and it was delightful to see Henrys child like joy. I never saw any one made so happy by a new possession. He said nothing could have been so acceptable. After we had heard its performance he said he must hasten to exhibit it to his sisters & mother. My heart really warmed with sympathy, and admiration at his whole demeanour on the occasion—and I like human nature better than I did. . . . Here is Mother just come in from church—where she affirms she saw Henry in your uppermost seat, not without "astonishment." It must be that he is converted to the right doctrine. I had a conversation with him a few days since on his heresies—but had no expectation of so speedy a result. . . .

To Ralph Waldo Emerson, 12 February 1843

Henrys Lecture pleased me much—and I have reason to believe others liked it. Henry tells me he is so happy as to have received Mr [John S.] *Keyes's* suffrage and the Concord paper has spoken well of it. I think you would have been a well pleased listener. I should like to hear it two or three times more. Henry ought to be known as a man who can give a Lecture. You must advertise him to the extent of your power. A few Lyceum fees would satisfy his moderate wants—to say nothing of the improvement and happiness it would give both him & his fellow creatures if he could utter what is "most within him"—and be heard. . . . I think you have made Henry wait a rea-sonable—or *un*reasonable time for an answer to his letter.

To Ralph Waldo Emerson, [17 May 1848]

Henry has helped Colombe remove the Apple tree, and has set out some of the pear trees from the heater-piece, in the garden or yard. He has planted the pears[1]—of which you, dear husband, will gather and eat the fruit, I hope. . . . Eddy is having his go-to-bed frolic with Henry, & has just in-formed me that Mr T. has first swallowed a book, then pulled it out of his (Eddy's) nose, then put it into his (Mr T.'s) "pantalettes." I tell Henry I shall send you word he is in his second childhood, a wearer of pantalettes. He says it is so, according to the younger Edda; the poetic, not the prose Edda. . . .

Note

1. The word *pears* was omitted from the published version of this letter in Delores Bird Carpenter's edition of *The Selected Letters of Lidian Jackson Emerson* (Columbia:

University of Missouri Press, 1987), 153. I have restored it here based on a review of the manuscript letter; see Lidian Emerson to Ralph Waldo Emerson, [17 May 1848], bMS Am 1280.235 (619), Emerson Family Papers, Houghton Library, Harvard University.

Lidian Jackson Emerson, *The Selected Letters of Lidian Jackson Emerson,* ed. Delores Bird Carpenter (Columbia: University of Missouri Press, 1987), 99, 118, 128–29, 153. Lidian Emerson to Ralph Waldo Emerson, [17 May 1848], bMS Am 1280.235 (619), Emerson Family Papers, Houghton Library, Harvard University.

[Thoreau at Walden in 1847]

Abigail May Alcott

> Abolitionist and social worker Abigail May Alcott (1800–1877) married Tran-
> scendentalist educator Amos Bronson Alcott in 1830. Together they raised
> four daughters, including the popular author Louisa May Alcott. The entire
> Alcott family shared a close friendship with Henry Thoreau, whom they knew
> well during the years they lived in Concord, Massachusetts, in the 1840s, and
> from 1857 on. These brief excerpts from Alcott's letters to her brother, Sam-
> uel Joseph May, demonstrate that she shared her husband's admiration for
> Thoreau's Walden experiment.

To Samuel J. May, 8 February 1847

Mr. Alcott thinks we shall never be safe until we get a Hut on Walden
Pond where with our Beans Books and Peace we shall live honest and
independent—But Habits are Tyrants as well as Laws and Customs I do
think time, Labour well devised and conscientious simplicity of life—will
keep us afloat.

To Samuel J. May, 18 March 1847

Thoreau came and read to them his lecture on his "Diogenes life"—His
hut is little larger than tradition reports the Philosopher's to have been but
I doubt if the sage lived a more temperate wise life than this Hero of the
19 century—He read the 1st part—and in the evening we all went up to the
Lyceum and heard the 2d part—If he does not print it I will get Anna to
copy in a legible hand some parts of it for your special use—I know you will
feel with me it is no small boon to live in the same age with so experimental
and true a Man—surely he who teaches us how to *live truly* is the Phylan-
thropist the Saviour of mankind.

Abigail May Alcott to Samuel J. May, 8 February and 18 March 1847, MS Am 1130.9 (25),
Amos Bronson Alcott Papers, Letterbooks of Amos Bronson Alcott, Houghton Library,
Harvard University.

[Journal and Epistolary Remarks on Thoreau, 1847–1859]

AMOS BRONSON ALCOTT

March 1847

Thoreau's is a walking Muse, winged at the anklets and rhyming her steps. The ruddiest and nimblest genius that has trodden our woods, he comes amidst mists and exhalations, his locks dripping with moisture, in the sonorous rains of an ever-lyric day. His genius insinuates itself at every pore of us, and eliminates us into the old elements again. A wood-nymph, he abides on the earth, and is a sylvan soul. If he could but clap wings to his shoulders or brow and spring forthright into the cope above sometimes, instead of beating the bush and measuring his tread along the marsh-sides and the river's sedge and sand, and taking us to some Maine or Indian wilderness, and peopling the woods with the Sileni and all the dryads!

But this fits him all the better for his special task of delineating these yet unspoiled American things, and of inspiring us with a sense of their homelier beauties—opening to us the riches of a nation scarcely yet discovered by her own population.

In this respect the contrast is striking between him and Emerson, whose Natures—caught, it is true, from our own woods—are never American, nor New English, which were better, but some fancied realm, some Atlantides of this Columbia, very clearly discernible to him but not by us; and our pleasure comes laden with the spoils this princely genius brings home, of the shores and climates of his far-off Indies, for our solace and refreshment—spices and gems, and the airs of Araby the Blessed. . . .

Thoreau took his position in Nature, where he was in deed and in spirit—a genius of the natural world, a savage mind amidst savage faculties, yet adorned with the graces of a civilization which he disowned, but celebrating thereby Nature still. . . .

16 March 1847

This evening I pass with Thoreau at his hermitage on Walden, and he reads me some passages from his MS [manuscript] volume which he is preparing to print some day entitled 'A Week on the Concord and Merrimack Rivers.' . . . It is a Virgil and Gilbert White and Yankee settler all, singing his prose-poems with remembrance of his reading and his experiences in the woods and road-paths by way of episode and variety—portraying of a dreamland lying wild and yet unvisited here in New England, and still remote from everybody but the bold dreamer himself. . . .

The book is purely American, fragrant with the lives of New England woods and streams, and could have been written nowhere else. It preserves to us whatever of the wild and mystic remains to us along our brooksides and rivers, and is written in a style as picturesque and flowing as the streams he sails on. . . . There is a toughness too, and a sinewy vigor, as of roots and the strength that comes of feeding on wild meats, and the moist lustres of the fishes in the bed below.

[7]

It has the merit, moreover, that somehow, despite all presumptions to the contrary, the sod and sap and fibre and flavour of New England have found at last a clear relation to the literature of other and classic lands, and we drink off here the quintessence also of literature the coolest and freshest. . . .

Especially am I touched by this soundness, this aboriginal vigour, as if a man had once more come into Nature. . . . Moreover, there is business here for the naturalist's notice—facts abundant in these pages, of leaves, lakes, rivulets, and old fields and hillsides. Such animals and fishes as he can surprise! Plants and stones hitherto untabled in the books! And here the husbandman and huntsman are helped in their callings—the former especially, to see for the first time . . . the farms they call theirs and somehow cultivate, or desolate rather in their shiftless economics. . . .

26 January 1848

Heard Thoreau's lecture before the Lyceum on the relation of the individual to the State—an admirable statement of the rights of the individual to self-government, and an attentive audience. His allusions to the Mexican War, to Mr. Hoar's expulsion from Carolina, his own imprisonment in Concord Jail for refusal to pay his tax, Mr. Hoar's payment of mine when taken to prison for a similar refusal, were all pertinent, well considered, and reasoned. I took great pleasure in this deed of Thoreau's.

22 January 1851

A sylvan man accomplished in the virtues of an aboriginal civility, and quite superior to the urbanities of cities, Thoreau is himself a wood, and its inhabitants. There is more in him of sod and shade and sky lights, of the genuine mold and moistures of the green grey earth, than in any person I know. Self dependent and sagacious as any denizen of the elements, he has the key to every animal's brain, every flower and shrub; and were an Indian to flower forth, and reveal the secrets hidden in the wilds of his cranium, it would not be more surprising than the speech of this Sylvanus.

He belongs to the Homeric age, and is older than fields and gardens; as virile and talented as Homer's heroes, and the elements. He seems alone, of all the men I have known, to be a native New Englander,—as much so as the oak, or granite ledge; and I would rather send him to London or Vienna or Berlin, as a specimen of American genius spontaneous and unmixed, than anyone else. . . . Here is coloring for half a dozen Socialisms. It stands out in layers and clots, like carbuncles, to give force and homeliness to the otherwise feminine lineaments. This man is the independent of independents—is, indeed, the sole signer of the Declaration, and a Revolution in himself—a more than '76—having got beyond the signing to the doing it out fully. Concord jail could not keep him safely. . . . Lately he has taken to surveying as well as authorship, and makes the compass pay for his book on "The Concord and Merrimak Rivers," which the public is slow to take off his hands. . . . But author and book can well afford to wait.

9 June 1851

I sometimes say of T.[horeau] that he is the purest of our moralists, and the best republican in the Republic—viz., the republican at home. A little over-confident and somewhat stiffly individual, perhaps,—dropping society clean out of his theory, while practically standing friendly in his own strict sense of friendship—there is about him a nobleness and integrity of bearing that make possible and actual the virtues of Rome and Sparta. . . .

17 August 1851

Thoreau has the profoundest passion for the aboriginal in Nature of any man I have known; and had the sentiment of humanity been equally strong and tender he might have written pastorals that Virgil and Theocritus would have envied him the authorship of. As it is, he has come nearer the primitive simplicity of the antique than any of our poets, and touched the fields and forests and streams of Concord with a classic interest that can never fade. . . .

5 November 1851

I meet nobody whose thoughts are so invigorating as his [Thoreau's], and who comes so scented of mountain breezes and springs, so like a luxuriant clod from under forest leaves, moist and mossy with earth-spirits. His company is tonic, never insipid, like ice-water in the dog days to the parched citizen pent in chambers and under brazen ceilings. . . .

10 November 1856

This morning we call on [Walt] Whitman, Mrs. Tyndall accompanying us to whet her curiosity on the demigod. . . .

I hoped to put him in communication direct with Thoreau . . . but each seemed planted fast in reserves, surveying the other curiously,—like two beasts, each wondering what the other would do, whether to snap or run; and it came to no more than cold compliments between them. Whether Thoreau was meditating the possibility of Walt's stealing away his "out-of-doors" for some sinister ends, poetic or pecuniary, I could not well divine, nor was very curious to know; or whether Walt suspected or not that he had here, for once, and the first time, found his match and more at smelling out "all Nature," a sagacity potent, penetrating and peerless as his own, if indeed not more piercing and profound, finer and more formidable. I cannot say. At all events, our stay was not long[.] . . .

5 November 1858

[Thoreau is] an out-of-doors man, and with doors opening on all sides of him, slides in slides, to admit her to his intelligence. His senses seem doubled and give him access to secrets not read easily by other men. His observation is wonderful, his sagacity like a bee and beaver, the dog and the deer—the most gifted in this way of any mind I have known, and the peer of the backwoodsman and Indian. . . .

I am proud of him. I should say he inspired love, if indeed the sentiment he awakens did not seem to partake of something yet purer, if that were possible, and as yet nameless from its rarity and excellency. Certainly he is better poised and more nearly self-sufficient than other men.

9 March 1859

At Emerson's with my wife. [William Ellery] Channing is there and some young people of the village. Thoreau reads us his paper on "Autumnal Tints." It is admirable, the last work of our poet-naturalist, and Seer of the Seasons. I think he stands nearest nature and to the mastery of her subtler secrets than any mind I have known; of a genius so penetrating, yet so holy, that in discriminating plant, animal, cloud, rock, any colour, or whatsoever nature shows, he wounds never, nor rends; as gentle as a maiden and as tender is his glance, his touch, his tread. Certain it is we had never seen leaves *before,* the chemistry of evenings and mornings, of twilight, of autumn's comings and goings, her opulence of foliage, the ways she woos and wins the moral sentiment and the mind through all her changes of leaf and landscapes. And then his uses of the conventions of society in so witty ways to exalt and dignify Nature, his Beloved, the pleasure in common things, and the surprizes along trodden and plain ways. A leaf becomes a Cosmos, a Genesis, and Paradise preserved, in his wonderful treatment of its spirit and parts united.

We sit till 10, and come home edifyed, entertained by this wizard townsman of ours. It was fairie land, and the Elysium of Autumn Season in Fancy and the thoughts while we listened. . . .

21 August 1859

Henry Thoreau is here and spends the evening conversing in his remarkable way on Nature and naturalists. I think him the naturalist by birth and genius, seeing and judging by instinct and first sight, as none other I have known. I remark this in Thoreau, that he discerns objects individually and apart, never in groups and collectively, as a whole, as the artist does. Nature exists separately to him and individually. He never theorizes; he sees only and describes; yet, by a seventh sense as it were, dealing with facts shooting forth from his mind and mythologically, so that his page is a creation. His fancy is ever the complement of his understanding, and finishes Nature to the senses even. If he had less of fancy, he would be the prose naturalist and no more; and had he less of understanding he would be a poet—if, indeed, with all this mastery of things concrete and sensible, he be not a poet, as Homer was.

28 January 1861

I see him [Thoreau] this morning and find his hoarseness forbids his going out as usual. 'Tis a serious thing to one who has been less a housekeeper than any man in town, has lived out of doors for the best part of his life, has harvested more wind and storm, sun and sky, and has more weather in him, than any—night and day abroad with his leash of keen senses, hounding any game stirring, and running it down for certain, to be spread on the dresser of his page before he sleeps and served as a feast of wild meats to all sound intelligences like his. If any can make game for his confinement it must be himself, and for solace, if sauce of the sort is desired by one so healthy as he has seemed hitherto. We have been accustomed to consider him the salt of things so long that we are loath to believe it has lost savor; since if it has, then "Pan is dead" and Nature ails throughout. . . .

[11]

1 March 1861

[H. G. O.] Blake and [Theophilus] Brown are here. They come to see Thoreau, who has walked out with Channing once or twice in the last days, and seems a little better. These men have something of the disciple's faith in their master's thoughts, and come sometimes on pilgrimage to Concord for an interview with him. This confidence in persons, this love of the mind, enthusiasm for a great man's thoughts, is a promising trait in anyone, a disposition always graceful to witness, and is far too rarely seen in our times of personal indifference, if not of confessed unbelief in Persons and Ideas. I know of nothing more creditable to Thoreau than this thoughtful regard and constancy by which he has held for years some of the best persons of his time. They are not many, to be sure, but do credit alike to him and themselves.

To Daniel Ricketson, 10 February 1862

You may not have been informed of the state of Henry's health this winter, and will be sorry to hear that he grows feebler day by day, and is evidently failing and fading from our sight. He gets some sleep, has a pretty good appetite, reads at intervals, takes notes of his readings, and likes to see his friends, conversing however with some difficulty as his voice partakes of his general debility.

We had thought this oldest inhabitant of our planet would have chosen to stay and see it fairly dismissed into the Chaos out of which he has brought so many precious jewels, gifts to friends to mankind generally, . . . But his work is nearly done for us here, and our woods and fields seem sorrowing, though not in sombre but in the robes of white most becoming the purity and probity that they have known so long and are soon to miss. There has been none such since Pliny, and it will be long before there comes his like:—the most knowing and wonderful worthy of his time. . . .

The Journals of Bronson Alcott, ed. Odell Shepard (Boston: Little, Brown, 1938), 193–95, 213–14, 201, 238, 250, 253, 257, 290–91, 309, 319, 333, 337. Amos Bronson Alcott Journal for 9 March 1859, Journals and diaries, MS Am 1130.12 (29), Houghton Library, Harvard University. The Letters of A. Bronson Alcott, ed. Richard L. Herrnstadt (Ames: Iowa State University Press, 1969), 326–27.

[Reflections on Thoreau through the Years]

Ralph Waldo Emerson

Transcendentalist author and speaker Ralph Waldo Emerson (1803–1882) first met Thoreau in 1837, shortly after Emerson had moved to Concord with his second wife, Lidian Jackson Emerson, and twenty-year-old Thoreau had just graduated from Harvard. According to Thoreau, Emerson asked him 'What are you doing now?' . . . 'Do you keep a journal?' So I make my first entry to-day," he recorded, about what became a meticulous, highly crafted lifelong practice of journalizing (*PEJ*, 1:5). Although their relations evolved over the next several years from dear to distant friend, Emerson's influence on Thoreau's development as an author and a thinker is undeniable. In contrast to the disappointed, static individual whom Emerson memorialized in the eulogy he delivered at Thoreau's funeral, his journal notebooks and correspondence reveal a dynamic friendship, editorial partnership, and, eventually, disenchanted relationship. Especially clear in the early years of their acquaintance is Emerson and his family's pleasure in Thoreau's company. In June 1841, he invites Thoreau to "come up to the Cliff this P.m. at any hour convenient to you where our ladies will be greatly gratified to see you & the more they say if you will bring your flute for the echo's sake; though now the wind blows." Even in 1856, well after their friendship had cooled, Emerson valued exploring Concord's environs with Thoreau: "A walk again with Henry, & found *Solidago Odora*. . . . and a tall shrub unknown to Henry. . . . But I was taken with the aspects of the forest, & thought to Nero advertising for a luxury a walk in the woods should have been offered. 'Tis one of the secrets for dodging old age" (*Letters*, 7:455–56; *Journals and Miscellaneous Notebooks*, 14:110).

Letters and journal entries reveal how often Emerson directed Thoreau to handle sensitive matters, from searching for the literary and personal effects of Margaret Fuller after she and her family perished in a shipwreck in 1850, to handling the funeral arrangements when Bulkeley Emerson, Waldo's long-ill brother, died in 1859. On more mundane and routine matters, Emerson called on Thoreau to review proofs for the Transcendentalist periodical the *Dial*; indeed, he put him in charge of editing the entire volume for April 1843 (Emerson, *Letters*, 4:219, 5:149; Harding, *Days*, 117). When Emerson was en route west to lecture in 1855, he tasked Thoreau with facilitating affairs related to the publication of *English Traits:* "I must ask you to correct the proofs of this or these chapters. . . . If anything puts it out of your power to help me at this pinch, you must dig up Channing out of his earths, and hold him steady to this beneficence" (Thoreau, *Correspondence,* 403–4). As a property surveyor, Thoreau assisted Emerson in attempting to settle at least one long-standing dispute with a Concord neighbor; both his availability and trustworthiness made Thoreau the all-purpose solution to a variety of Emerson's needs— gardener, house and family companion, editorial assistant, and proofreader (Emerson, *Journals and Miscellaneous Notebooks,* 12:212–13).

Inescapably obvious in these private writings is what Robert Sattelmeyer calls Emerson's "patronizing and somewhat proprietary attitude toward Thoreau" ("When He Became My Enemy," 192)—as evident in both the recurrent personal pronoun, "*my* young Henry T." and "*my* young contemporaries, T[horeau]. and C[hanning]," as well as the imperative word choice: "You *must* go to Mr Lane with my affectionate respects and tell him that I depend on his most important aid for the new number" of the *Dial* (emphasis added) (*Journals and Miscellaneous Notebooks,* 5:460, 7:266; Thoreau, *Correspondence,* 85). In this same letter from February 1843, Emerson presumes that Thoreau has forgotten Emerson's previous "most rude & snappish speech" (85). Within a few years, these perhaps paternalistic references had become more pointedly critical. By 1847, Emerson reflects that "T. sometimes appears only as a gen d'arme[,] good to knock down a cockney with, but without that power to cheer & establish, which makes the value of a friend." Likely describing Thoreau and again adopting the possessive pronoun, he notes that "the man of the world bows with a vertical movement of the head, up & down. My Stoic used a horizontal Salutation, as if always saying No." By the time Thoreau died in 1862, Emerson had fixed this model of Thoreau as a decided Stoic, a man "rarely tender, as if he did not feel himself except in opposition" (*Journals and Miscellaneous Notebooks,* 14:130–31; Myerson, "Emerson's 'Thoreau,'" 39). Despite journal entries subsequent to Thoreau's death that reveal Emerson's more considered, less certain opinions, these views remained largely private.

In the selections below, journal entries are preceded by a date. Excerpts from letters are preceded by the name of the correspondent and the date. Square brackets indicate speculative dates for journal entries, as determined by the editors of Emerson's *Journals and Miscellaneous Notebooks.*

To William Emerson, 1 June 1841

Our houschold is now enlarged by the presence of Mary Russell for the summer; of Margaret Fuller for the last fortnight; & of Henry Thoreau who may stay with me a year. I do not remember if I have told you about him: but he is to have his board &c for what labor he chooses to do: and he is thus far a great benefactor & physician to me for he is an indefatigable & a very skilful laborer & I work with him as I should not without him. . . . Thoreau is a scholar & a poet & as full of buds of promise as a young apple tree. . . .

6 June [1841]

Then the good river-god has taken the form of my valiant Henry Thoreau here & introduced me to the riches of his shadowy starlit[,] moonlit stream, a lovely new world lying as close & yet as unknown to this vulgar trite one of streets & shops as death to life or poetry to prose. Through one field only we went to the boat & then left all time, all science, all history behind us and entered into Nature with one stroke of a paddle. Take care, good friend! I said, as I looked west into the sunset overhead & underneath, & he with his face toward me rowed towards it,—take care; you know not what you do, dipping your wooden oar into this enchanted liquid, painted with all reds & purples & yellows which glows under & behind you. Presently this glory faded & the stars came & said "Here we are," & began to cast such private & ineffable beams as to stop all conversation. . . .

To Rufus Wilmot Griswold, 25 September 1841

Will you allow me to call your attention to the few pieces in the Dial signed H. D. T. (or, by mistake, D. H. T.) which were written by Henry D. Thoreau, of this town, a graduate of Cambridge in the year 1837. Unless I am greatly mistaken, Mr. Thoreau already deserves and will more and more deserve your attention as a writer of American Poetry. . . .

[1843]

H. D. T. sends me a paper with the old fault of unlimited contradiction. The trick of his rhetoric is soon learned. It consists in substituting for the obvious word & thought its diametrical antagonist. He praises wild mountains & winter forests for their domestic air; snow & ice for their warmth;

villagers & wood choppers for their urbanity[;] and the wilderness for resembling Rome & Paris. With the constant inclination to dispraise cities & civilization, he yet can find no way to honour woods & woodmen except by paralleling them with towns & townsmen. W[illiam] E[llery] C[hanning] declares the piece is excellent: but it makes me nervous & wretched to read it, with all its merits.

To William Emerson, 6 May 1843

I have advanced Henry Thoreau $10.00 more, since I wrote before, & this sum having been expended in outfit, I paid him last night $7.00 for travelling expenses, so that I charge you with 17.— And now goes our brave youth into the new house, the new connexion, the new City. I am sure no truer & no purer person lives in wide New York; and he is a bold & a profound thinker though he may easily chance to pester you with some accidental crotchets and perhaps a village exaggeration of the value of facts. Yet I confide, if you should content each other, in Willie's soon coming to value him for his real power to serve & instruct him. . . .

[1844]

H. D. T. said, he knew but one secret which was to do one thing at a time, and though he has his evenings for study, if he was in the day inventing machines for sawing his plumbago, he invents wheels all the evening & night also; and if this week he has some good reading & thoughts before him, his brain runs on that all day, whilst pencils pass through his hands.

[1844, 1845]

H. T's conversation consisted of a continual coining of the present moment into a sentence & offering it to me. I compared it to a boy who from the universal snow lying on the earth gathers up a little in his hand, rolls it into a ball, & flings it at me.

[1844, 1845]

H. D. T. said that the other world was all his art; that his pencils would draw no other; that his jackknife would cut nothing else. He does not use it as a means. Henry is a good substantial childe, not encumbered with himself. He has no troublesome memory, no wake, but lives extempore, &

brings today a new proposition as radical & revolutionary as that of yesterday, but different. The only man of leisure in the town. He is a good Abbot Samson: & carries counsel in his breast. If I cannot show his performance much more manifest than that of the other grand promisers, at least I can see that with his practical faculty, he has declined all the kingdoms of this world. Satan has no bribe for him.

To Charles King Newcomb, 16 July 1846

In a short time, if Wiley & Putnam smile, you shall have Henry Thoreau's "Excursion on Concord & Merrimack rivers," a seven days' voyage in as many chapters, pastoral as Isaak Walton, spicy as flagroot, broad & deep as Menu. He read me some of it under an oak on the river bank the other afternoon, and invigorated me. . . .

To Evert Augustus Duyckinck, 12 March 1847

Mr Henry D. Thoreau of this town has just completed a book of extraordinary merit, which he wishes to publish. It purports to be the account of "An Excursion on the Concord & Merrimack Rivers," which he made some time ago in company with his brother, in a boat built by themselves. The book contains about the same quantity of matter for printing as Dickens's Pictures of Italy. I have represented to Mr Thoreau, that his best course would undoubtedly be, to send the book to you, to be printed by Wiley & Putnam, that it may have a good edition & wide publishing.

This book has many merits. It will be as attractive to *lovers of nature,* in every sense, that is, to naturalists, and to poets, as Isaak Walton. It will be attractive to scholars for its excellent literature, & to all thoughtful persons for its originality & profoundness. The narrative of the little voyage, though faithful, is a very slender thread for such big beads & ingots as are strung on it. It is really a book of the results of the studies of years.

Would you like to print this book into your American Library? It is quite ready, & the whole can be sent you at once. It has never yet been offered to any publisher. If you wish to see the MS. [manuscript] I suppose Mr Thoreau would readily send it to you. I am only desirous that you should propose to him good terms, & give his book the great advantages of being known which your circulation ensures.

Mr Thoreau is the author of an Article on Carlyle, now printed & printing in Graham's last & coming Magazine, & of some papers in the Dial; but he has done nothing half so good as his new book. He is well known to Mr Hawthorn also.

To William Henry Furness, 6 August 1847

Now I write because Henry D. Thoreau has a book to print. Henry D. Thoreau is a great man in Concord, a man of original genius & character who knows Greek & knows Indian also,—not the language quite as well as John Eliot—but the history monuments & genius of the Sachems, being a pretty good Sachem himself, master of all woodcraft, & an intimate associate of the birds, beasts, & fishes, of this region. I could tell you many a good story of his forest life.—He has written what he calls, "A Week on the Concord & Merrimack Rivers," which is an account of an excursion made by himself & his brother (in a boat which he built) some time ago, from Concord, Mass., down the Concord river & up the Merrimack, to Concord N. H.—I think it a book of wonderful merit, which is to go far & last long. It will remind you of Isaak Walton, and, if it have not all his sweetness, it is rich, as he is not, in profound thought.—Thoreau sent the manuscript lately to Duyckinck,— Wiley & Putnam's literary Editor, who examined it & "gave a favorable opinion of it to W. & P." They have however declined publishing it. And I have promised Thoreau that I would inquire publishing it. And I have before we begin to set our own types. Would Mr Hart, or Mr Kay like to see such a manuscript? It will make a book as big as my First Series of Essays. They shall have it on half profits, or on any reasonable terms. Thoreau is mainly bent on having it printed in a cheap form for a large circulation. . . .

[1848]

Henry Thoreau is like the woodgod who solicits the wandering poet & draws him into antres vast & desarts idle, & bereaves him of his memory, & leaves him naked, plaiting vines & with twigs in his hand. Very seductive are the first steps from the town to the woods, but the End is want & madness—.

[1853]

H[enry] is military
H[enry Thoreau] seemed stubborn & implacable; always manly & wise, but rarely sweet. One would say that as Webster could never speak without

an antagonist, so H. does not feel himself except in opposition. He wants a fallacy to expose, a blunder to pillory, requires a little sense of victory, a roll of the drums, to call his powers into full exercise[.]

[1853]

Sylvan [Henry Thoreau] could go wherever woods & waters were & no man was asked for leave. Once or twice the farmer withstood, but it was to no purpose,—he could as easily prevent the sparrows or tortoises. It was their land before it was his, & their title was precedent. S. knew what was on their land, & they did not; & he sometimes brought them ostentatiously gifts of flowers or fruits or shrubs which they would gladly have paid great prices for, & did not tell them that he took them from their own woods.

Moreover the very time at which he used their land & water (for his boat glided like a trout everywhere unseen,) was in hours when they were sound asleep. Long before they were awake he went up & down to survey like a sovereign his possessions, & he passed onward, & left them before the farmer came out of doors. Indeed it was the common opinion of the boys that Mr T[horeau] made Concord.

To George Partridge Bradford, 28 August 1854

The House of Lords have most unseasonably reversed Lord Campbells copyright interpretations; bad for Thoreau, bad for me, yet I wish it may drive us to granting foreign copyright which would no doubt restore this Eng. privilege. All American kind are delighted with "Walden" as far as they have dared say, The little pond sinks in these very days as tremulous at its human fame. I do not know if the book has come to you yet;—but it is cheerful, sparkling, readable, with all kinds of merits, & rising some-times to very great heights. We account Henry the undoubted King of all American lions. He is walking up & down Concord, firm-looking, but in a tremble of great expectation. . . .

21 May [1856]

Yesterday to the Sawmill Brook with Henry. He was in search of yellow violet (pubescens) and menyanthes which he waded into the water for. & which he concluded, on examination, had been out five days. Having found his flowers, he drew out of his breast pocket his diary & read the names of all the plants that should bloom on this day, 20 May; whereof he keeps account as a banker when his notes fall due. . . . Then we diverged to the brook, where was viburnum dentatum, arrowhead. But his attention was drawn to the redstart which flew about with its *cheah cheah chevet*, & presently to two fine grosbeaks[,] rosebreasted, whose brilliant scarlet "made the rash gazer wipe his eye," & which he brought nearer with his spy glass, & whose fine clear note he compares to that of a "tanager who has got rid of his hoarseness," then he heard a note which he calls that of the nightwarbler, a bird he has never identified, has been in search of for twelve years; which, always, when he sees, is in the act of diving down into a tree or bush, & which 'tis vain to seek; the only bird that sings indifferently by night & by day. I told him, he must beware of finding & booking him, lest life should have nothing more to show him. He said, "What you seek in vain for half your life, one day you come full upon all the family at dinner.—You seek him like a dream, and as soon as you find him, you become his prey." He thinks he could tell by the flowers what day of the month it is, within two days. We found saxifraga Pennsylvanica and chrysosplenium oppositifolium, by Everett's spring, and stellaria & cerastium and arabis rhemboidea & veronica anagallis, which he thinks handsomer than the cultivated *veronica, forget me not. Solidago odora,* he says, is common in Concord, & penny royal he gathers in quantity as *herbs* every season. *Shad blossom* is no longer a *pyrus,* which is now confined to choke berry. . . .

[1857, 1858]

I found Henry T. yesterday in my woods. He thought nothing to be hoped from you, if this bit of mould under your feet was not sweeter to you to eat, than any other in this world, or in any world. We talked of the willows. He says, 'tis impossible to tell when they push the bud (which so marks the arrival of spring) out of its dark scales. It is done & doing all winter. It is begun in the previous autumn. It seems one steady push from autumn to spring. I say, How divine these studies! Here there is no taint of mortality. . . .

11 May [1858]

Yesterday with Henry T. at the pond saw the creeper *vesey vesey vesey. Yorick is the veery, or Wilson's Thrush.* . . . I hear the account of the man who lives in the wilderness of Maine with respect, but with despair. It needs the doing hand to make the seeing eye, & my imbecile hands leave me always helpless & ignorant, after so many years in the country. . . . I tell him that a man was not made to live in a swamp, but a frog.* The charm which Henry T. uses for bird & frog & mink, is patience. They will not come to him, or show him aught, until he becomes a log among the logs, sitting still for hours in the same place; then they come around him & to him, & show themselves at home. . . .

*If God meant him to live in a swamp, he would have made him a frog.

[1858]

My dear Henry,

A frog was made to live in a swamp, but a man was not made to live in a swamp. Yours ever,

R.

June [1862]

Henry T[horeau]. remains erect, calm, self-subsistent before me, and I read him not only truly in his Journal, but he is not long out of mind when I walk, and, as today, row upon the pond. He chose wisely no doubt for himself to be the bachelor of thought & nature that he was,—how near to the old monks in their ascetic religion! He had no talent for wealth, & knew how to be poor without the least hint of squalor or inelegance.

Perhaps he fell, all of us do, into his way of living, without forecasting it much, but approved & confirmed it with later wisdom. . . .

[1863]

In reading Henry Thoreau's Journal, I am very sensible of the vigor of his constitution. That oaken strength which I noted whenever he walked or worked or surveyed wood lots, the same unhesitating hand with which a field-laborer accosts a piece of work which I should shun as a waste of strength, Henry shows in his literary task. He has muscle, & ventures on & performs feats which I am forced to decline. In reading him, I find the same thoughts, the same spirit that is in me, but he takes a step beyond, & illustrates by excellent images that which I should have conveyed in a sleepy generality. 'Tis as if I went into a gymnasium & saw youths leap, climb, & swing with a force unapproachable,—though their feats are only continuations of my initial grapplings & jumps.

To James Elliot Cabot, 29 December 1863

I have borrowed of Miss Thoreau a volume of her brother's MSS. [manuscripts]—taken almost at random from those I have read,—to send you: it will be as good a specimen probably as any. You will find the handwriting hard to read at first, with abbreviations,—*appy* for apparently, *mts* for mountains, &c, but I got through several volumes with ever mounting estimation, though I have postponed further readings for the present. I need not say to you, that Miss Thoreau values these books religiously, and I have assured her they would be perfectly safe in your hands. I am delighted to have you see one, and perhaps you will suggest what can be done with them.

To George Stewart Jr., 22 January 1877

Thoreau was a superior genius. I read his books and manuscripts always with new surprise at the range of his topics and the novelty and depth of his thought. A man of large reading, of quick perception, of great practical courage and ability,—who grew greater every day, and, had his short life been prolonged would have found few equals to the power and wealth of his mind. . . .

The Journals and Miscellaneous Notebooks of Ralph Waldo Emerson, 16 vols., ed. William H. Gilman et al. (Cambridge: Belknap Press of Harvard University Press, 1960–82), 7:454; 9:9–10, 77, 101–2, 103; 10:106–7, 344; 13:183, 187; 14:90–91, 195, 203, 204, 15:261–62, 352–53. *The Letters of Ralph Waldo Emerson*, 10 vols., ed. Ralph L. Rusk and Eleanor M. Tilton (New York: Columbia University Press, 1939–95), 2:402; 7:473; 3:172, 338, 384; 8:121–22; 4:459–60; 5:344; 6:303.

[Promoting Thoreau, 1846–1855]

Horace Greeley

Originally from New Hampshire, editor and political reformer Horace Greeley (1811–1872) came to New York in 1831. Ten years later, he founded and edited the *New York Tribune,* one of the most influential newspapers of its day, and in whose editorials he promoted a range of liberal and reform causes. He and Thoreau met in 1843; thereafter Greeley became an important promoter of Thoreau's authorship. Not only did he note forthcoming lectures and review books on publication, but Greeley also acted as Thoreau's literary agent with various periodical editors, including Rufus Griswold, George Rex Graham, George Palmer Putnam, and George William Curtis. His reviews of *A Week* and *Walden* drew attention to both. In numerous letters to Thoreau over the years, Greeley exhibits promotional zeal and offers unsolicited advice along with expressing frustration with what clearly seemed to him, at times, Thoreau's overly principled stand on not making editorial changes to suit public taste. In 1855 and 1856, Greeley tried to persuade Thoreau to move to New York and tutor his children, but Thoreau ultimately declined the offer. Unlike others who knew Thoreau as well as he did, Greeley left no sustained record of his thoughts on Thoreau—as a writer or friend.

To Henry D. Thoreau, 16 August 1846

Believe me when I say that I *mean* to do the errand you have asked of me, and that soon. But I am not sanguine of success, and have hardly a hope that it will be immediate if ever. I hardly know a soul that could publish your article all at once, and "To be continued" are words shunned like a pestilence. But I know you have written a good thing about Carlyle—too solidly good, I fear, to be profitable to yourself or attractive to publishers. Didst thou ever, O my friend! ponder on the significance and cogency of the assurance, "Ye cannot serve God and Mammon," as applicable to Literature—applicable, indeed, to all things whatsoever. God grant us grace to endeavor to serve Him rather than Mammon—that ought to suffice us. In my poor judgment, if any thing is calculated to make a scoundrel of an honest man, writing to sell is that very particular thing.

To Henry D. Thoreau, 5 February 1847

. . . Your article is this moment in type, and will appear about the 20th inst. as *the leading article* in Graham's Mag. for next month. Now don't object to this, nor be unreasonably sensitive at the delay. It is immensely more important to you that the article should appear thus (that is, if you have any literary aspirations,) than it is that you should make a few dollars by issuing it in some other way. As to lecturing, you have been at perfect liberty to deliver it as a lecture a hundred times if you had chosen—the more the better. It is really a good thing, and I will see that Graham pays you fairly for it. But its appearance there is worth far more to you than money.

I know there has been too much delay, and have done my best to obviate it. But I could not. A Magazine that pays, and which it is desirable to be known as a contributor to, is always crowded with articles, and has to postpone some for others of even less merit. I do this myself with good things that I am not required to pay for.

Thoreau, do not think hard of Graham. Do not try to stop the publication of your article. It is best as it is. . . .

To Henry D. Thoreau, 17 April 1848

I enclose you $25 for your article on Maine Scenery, as promised. I know it is worth more though I have not yet found time to read it; but I have tried once to sell it without success. It is rather long for my columns and too fine for the million; but I consider it a cheap bargain, and shall print it myself if I do not dispose of it to better advantage. You will not of course consider yourself under any sort of obligation to me, for my offer was in the way of business and I have got more than the worth of my money. Send me a line acknowledging the receipt of the money, and say if all is right between us. . . .

If you will write me two or three articles in the course of the summer, I think I can dispose of them for your benefit. But write not more than half as long as your article just sent me, for that is too long for the Magazines. . . .

What about your book? Is any thing going on about it now? Why did not Emerson try it in England? I think the Howitts could get it favorably before the British public. If you can suggest any way wherein I can put it forward, do not hesitate, but command me.

To Henry D. Thoreau, 2 January 1853

I am sorry you and C[urtis] cannot agree so as to have your whole [manuscript] printed. It will be worth nothing elsewhere after having partly appeared in Putnam's. I think it is a mistake to conceal the authorship of the several articles, making them all (so to speak) *editorial;* but *if* that is done, don't you see that the elimination of very flagrant heresies (like your defiant Pantheism) becomes a necessity? If you had withdrawn your MS., on account of the abominable misprints in the first number, your ground would have been far more tenable.

However, do what you will.

To Henry D. Thoreau, 6 March 1854

Thoreau, I want you to do something on *my* urgency. I want you to collect and arrange your "Miscellanies" and send them to me. Put in "Ktaadn," "Carlyle," "A Winter Walk," "Canada," etc., and I will try to find a publisher who will bring them out at his own risk, and (I hope) to your ultimate profit. If you have anything new to put with them, very well; but let me have about a 12mo volume whenever you can get it ready, and see if there is not something to your credit in the bank of Fortune.

To Henry D. Thoreau, 23 March 1854

I am glad your "Walden" is coming out. *I* shall announce it at once, whether Ticknor does or not.

I am in no hurry now about your Miscellanies; take your time, select a good title, and prepare your articles deliberately and finally. Then if Ticknor will give you something worth having, let him have this too; if proffering it to him is to glut your market, let it come to me. But take your time. I was only thinking you were hybernating when you ought to be doing something. I referred (without naming you) to your 'Walden' experience in my lecture on "Self-Culture," with which I have bored ever so many audiences. This episode excited much interest and I have repeatedly been asked who it is that I refer to.

To Henry D. Thoreau, 17 August 1855

There is a very small class in England who ought to know what you have written, and for whose sake I want a few copies of "Walden" sent to certain periodicals over the water—for instance, to

Westminster Review . . .

The Reasoner . . .

Dickens's Household Words . . .

I feel sure your publishers would not throw away copies sent to these periodicals; especially if your "Week on the Concord and Merrimac" could accompany them. Chapman, Ed Westminster Rev. expressed surprise to me that your book had not been sent to him, and I could find very few who had read or seen it. If a new edition should be called for, try to have it better known in Europe; but have a few copies sent to those worthy of it at all events.

Horace Greeley to Henry D. Thoreau, *The Correspondence of Henry David Thoreau,* ed. Walter Harding and Carl Bode (New York: New York University Press, 1958), 169–70, 174, 218–19, 293, 323–24, 324–25, 380.

[Journal and Epistolary Comments on Thoreau, 1842–1854]

Nathaniel Hawthorne

Along with Waldo Emerson and Thoreau, Nathaniel Hawthorne (1804–1864) completes the triad of Concord authors most famous today. He lived in Concord three times during his adult life, first renting the historic Old Manse with his bride, Sophia Peabody, shortly after their wedding in the summer of 1842. As a wedding gift to the couple, Henry Thoreau assisted local African American handyman and gardener Jack Garrison in planting the large garden on the Manse's expansive front lawn. Both Hawthorne's letters and journal commentary reflect generally ambivalent opinions of Thoreau, whose behavior and manners he found distasteful but whose writings he recommended, albeit unevenly. Hawthorne most admired Thoreau's firm individualism, which he credited with preventing Thoreau from coming too strongly under the Transcendentalists' spell.

Excluding his enjoyment of a few canoe outings with Thoreau, Hawthorne differed from Emerson and others who found Thoreau most likable as nature guide. Describing a walk to Gowing's Swamp with Hawthorne and Thoreau, William Ellery Channing relates Hawthorne's unexpectedly disappointing behavior: "It was a choice walk, to which Thoreau and I did not invite everybody. When we reached the place Hawthorne said nothing, but just glanced about him and remarked: 'Let us get out of this dreadful hole!'" (qtd. in Sanborn, *Recollections*, 2:526). When he and Sophia lived in Salem, Massachusetts, in the mid-1840s, Hawthorne arranged for Thoreau to give two lectures there. But when *Walden* was published he found as much to damn as to praise, writing to British editor Richard M. Milnes that "'Walden' and 'Concord River,' are by a very remarkable man; but I hardly hope you will read his books, unless for the observation of nature contained in them—which is wonderfully accurate. I sometimes fancy it a characteristic of American books, that it generally requires an effort to read them; there is hardly ever one that carries the reader away with it; and few that a man of weak resolution can get to the end of" (*Letters*, 3:277). In what seems one of his most sincere reflections,

Hawthorne expressed disappointment when Thoreau departed Concord for New York in 1843: "I should like to have him remain here; he being one of the few persons, I think, with whom to hold intercourse is like hearing the wind among the boughs of a forest-tree; and with all this wild freedom, there is high and classic cultivation in him too" (*American Notebooks*, 369).

In the selections below, journal entries are preceded by a date. Excerpts from letters are preceded by the name of the correspondent and the date.

1 September [1842]

Mr. Thorow dined with us yesterday. He is a singular character—a young man with much of wild original nature still remaining in him; and so far as he is sophisticated, it is in a way and method of his own. He is as ugly as sin, long-nosed, queer-mouthed, and with uncouth and somewhat rustic, although courteous manners, corresponding very well with such an exterior. But his ugliness is of an honest and agreeable fashion, and becomes him much better than beauty. He was educated, I believe, at Cambridge, and formerly kept school in this town; but for two or three years back, he has repudiated all regular modes of getting a living, and seems inclined to lead a sort of Indian life among civilized men—an Indian life, I mean, as respects the absence of any systematic effort for a livelihood. He has been for sometime an inmate of Mr. Emerson's family; and, in requital, he labors in the garden, and performs such other offices as may suit him—being entertained by Mr. Emerson for the sake of what true manhood there is in him. Mr. Thorow is a keen and delicate observer of nature—a genuine observer, which, I suspect, is almost as rare a character as even an original poet; and Nature, in return for his love, seems to adopt him as her especial child, and shows him secrets which few others are allowed to witness. He is familiar with beast, fish, fowl, and reptile, and has strange stories to tell of adventures, and friendly passages with these lower brethren of mortality. Herb and flower, likewise, wherever they grow, whether in garden or wild wood, are his familiar friends. He is also on intimate terms with the clouds, and can tell the portents of storms. It is a characteristic trait, that he has a great regard for the memory of the Indian tribes, whose wild life would have suited him so well; and strange to say, he seldom walks over a ploughed field without picking up an arrow-point, a spear-head, or other relic of the red men—as if their spirits willed him to be the inheritor of their simple wealth.

With all this he has more than a tincture of literature—a deep and true taste for poetry, especially the elder poets, although more exclusive than is desirable, like all other Transcendentalists, so far as I am acquainted with them. He is a good writer—at least, he has written one good article, a rambling disquisition on Natural History in the last Dial,—which, he says, was chiefly made up from journals of his own observations. Methinks this article gives a very fair image of his mind and character—so true, minute, and literal in observation, yet giving the spirit as well as letter of what he sees, even as a lake reflects its wooded banks, showing every leaf, yet giving the wild beauty of the whole scene;—then there are passages in the article of cloudy and dreamy metaphysics, partly affected, and partly the natural exhalations of his intellect;—and also passages where his thoughts seem to measure and attune themselves into spontaneous verse, as they rightfully may, since there is real poetry in him. There is a basis of good sense and moral truth, too, throughout the article, which also is a reflection of his character; for he is not unwise to think and feel, however imperfect in his own mode of action. On the whole, I find him a healthy and wholesome man to know.

After dinner (at which we cut the first water-melon and musk melon that our garden has ripened) Mr. Thorow and I walked up the bank of the river; and, at a certain point, he shouted for his boat. Forthwith, a young man paddled it across the river, and Mr. Thorow and I voyaged further up the stream, which soon became more beautiful than any picture, with its dark and quiet sheet of water, half shaded, half sunny, between high and wooded banks. The late rains have swollen the stream so much, that many trees are standing up to their knees, as it were, in the water; and boughs, which lately swung high in air, now dip and drink deep of the passing wave. As to the poor cardinals, which glowed upon the bank, a few days since, I could see only a few of their scarlet caps, peeping above the water. Mr. Thorow managed the boat so perfectly, either with two paddles or with one, that it seemed instinct with his own will, and to require no physical effort to guide it. He said that, when some Indians visited Concord a few years since, he found that he had acquired, without a teacher, their precise method of propelling and steering a canoe. Nevertheless, being in want of money, the poor fellow was desirous of selling the boat, of which he is so fit a pilot, and which was built by his own hands; so I agreed to give him his price (only seven dollars) and accordingly became possessor of the Musketaquid. I wish I could acquire the aquatic skill of its original owner at as reasonable a rate.

2 September [1842]

Yesterday afternoon, while my wife, and Louisa, and I, were gathering the windfallen apples in our orchard, Mr. Thorow arrived with the boat. The adjacent meadow being overflowed by the rise of the stream, he had rowed directly to the foot of the orchard, and landed at the bars, after floating over forty or fifty yards of water, where people were making hay, a week or two since. I entered the boat with him, in order to have the benefit of a lesson in rowing and paddling. My little wife, who was looking on, cannot feel very proud of her husband's proficiency. I managed, indeed, to propel the boat by rowing with two oars; but the use of the single paddle is quite beyond my present skill. Mr. Thorow had assured me that it was only necessary to will the boat to go in any particular direction, and she would immediately take that course, as if imbued with the spirit of the steersman. It may be so with him, but certainly not with me; the boat seemed to be bewitched, and turned its head to every point of the compass except the right one. He then took the paddle himself, and though I could observe nothing peculiar in his management of it, the Musketaquid immediately became as docile as a trained steed. I suspect that she has not yet transferred her affections from her old master to her new one. By and bye, when we are better acquainted, she will grow more tractable; . . . It is not very likely that I shall make such long voyages in her as Mr. Thorow has. He once followed our river down to the Merrimack, and thence, I believe, to Newburyport—a voyage of about eighty miles, in this little vessel. . . .

To Epes Sargent, 21 October 1842

There is a gentleman in this town by the name of Thoreau, a graduate of Cambridge, and a fine scholar, especially in old English literature—but withal a wild, irregular, Indian-like sort of fellow, who can find no occupation in life that suits him. He writes; and sometimes—often, for aught I know—very well indeed. He is somewhat tinctured with Transcendentalism; but I think him capable of becoming a very valuable contributor to your Magazine. In the Dial for July, there is an article on the Natural

History of this part of the country, which will give you an idea of him as a genuine and exquisite observer of nature—a character almost as rare as that of a true poet. A series of such articles would be a new feature in Magazine-literature, and perhaps a popular one; and, not improbably, he might give them a more popular tone than the one in the Dial. Would it not be worth while to try Mr. Thoreau's pen? He writes poetry also—for instance, "To the Maiden in the East"—"The Summer Rain"—and other pieces, in the Dial for October, which seem to be very careless and imperfect, but as true as bird-notes. The man has stuff in him to make a reputation of; and I wish that you might find it consistent with your interest to aid him in attaining that object. In common with the rest of the public, I shall look for character and individuality in the Magazine which you are to edit; and it seems to me that this Mr. Thoreau might do something towards marking it out from the ordinary catalogue of such publications.

To E[vert] A. Duyckinck, 1 July 1845

As for Thoreau, there is one chance in a thousand that he might write a most excellent and readable book; but I should be sorry to take the responsibility, either towards you or him, of stirring him up to write anything for the series. He is the most unmalleable fellow alive—the most tedious, tiresome, and intolerable—the narrowest and most notional—and yet, true as all this is, he has great qualities of intellect and character. The only way, however, in which he could ever approach the popular mind, would be by writing a book of simple observation of nature, somewhat in the vein of White's History of Selborne. . . .

To Richard M. Milnes, 18 November 1854

I have known Thoreau a good many years; but it would be quite impossible to comprise him within this little sheet of note-paper. He is an excellent scholar, and a man of most various capacity; insomuch that he could make his part good in any way of life, from the most barbarous to the most civilized. But there is more of the Indian in him, I think, than of any other kind of man. He despises the world, and all that it has to offer, and, like other humorists, is an intolerable bore. I shall cause it to be made known to him that you sat up till two oclock, reading his book; and he will pretend that it is of no consequence, but will never forget it. I ought not to forbear saying that he is an upright, conscientious, and courageous man, of whom it is impossible to conceive anything but the highest integrity. Still, he is not an agreeable person; and in his presence one feels ashamed of having any money, or a house to live in, or so much as two coats to wear, or of having written a book that the public will read—his own mode of life being so unsparing a criticism on all other modes, such as the world approves. I wish anything could be done to make his books known to the English public; for certainly they deserve it, being the work of a true man and full of true thought. You must not think that he is a particular friend of mine. I do not speak with quite this freedom of my friends. We have never been intimate; though my home is near his residence.

Nathaniel Hawthorne, *The American Notebooks,* ed. Claude M. Simpson (Columbus: Ohio State University Press, 1972), 353–57. Nathaniel Hawthorne, *The Letters,* 6 vols., ed. Thomas Woodson et al. (Columbus: Ohio State University Press, 1984–87), 1:656–57, 2:106, 3:279–80.

[News of the Thoreau Family in 1849 and 1857]

MARIA THOREAU

One of several family members who lived in the extended Thoreau household during Henry's life, Maria Thoreau (1794–1881) was the last survivor of John Thoreau's family. She has been characterized as "a sharp and brilliant soul, a great talker, with very decided opinions upon religion, politics and the world in general. . . . [B]risk and energetic, and most firmly entrenched in her own opinions and principles." According to Eben Loomis and others, Maria Thoreau was the veiled woman who showed up at jailer Samuel Staples's home one night in late July 1846 to pay Henry's delinquent poll tax, therefore sparing her nephew more than one night in the Middlesex County jail (Todd, 11; Oehlschlaeger and Hendrick, 197–202). In his journal on 27 March 1853, Henry records Maria's comments at his not having read a book she'd recommended: "Think of it, he stood haf an hour today to hear the frogs croak, and he would'nt read the life of Chalmers—" (*PEJ*, 6:41).¹ During the theological schism of 1826, Maria and her sisters, Jane and Elizabeth, were the only Thoreau family members to leave Rev. Ezra Ripley's First Unitarian Church to join the newly formed Trinitarian Church in Concord. Although an abolitionist and founding member of the Concord Female Anti-Slavery Society, Maria disdained many of William Lloyd Garrison's more radical ideas, particularly his anti-Sabbath stance. Her correspondence with close friends Mary Wilder and Prudence Ward details family life, including Henry and his siblings' activities. She expresses decided opinions on Henry's writings, philosophy, and lectures; thanks to her wide-ranging missives, we also learn the family's reaction to Sophia Foord's ill-fated proposal of marriage to Henry. As *A Week* was in press, Maria's "fear [that] it will not sell well," proved all too accurate (Thoreau, Letter to Ward, 15 March 1849).

To Prudence Ward, 28 February 1849

Today Henry has gone to Salem to read another lecture they seem to be wonderfully taken with him there, and next month he is to go to Portland to deliver the same, and George wants him to keep on to Bangor they want to have him there, and if their funds will hold out they intend to send for him they give 25 dollars, and at Salem and Portland 20—he is preparing his Book for the press and the title is to be, Waldien (I dont know how to spell it) or life in the woods I think the title will take if the Book dont.—I was quite amused with what Sophia told me her mother said about it the other day, she poor girl was lying in bed with a sick head ache when she overheard Cynthia (who has grown rather nervous of late) telling over her troubles to Mrs Dunbar, after speaking of her own and Helen's sickness, she says . . . and Henry is putting things into his Book that never ought to be put there, . . . you know I have said, there were parts of it that sounded to me very much like blasphemy, and I did not believe they would publish it, on reading it to Helen the other day Sophia told me, she made the same remark, and coming from her, Henry was much surprised, and said she did not understand it, but still I fear they will not persuade him to leave it out, by the way, have you heard what a strange story there was about Miss Ford, and Henry, Mrs Brooks said at the convention, a lady came to her and inquired, if it was true, that Miss F—had committed, or was going to commit suicide on account of H— Thoreau, what a ridiculous story this is. When it was told to H— he made no remark at all, and we cannot find out from him any thing about it, for a while, they corresponded, and Sophia said that she recollected one day on the reception of a letter she heard H— say, he should'nt answer it, or he must put a stop to this, some such thing she could'nt exactly tell what. . . .

To Prudence Ward, 1 May 1849

Mr Emerson gave us his last lecture on Wednesday evening, and much good may it do those who understand it. Henry has been to Worcester twice and is going again next Friday tho', I understood one of the papers there criticised the first lecture very severely. Henry says he does not know what they will say to the last, for that, they will not like, (it is the one I was so disgusted with, but the next one they may like better, however it was there own proposition to have him come, and I think they will have enough of him, his last proof sheet went to Boston yesterday so I suppose his Book will soon be forthcoming.

To Mary Wilder, 18 August 1857

Henry returned from his *tramp* being absent about a fortnight, he had a fine time only one night was very anxious about Edward Hoar who you know accompanied him, for he was *lost,* it appears that the Indian in his boat spoke to Henry requiring some assistance, and he *turned back* to afford it, which Edward not perceiving kept on, and was soon lost in the mazes of the forest, but he had the precaution as soon as he found he could not overtake Henry to stop where he was, in the meanwhile H. soon discovered his absence, and commenced searching for him, but it was a dark lowering afternoon and soon it was too dark to prosecute the search that night, for their own safety was involved so they incampt, and after passing a most anxious night *thinking* he heard Edward's voice at intervals through the whole of it (which *was a mistake*), he early in the morning started again *without breakfast* which the Indian did not like so well, and found him a mile and an half ahead standing by the lake, he had written a note and hung it on a tree, telling what his intentions were. I believe he meant to continue on to Moose Lake hoping to find Henry there, but I fear even if he found the way he would have got pretty hungry by that time as H. had the provisions with him it was a narrow escape, Henry said he expected every moment in his search to come upon his dead body at the foot of some cliff as the rout was precipitous and Edward is very near sighted. . . .

Mr. Emerson has *eight young* ladies staying at his house daughters of Agassiz, Felton, Ward and others, and he wishing to entertain them projected a sail on the river last Saturday afternoon. he wished Henry to accompany them, but he was engaged, so three young gentlemen went, there were four boats, two of the young ladies was to row one of them, well, they started at half past four, and at half past nine Mr. E. called in great trouble to get Henry to get out his boat to go in search of them as he had seen nothing of them, they had not *returned* and he feared some accident had happened, the night was dark and H. and Mr. E set sail with lanterns sending a man by the road with a carriage, it was an anxious hour for all of us as we could not conjecture what had happened, and great was our relief when H. returned and reported all safe.

Note

1. A second edition of William Hann's *Life of Thomas Chalmers,* edited by James C. Moffat, was published in 1853.

Maria Thoreau to Prudence Ward, 28 February and 1 May 1849, Thoreau-Sewall Papers, the Huntington Library, San Marino, CA. Maria Thoreau to Mary Wilder, 18 August 1857, Loomis-Wilder Family Papers, Special Collections, Yale Univerity Library, New Haven, CT.

[A Day with Thoreau and Emerson in 1852]

JOHN ALBEE

In May 1852, poet and literary critic John Albee (1833–1915) paid a visit to Waldo Emerson, which he later described in his *Remembrances of Emerson*, published in 1901. Thoreau figures prominently in this account, as a quasi-member of the family, in the domestic scenes with the Emerson children as well as in the adults' discussion. Albee presents a spontaneous view of Thoreau, including an example of his recurring ridicule of the uselessness of a Harvard education. Albee's depiction of both Emerson's deference to and occasional teasing of Thoreau also evidences the tenor of this relationship by the early 1850s.

THOREAU WAS already there. I think he had ended his experiment at Walden Pond some years before. Thoreau was dressed, I remember, in a plain, neat suit of dark clothes, not quite black. He had a healthy, out-of-door appearance, and looked like a respectable husbandman. He was rather silent; when he spoke, it was in either a critical or a witty vein. I did not know who or what he was; and I find in my old diary of the day that I spelled his rare name phonetically, and heard afterward that he was a man who had been a hermit. I observed that he was much at home with Emerson; and as he remained through the afternoon and evening, and I left him still at the fireside, he appeared to me to belong in some way to the household. I observed also that Emerson continually deferred to him and seemed to anticipate his view, preparing himself obviously for a quiet laugh at Thoreau's negative and biting criticisms, especially in regard to education and educational institutions. He was clearly fond of Thoreau; but whether in a human way, or as an amusement, I could not then make out. Dear, indeed, as I have since learned, was Thoreau to that household; where his memory is kept green, where Emerson's children still speak of him as their elder brother. In the evening Thoreau devoted himself wholly to the children and the parching of corn by the open fire. I think he made himself very entertaining to them. Emerson was talking to me, and I was only conscious of Thoreau's presence as we are of those about us but not engaged with us. A very pretty picture remains in my memory of Thoreau leaning over the fire with a fair girl on either side, which somehow did not comport with the subsequent story I heard of his being a hermit. Parched corn had for him a fascination beyond the prospect of something to eat. He says in one of his books that some dishes recommend themselves to our imaginations as well as palates. . . .

I never saw Thoreau again until I heard him in Boston Music Hall deliver his impassioned eulogy on John Brown. Meantime the "Week on the Concord and Merrimac Rivers" had become one of my favorite books; and I have atoned for my youthful and untimely want of recognition by bringing from my ocean beach a smooth pebble to his cairn at Walden. . . .

In the conversation of an afternoon and evening it is impossible to relate all that was said; one thinks he never shall forget a word of such a memorable day; but at length it becomes overlaid in the chambers of the memory and only reappears when uncalled for. I find set down in my diary of the day two or three things which a thousand observers have remarked: that Emerson spoke in a mild, peculiar manner, justifying the text of Thoreau, that you must be calm before you can utter oracles; that he often hesitated for a word, but it was the right one he waited for; that he sometimes expressed himself mystically, and like a book. This meant, I suppose, that the style and subjects were novel to me, being then only used to the slang of schoolboys and the magisterial manner of pedagogues. He seldom looked the person addressed in the eye, and rarely put direct questions. I fancy this was a part of his extreme delicacy of manner.

As soon as I could I introduced the problem I came to propound—what course a young man must take to get the best kind of education. Emerson pleaded always for the college; said he himself entered at fourteen. This aroused the wrath of Thoreau, who would not allow any good to the college course. And here it seemed to me Emerson said things on purpose to draw Thoreau's fire and to amuse himself. When the curriculum at Cambridge was alluded to, and Emerson casually remarked that most of the branches were taught there, Thoreau seized one of his opportunities and replied: "Yes, indeed, all the branches and none of the roots." At this Emerson laughed heartily. So without conclusions, or more light than the assertions of two representative men can give, I heard agitated for an hour my momentous question. . . .

I found myself involuntarily coinciding with Emerson's views rather than Thoreau's whimsical opinions. Yet Thoreau had been to college; but at some strange epoch in his life he had broken with his past and many of the traditions and conventions of his contemporaries. He had resolved to live according to Nature; and had the usual desire to publish the fact and explain the proceeding. It had never, however, the tone of apology; and it is our good fortune that he was not too singularly great to feel the need of communicating himself to his kind. Never has any writer so identified himself with Nature and so constantly used it as the symbol of his interior life. It is sometimes difficult to distinguish Thoreau from his companions, the woods, the woodchucks, and muskrats, the birds, the pond and the river. An inspired prescience foretold where to find the flower he wanted, and how to lure the little Musketaquid perch to his hand. Rare plants bloomed when he arrived at their secret hiding-places as if they had made an appointment with him; and the birds knew their lover's old cap and never mistook his telescope for a gun. In his intercourse with nature his pilot was some prophetic thought which led him by sure instinct to its sympathetic analogon in nature. It was natural, therefore, that to such a man systems of education should seem hindrances; they interposed another's will across the track of one's native intuitions. To shake off such substitutes with all their baggage was his prime intention. . . .

He [Emerson] said we needed some great poets, orators. He was always looking out for them, and was sure the new generation of young men would contain some. Thoreau here remarked he had found one, in the woods, but it had feathers and had not been to Harvard College. Still it had a voice and an aerial inclination, which was pretty much all that was needed. "Let us cage it," said Emerson. "That is just the way the world always spoils its poets," responded Thoreau. Then Thoreau, as usual, had the last word; there was a laugh, in which for the first time he joined heartily, as the perquisite of the victor. Then we went in to tea in right good humor.

John Albee, *Remembrances of Emerson* (New York: Robert G. Cooke, 1901), 18–22, 24–25, 31–32.

[Memories of Thoreau, 1857 and 1860]

Ellen Tucker Emerson

Ellen Tucker Emerson (1839–1909) was the elder daughter of Ralph Waldo and Lidian Emerson. Like her siblings, she prized Thoreau's visits and games as well as his prowess in leading "huckleberryings" and other outdoor excursions (Ellen Tucker Emerson, *Life*, 107). Her letters to Waldo and Edward Emerson offer a sample of life in the Emerson household during Thoreau's visits. Thoreau's own fondness for Ellen is reflected in a letter he sent to ten-year-old Ellen when she was vacationing in New York. Updating her on Concord and family news, Thoreau described her brother's new fishing pole, her sister's berry-picking, and related that "the white-lillies are in blossom, and the john'swort and goldenrod are beginning to come out" before closing with the advice that Ellen "must see the sun rise out of the ocean before you come home." Two years before, he had written to Waldo Emerson that he and Ellen "have a good understanding—I appreciate her genuineness" (*Correspondence*, 245–46, 199).

To Ralph Waldo Emerson, 17 January 1857

Mr Thoreau has been here twice this week, once to dinner and once to tea. He went to have his Ambrotype taken to-day and such a shocking, spectral, spectral, black and white picture as Eddy brought home in triumph was never seen. I am to carry it back and poor Mr Thoreau has got to go again. . . .

To Ralph Waldo Emerson, 22 January 1857

Mr Thoreau was here night before last and Eddy illuminated his snow cave and called out to us; we couldn't hear what he said though we were close at the mouth of the cave and Mr Thoreau said "Speak louder" so Eddy spoke again and we could hear some very feeble words. Then Mr Thoreau told him to holla as loud as he could, but we heard only very weak squeaks. Then Mr Thoreau was very surprised, as he said he could hardly believe Eddy was calling loud, and he went in himself and shouted and it sounded as if someone was in trouble over the brook near Mr Stow's. And Edie went in and peeped and that sounded very feeble. Mr Thoreau thought that the snow sucked up the sound. Then he said he should like to see how transparent snow was, and we dug into the snow-drift a hole with one side 4 inches thick and one 14 and about 6 inches from the top, then we put the lamp in and walled it up with a block of snow eight inches thick, through the four inches one could see to read, through the fourteen the lamp shone bright and shining like a lantern—a Norwegian would think it was a Troll-mount. Mr Thoreau was quite delighted and so we all were with our experiments. We tried to wall up the lamp air tight, but in spite of thick walls it burned bright. . . .

To Edward Emerson, 11 August 1860

Here at home the greatest event of the week was Mr Thoreau's arrival last night for he was extremely interesting on the subject of Monadnoc so that we all wanted to set off directly and go there, taking him for guide. All tea-time Mr Thoreau told most wonderful stories of the rocks etc. that were to be seen there, and of the profusion of berries. Then after tea I went out to see about the milk, and coming back, found Father and Milcah in full pursuit of something, nobody knew what, which seemed to rustle inside the chimney, or behind the closet-door, but couldn't be found to the surprise of everybody and the extreme excitement of Milcah. Presently it began again louder than ever, just as I came to the mantle-piece and I was sure it was behind the "School of Philosophers," which I lifted and there was a bat. Mr Thoreau was immediately anxious to see it, and everybody came round but Bat began to fly round in circles and all watched him. At last, Mr T. caught him and he began to grin and chatter and gnash his teeth with rage, and Mother said "There, Batty, you shall have something to bite if it will make you feel better, I'm sure," and presented her little finger which didn't seem to satisfy him particularly, but at last he did bite it and hurt a little. He was then confined under a glass-dish and Mr Thoreau got the Report on such creatures and identified him as a "hoary bat," and he was afterwards liberated. The Family went into the parlour and Mr Thoreau proceeded to tell us more about the Mountain, till we were all on fire to go. . . .

To Edward Emerson, 1 July 1862

Father is constantly engaged now in writing and reading about Mr Thoreau and you had better keep a mem[o] of what you will ask for when you get home, and put down on it Mr Channing's quotations from Mr Thoreau's journal. They are very nice and Father likes to read them. One of them Father considers a question for a game party. "Some circumstantial evidence is very strong, as when you find a trout in the milk." Father wanted I should ask the gameparty what that proved. I saw the moment I heard it and considered it so self evident as to be not worth mentioning, and long afterward Mother said "Or a mouse." Then I explained to her that wasn't the same thing, that it meant the milk was watered. Whereupon Father said he hadn't thought of that before, of course that was right. I was amazed that he shouldn't have seen it, but on trying the experiment I find that very few people do. . . .[1]

Note

1. Although Ellen Emerson is one of the earliest to appreciate Thoreau's reference to "a trout in the milk," it was perhaps most famously cited by Sherlock Holmes in "The Adventures of the Noble Bachelor": "Circumstantial evidence is occasionally very convincing, as when you find a trout in the milk, to quote Thoreau's example" (A. Conan Doyle, *The Adventures of Sherlock Holmes* [London: George Newnes, 1892], 248).

Ellen Tucker Emerson, *The Letters of Ellen Tucker Emerson,* 2 vols., ed. Edith E. W. Gregg (Kent, OH: Kent State University Press, 1982), 1:125, 127–28, 216–17, 274.

[Childhood with Thoreau,
as Remembered in 1882]

[EDITH EMERSON FORBES]

Edith Emerson Forbes (1841–1929) was the younger of Waldo and Lidian Emerson's two daughters. She married William Hathaway Forbes in 1865. Despite a breach in her family's friendship with Franklin Benjamin Sanborn after she rejected his marriage proposal in 1861, Forbes responded to his request for her memories of Thoreau by sending this reminiscence, which Sanborn included in his 1882 biography, *Henry D. Thoreau*. Like her brother, Edward, and sister, Ellen, Edith Forbes fondly recalls Thoreau's paternal steadiness in her life, particularly the warmth of domestic scenes that took place during Thoreau's lengthy stays with her family in the 1840s as well as his regular evening visits. Her mother's correspondence amplifies these memories: "Edith is looking most beautifully as she dances with Henry [Thoreau] or lays her innocent head on his music box that she may drink yet deeper of its sweetness. . . . [T]he cherub face appears above the screen for Uncle Henry takes care that Edie shall take as high flights in Papa's absence as ever—she rides on his shoulder or is held high up in the air—I think he adds to her happiness, and she no less to his" (Lidian Jackson Emerson, *Selected Letters*, 121–22). Pointedly, all three Emerson children specifically cherish Thoreau as huckleberry party orchestrator par excellence, countering their father's trivializing of this role in his eulogy of Thoreau.

"THE TIME WHEN Mr. Thoreau was our more intimate playfellow must have been in the years from 1850 to 1855. He used to come in, at dusk, as my brother and I sat on the rug before the dining-room fire, and, taking the great green rocking-chair, he would tell us stories. Those I remember were his own adventures, as a child. He began with telling us of the different houses he had lived in, and what he could remember about each. The house where he was born was on the Virginia road, near the old Bedford road. The only thing he remembered about that house was that from its windows he saw a flock of geese walking along in a row on the other side of the road; but to show what a long memory he had, when he told his mother of this, she said the only time he could have seen that sight was, when he was about eight months old, for they left that house then. Soon after, he lived in the old house on the Lexington road, nearly opposite Mr. Emerson's. There he was tossed by a cow as he played near the door, in his red flannel dress,—and so on, with a story for every house. He used to delight us with the adventures of a brood of fall chickens, which slept at night in a tall old fashioned fig-drum in the kitchen, and as their bed was not changed when they grew larger, they packed themselves every night each in its own place, and grew up, not shapely, but shaped to each other and the drum, like figs!

"Sometimes he would play juggler tricks for us, and swallow his knife and produce it again from our ears or noses. We usually ran to bring some apples for him as soon as he came in, and often he would cut one in halves in fine points that scarcely showed on close examination, and then the joke was to ask Father to break it for us and see it fall to pieces in his hands. But perhaps the evenings most charming were those when he brought some ears of pop-corn in his pocket and headed an expedition to the garret to hunt out the old brass warming-pan; in which he would put the corn, and hold it out and shake it over the fire till it was heated through, and at last, as we listened, the rattling changed to popping. When this became very brisk, he would hold the pan over the rug and lift the lid, and a beautiful fountain of the white corn flew all over us. It required both strength and patience to hold out the heavy warming-pan at arm's length so long, and no one else ever gave us that pleasure.

"I remember his singing 'Tom Bowline' to us, and also playing on his flute, but that was earlier. In the summer he used to make willow whistles, and trumpets out of the stems of squash leaves, and onion leaves. When he found fine berries during his walks, he always remembered us, and came to arrange a huckleberrying for us. He took charge of the 'hay rigging' with the load of children, who sat on the floor which was spread with hay, covered with a buffalo-robe; he sat on a board placed across the front and drove, and led the frolic with his jokes and laughter as we jolted along, while the elders of the family accompanied us in a 'carryall.' Either he had great tact and skill in managing us and keeping our spirits and play within bounds, or else he became a child in sympathy with us, for I do not remember a check or reproof from him, no matter how noisy we were. He always was most kind to me and made it his especial care to establish me in the 'thickest places,' as we used to call them. Those sunny afternoons are bright memories, and the lamb-kill flowers and sweet 'everlasting,' always recall them and his kind care. Once in awhile he took us on the river in his boat, a rare pleasure then; and I remember one brilliant autumn afternoon, when he took us to gather the wild grapes overhanging the river, and we brought home a load of crimson and golden boughs as well. He never took us to walk with him, but sometimes joined us for a little way, if he met us in the woods on Sunday afternoons. He made those few steps memorable by showing us many wonders in so short a space: perhaps the only chincapin oak in Concord, so hidden that no one but himself could have discovered it—or some remarkable bird, or nest, or flower. He took great interest in my garden of wild flowers, and used to bring me seeds, or roots, of rare plants. In his last illness it did not occur to us that he would care to see us, but his sister told my mother that he watched us from the window as we passed, and said: 'Why don't they come to see me? I love them as if they were my own.' After that we went often, and he always made us so welcome that we liked to go. I remember our last meetings with as much pleasure as the old play-days."

Edith Emerson Forbes, qtd. in F. B. Sanborn, *Henry D. Thoreau* (Boston: Houghton, Mifflin, 1882), 270–73.

[Considerations of Thoreau's Death, 1862]

Sophia E. Thoreau, Caroline Wells Healey Dall, Sophia Peabody Hawthorne, and Sarah Alden Bradford Ripley

Thoreau's death on 6 May 1862 inspired poignant letters by activist and author Caroline Wells Healey Dall (1822–1912), artist and neighbor Sophia Peabody Hawthorne (1809–1871), friend and neighbor Sarah Alden Bradford Ripley (1793–1867), and Sophia Elizabeth Thoreau (1819–1876), the youngest of the four Thoreau children and the only sibling to outlive Henry.

A teacher and an abolitionist, Sophia Thoreau shared her brother's interests in social reform and in natural history. Together, they collected botanical specimens, which she carefully identified and preserved in scrapbooks. Author Irving Allen describes Sophia as sharing with her brother "a certain weight and gravity of thought and utterance"; he calls attention especially to sister and brother as "pre-eminent and sincere *reformers* in an era and an atmosphere where reformers were radical by a sort of necessity of environment" ("American Women to Whom the World Is Indebted," 988). No one was more adamant and resolute in preserving her brother's reputation than Sophia Thoreau. Her careful assistance in the months immediately preceding his death allowed Henry Thoreau to compile and prepare several natural history articles for posthumous publication in the *Atlantic Monthly*. With Waldo Emerson and Ellery Channing, Sophia coedited a number of Henry's unpublished letters and other manuscripts, including *The Maine Woods* and *Cape Cod*. Her letter below to Henry's close friend Daniel Ricketson draws attention to her brother's ability during his final days to keep his mind alive as well as to appreciate the comfort offered at this time by friends and neighbors.

To Daniel Ricketson, 20 May 1862

Profound joy mingles with my grief. I feel as if something very beautiful had happened, not death; although Henry is with us no longer, yet the memory of his sweet and virtuous soul must ever cheer and comfort me. My heart is filled with praise to God for the gift of such a brother, and may I never distrust the love and wisdom of Him who made him, and who has now called him to labor in more glorious fields than earth affords.

You ask for some particulars relating to Henry's illness. I feel like saying that Henry was never affected, never reached by it. I never before saw such a manifestation of the power of spirit over matter. Very often I have heard him tell his visitors that he enjoyed existence as well as ever. He remarked to me that there was as much comfort in perfect disease as in perfect health, the mind always conforming to the condition of the body. The thought of death, he said, could not begin to trouble him. His thoughts had entertained him all his life, and did still.

When he had wakeful nights, he would ask me to arrange the furniture so as to make fantastic shadows on the wall, and he wished his bed was in the form of a shell, that he might curl up in it. He considered occupation as necessary for the sick as for those in health, and has accomplished a vast amount of labor during the past few months in preparing some papers for the press. He did not cease to call for his manuscripts till the last day of his life.

During his long illness I never heard a murmur escape him, or the slightest wish expressed to remain with us; his perfect contentment was truly wonderful. None of his friends seemed to realize how very ill he was, so full of life and good cheer did he seem. One friend, as if by way of consolation, said to him, "Well, Mr. Thoreau, we must all go." Henry replied, "When I was a very little boy I learned that I must die, and I set that down, so of course I am not disappointed now. Death is as near to you as it is to me."

There is very much that I should like to write you about my precious brother, had I time and strength. I wish you to know how very gentle, lovely, and submissive he was in all his ways. His little study bed was brought down into our front parlor, when he could no longer walk with our assistance, and every arrangement pleased him. The devotion of his friends was most rare and touching; his room was made fragrant by the gift of flowers from young and old; fruit of every kind which the season afforded, and game of all sorts was sent him. It was really pathetic, the way in which the town was moved to minister to his comfort. Total strangers sent grateful messages, remembering the good he had done them. All this attention was fully appreciated and very gratifying to Henry; he would sometimes say,

"I should be ashamed to stay in this world after so much had been done for me, I could never repay my friends." And they so remembered him to the last. Only about two hours before he left us, Judge Hoar called with a bouquet of hyacinths fresh from his garden, which Henry smelled and said he liked, and a few minutes after he was gone, another friend came with a dish of his favorite jelly.

I can never be grateful enough for the gentle, easy exit which was granted him. At seven o'clock Tuesday morning he became restless and desired to be moved; dear mother, Aunt Louisa, and myself were with him; his self-possession did not forsake him. A little after eight he asked to be raised quite up, his breathing grew fainter and fainter, and without the slightest struggle, he left us at nine o'clock. . . .

> Caroline Wells Healey Dall was an author, a critic, an abolitionist, and a women's rights activist whose husband, Charles Henry Appleton Dall, was a Harvard classmate of Henry Thoreau. In her few journal comments about Thoreau, Dall offers a mixed reaction to his lectures and writings. She enjoyed "the descriptions of Nature" in *A Week* but echoed other critics in sensing that "the excursions into spirit . . . seem blasphemous." After reading *Walden*, Dall "tire[d] of Thoreau" and "doubt[ed] whether the world will be the better for the book" (*Selected Journals*, 286, 284). After hearing Thoreau deliver "Autumnal Tints" in Worcester in 1859, she enjoyed this "very charming report, but I did not carry away a very high idea of Thoreau himself." Given her own radical abolitionism, Dall's response to "A Plea for Captain John Brown" is curious. Despite being "on the whole a grand tribute to the truest American who has lived since George Washington," she judged portions of the speech itself "in very bad taste." A few weeks later, Thoreau enjoyed Dall's own lecture in Concord on "Lives of Noted Women," a positive reaction that for some reason surprised Dall (*Daughter of Boston*, 273, 286, 290). Notorious for biting and acerbic rebukes (Deese, "Introduction," xvii), Dall's characterization here of Thoreau's tongue as "a Damascus blade" is nicely ironic.

To Sophia Thoreau, 26 July 1862

Ever since Mr Thoreau's death, I have been hoping to come to Concord and express to you, with my own lips, the sympathy I felt. But circumstances beyond my control compel me however reluctantly to resign the hope.

I cannot let you think any longer that of all those who loved him I alone am silent. I know very well that no words of mine can do him honor. Those whom he loved have already borne away the sacred bier, and covered the worn out garment, beautiful because it had been his, with flowers—yet one word let me say. The idiosyncrasies of men, are their, and our—best possession. Thoreau alone seems to have fully felt this and did not disguise what was given him. *Many* have accepted him as a naturalist and praised his Walden Water. It is pleasant to *me* to remember him, as he stood by his own hearth—beloved of his mother and sister—and to record this once my estimate of his conversational power.

I have not met him often, but those times I shall never forget. I could never be a half hour in his company, without *hearing* what I could never forget. His tongue, like a Damascus blade, was hardly fit for ordinary use, but it shaped or severed at a blow—the substances which most weapons—do only *tear*.

No thinking would improve the words it wielded.

Remember me tenderly to your mother and believe you will always, for his sake as your own, be held in the sacred regard of your friend.

Artist Sophia Peabody Hawthorne married Nathaniel Hawthorne in July 1842, and moved with him to Concord, Massachusetts, where they lived until 1846, in 1852–3, and from 1860 until their deaths. Sophia's vivid rendering of the Concord authors ice-skating on the Concord River casts the nimble Thoreau and the gangling Emerson alongside her classically beautiful, if nearly inert, husband: "Henry Thoreau is an experienced skater, and was figuring dithyrambic dances and Bacchic leaps on the ice—very remarkable, but very ugly, methought. Next him followed Mr. Hawthorne, who, wrapped in his cloak, moved like a self-impelled Greek statue, stately and grave. Mr. Emerson closed the line, evidently too weary to hold himself erect, pitching head-foremost, half lying on the air" (qtd. in Lathrop, 53).

Sophia had found Thoreau "very interesting" (57) when they knew each other in Concord; when he lectured in Salem in 1848 at Nathaniel's invitation, she was charmed with both his lecture on "Student Life, in New England" and what seemed (to her) his transformation: "Mr. Thoreau has risen above all his arrogance of manner, and is as gentle, simple, ruddy, and meek as all geniuses should be; and now his great blue eyes fairly outshine, and put into shade a nose which I once thought must make him uncomely forever. His lecture was so enchanting,—such a revelation of nature in all its exquisite detail of wood-thrushes, squirrels, sunshine, mists, and shadows, fresh vernal odors, pine-tree ocean melodies,—that my ears rang with music, and I seemed to have been wandering through copse and dingle" (qtd. in

Sanborn, "Hawthorne and His Friends," 10). In these brief excerpts from letters to close friend Annie Fields, wife of Thoreau's publisher James T. Fields,
Sophia Hawthorne captures the essence of Thoreau's legacy, not only to her
personally, but to Concord itself.

To Annie Adams Fields, 7 May [1862]

On Friday also Mr Thoreau's funeral is to take place. He was Concord itself in one man—and his death makes a very large vacuum. I ought to be at
his funeral—for the sake of showing my deep respect and value for him to
others, though I could much better mourn him at home. . . .

To Annie Adams Fields [May 1862]

I suppose he [Thoreau] believed that beasts and reptiles, birds and fishes
fulfilled their ends, and that man generally came short. So he respected the
one and avoided the other. His alpine purity, his diamond truth, his stainless sincerity, his closeness to nature and faithful rendering—these are immortal beauties in him. He has now stepped out of his French body—and
his soul has taken up its fitting celestial manifestation. And he has doubtless found the Victoria Regia, which *would not* grow wild in Concord, even
though it were the birth place of Henry Thoreau! and though he declared
he should one day find it here. . . .

> The brilliant scholar Sarah Alden Bradford Ripley was Waldo Emerson's aunt
> and a friend of the Thoreau family, especially in the years after she and her
> husband, Samuel Ripley, moved back to his native Concord in 1846 to take
> up residence in the family home at the Old Manse. Sarah Ripley shared with
> Thoreau an abiding interest in natural history; he particularly enjoyed exam-
> ining her lichen collection and discussing works of natural history with her,
> including Darwin's *Origin of Species.*

To Sophia Thayer, [1862]

I went to call on Mr Thoreau yesterday for the first time since his sickness.
I was much moved at first to see him so changed, so wasted and feeble. But
he talked cheerfully about what the earliest Phylosopher had said about
health, and natural remedies. He was sitting in a large parlour, handsomely
furnished, the windows filled with flowers; himself in a handsome suit of
black clothes sitting in an easy chair, I do not think I should have recog-

nized him if I had fallen on him unawares. How much he has trusted to his life according to the natural laws. . . .

To Sophia Thayer, [6 May 1862]

This fine morning is sad for those of us who sympathize with the friends of Henry Thoreau the philosopher, and the woodman. He had his reason to the last and talked with his friends pleasantly and arranged his affairs; and at last passed in quiet sleep from this state of duty and responsibility to that which is behind the veil. His funeral service is to be at the church and Mr Emerson is to make an address. . . .

To [Cynthia] Thoreau, 20 May [1862]

I received last evening the token of remembrance from the Friend and the Philosopher, with a mingled feeling of sorrow and gratitude. What a loss to Concord! What a loss still greater to all who knew him intimately! But he has left many a relic in which he will reappear to those who understood and loved him. The books will be invaluable to me. . . .

Sophia E. Thoreau to Daniel Ricketson, qtd. in *Daniel Ricketson and His Friends: Letters Poems Sketches Etc.,* ed. Anna and Walton Ricketson (Boston: Houghton, Mifflin, 1902), 141–43.

Caroline H. Dall to Sophia E. Thoreau, 26 July 1862, Thoreau-Sewall Papers, Scrapbook HM 64967 (HT-25), Huntington Library, San Marino, CA.

Sophia Peabody Hawthorne to Annie Adams Fields, 7 May [1862] and [May 1862], Ms.C.1.11 (20 and 21), Rare Books and Manuscripts, Boston Public Library.

Sarah Alden Bradford Ripley to Sophia Thayer, [1862] and [6 May 1862], Sarah Alden Ripley Papers, MC180, folder 10, Schlesinger Library, Radcliffe Institute for Advanced Study, Harvard University. Sarah Alden Bradford Ripley to [Cynthia] Thoreau, 20 May [1862], Thoreau Family Correspondence, Vault A45, Thoreau, Unit 3, Special Collections, Concord Free Public Library, Concord, MA.

"Notice of the Death of Mr. Thoreau" (1862)

[Charles T. Jackson]

> Dr. Charles Thomas Jackson (1805–1880), brother of Lidian Jackson Emerson, was a physician and chemist who for many years served as an officer of the Boston Society of Natural History. In 1850, Thoreau became a corresponding member of the Society, which regularly acknowledged in its annual proceedings his donation of specimens and collections. Here, Jackson affirms the importance of Thoreau's studies and contributions to the organization.

HENRY D. THOREAU was distinguished for the great accuracy of his observations, and for the thoroughness with which he executed every research upon which he entered. He was esteemed as an accurate land surveyor, the only business upon which he ever entered for pay. As a botanist he was highly esteemed by those who are the best judges of the subject.

As an observer of the habits of animals he was unrivalled. He would wait all day, if it was necessary, for a bird to approach him. He said their curiosity would bring them to examine him if he would remain quiet long enough; and he generally managed to make familiar acquaintance with all living creatures he met with in his rambles through the forest. Thoreau had a genuine love of nature, and pursued natural history for his own gratification, and not with any ambitious views. He was greatly troubled to find that anything had escaped the observation of eminent naturalists, and seemed to be surprised that anything should have been left by them for him to discover.

Thoreau was a man of original genius, and very peculiar in his views of society and the ways of life. He was conscientiously scrupulous, and was opposed to aiding or abetting, even by a poll-tax, measures which he did not approve of, and therefore got into trouble occasionally with the constituted authorities of the town, who could not indulge him in his opposition to a tax because any part of it might go to support the militia; so they twice shut him up in the jail, from whence his friends took him by paying his tax against his protest.[1]

His published works are full of knowledge of the secrets of nature, and are enlivened by much quaint humor, and warmed with kindness towards all living beings. Those who knew Thoreau best loved and appreciated him most.

Dr. Jackson proposed the following resolutions, which were adopted:—

Resolved, That the Boston Society of Natural History has learned with profound regret the premature decease of their corresponding member, Henry D. Thoreau, of Concord, who was a most faithful and devoted student of nature, a keen and appreciating observer, whose researches, had longer life been granted him, promised important acquisitions to science.

Resolved, That a copy of this resolution be transmitted to the mother and sister of this eminent naturalist, with expressions of the warm sympathy of this Society in their great loss.

Dr. Jackson announced the donation of Mr. Thoreau's collections to the Society. These consisted of:

1. His collection of New England pressed plants, numbering more than one thousand species, arranged by himself, together with those western plants collected in his journey of 1861.
2. His collection of birds' eggs and nests, carefully identified by himself, composed of New England species.
3. The collection of Indian antiquities, consisting of stone implements and weapons (chiefly) found by himself in Concord.

Note

1. Jackson is mistaken; Thoreau spent only one night in jail, in late July 1846.

[Charles T. Jackson], *Proceedings of the Boston Society of Natural History* 9 (1865): 71–72.

"Thoreau's Flute" (1863)

[Louisa May Alcott]

The second of Bronson and Abigail Alcott's four daughters, Louisa May Alcott (1832–1888) was one of several Concord youngsters who adored Thoreau, whom she called her "wood god" for his stories, and as forest and river guide ("In Memoriam"). As a successful author, Alcott venerated Thoreau in her writings. In the poem below, he appears as a "savior" who will never truly die. Yet Alcott's use of him as the model for Adam Warwick in her 1864 novel, *Moods*, also demonstrates her adult understanding of Thoreau as a complex, romantic, and sympathetic figure. Following the *Atlantic Monthly*'s practice at the time, "Thoreau's Flute" was published without attribution, leading to a humorous incident in which Henry Wadsworth Longfellow mistakenly assumed that Waldo Emerson had written the poem. He eagerly brought out the magazine to show it to Louisa's father, Bronson Alcott, during a visit. Naturally, Bronson relished the opportunity to set Longfellow straight as to the author's true identity. Nan Cooke Carpenter provides the details for the neighborly collaboration that led to the poem's publication. Louisa's mother had first shared it with next-door neighbor Sophia Hawthorne, who sent it on to her friend Annie Adams Fields, wife of *Atlantic Monthly* editor James T. Fields. Before giving the poem to her husband to read, however, Annie Fields suggested two revisions to stanza one to improve the rhyme scheme, which Louisa promptly made. Originally, "Spring mourns as for untimely frost" read "Spring came to us in guise forlorn," and "The Genius of the wood is lost" had been "The genius of the wood is gone" (71–73). "Thoreau's Flute" was reprinted in various newspapers in 1863, including the *Boston Transcript* and the *Liberator*. In 1889, it also appeared in *A Library of American Literature*.

We, sighing, said, "Our Pan is dead;
   His pipe hangs mute beside the river;—
   Around it wistful sunbeams quiver,
But Music's airy voice is fled.
Spring mourns as for untimely frost;
   The bluebird chants a requiem;

The willow-blossom waits for him;—
The Genius of the wood is lost."

Then from the flute, untouched by hands,
    There came a low, harmonious breath:
    "For such as he there is no death;—
His life the eternal life commands;
Above man's aims his nature rose:
    The wisdom of a just content
    Made one small spot a continent,
And tuned to poetry Life's prose.

"Haunting the hills, the stream, the wild,
    Swallow and aster, lake and pine,
    To him grew human or divine,—
Fit mates for this large-hearted child.
Such homage Nature ne'er forgets,
    And yearly on the coverlid
    'Neath which her darling lieth hid
Will write his name in violets.

"To him no vain regrets belong,
    Whose soul, that finer instrument,
    Gave to the world no poor lament,
But wood-notes ever sweet and strong.
O lonely friend! he still will be
    A potent presence, though unseen,—
    Steadfast, sagacious, and serene:
Seek not for him,—he is with thee."

[Louisa May Alcott], "Thoreau's Flute," *Atlantic Monthly* 12 (September 1863): 280–81.

From "Thoreau" (1865)

[John Weiss]

John Weiss (1818–1879) was a Harvard classmate of Thoreau. A Unitarian minister, he was also an abolitionist and an author whose *Life and Correspondence of Theodore Parker* (1864) was the first biography of the famed Transcendentalist. As someone who knew Thoreau most of his life but wasn't a close friend, Weiss provides a critical look at the young college student, the fledgling writer, and the mature thinker. His rebuke of Waldo Emerson for decrying Thoreau's lack of ambition in his funeral eulogy stands as an early public corrective. Weiss excuses Thoreau's solitary habits as a college student as evidence that "he was already living on some Walden Pond, where he had run up a temporary shanty in the depths of his reserve." Weiss refers below to Thoreau's non-participation in the "Dunkin Rebellion," a student melee that took place at Harvard in 1834. His extended commentary on Thoreau's spirituality reflects an unusual tolerance, even from a liberal clergyman, and he weighs in on a continuing controversy in Thoreau studies: the extent to which he can be claimed as a religious thinker. In this article also appears Weiss's familiar avowal that Thoreau "saw more upon the ground than anybody suspected to be there."

UPON THE TABLET which friendship and delicate appreciation have raised to exhibit their record of Thoreau's genius, there is still space where a classmate's pen may leave some slight impressions, without claiming either advantage or authority to do so beyond a late but ever-deepening regard. This bids the thoughts return and drop themselves for holding-ground into some recollections of his collegiate career.

He would smile to overhear that word applied to the reserve and unaptness of his college life. He was not signalized by a plentiful distribution of the parts and honors which fall to the successful student. . . . We could sympathize with his tranquil indifference to college honors, but we did not suspect the fine genius that was developing under that impassive demeanor. Of his private tastes there is little of consequence to recall, excepting that he was devoted to the old English literature, and had a good many volumes of the poetry from Gower and Chaucer down through the era of Elizabeth. In this mine he worked with a quiet enthusiasm, diverting to it hours that should have sparkled with emulation in the divisions where other genius stood that never lived, like his, to ripen. . . .

We owe to those studies not named in the programme, the commencement of a quaint and simple style, and a flavor of old thinking, which appears through all the works of Thoreau. His earliest masters were thus the least artificial of the minds which have drawn from the well of undefiled English. And the phrase "mother-tongue" was cherished by him, and gained his early homage. He did not care for the modern languages; nor was he ever seriously attracted, by the literature which they express, to lay aside his English worthies. His mind was in native harmony with them, and it sometimes produces modern speculation in sentences and fragments of speech and turns of phrase that make you wonder if old Sir Thomas Brown, or Owen Feltham, or Norris, were lodging for awhile with him in their progress upon some transmigrating tour. We wonder if he alludes to the University when he says that he has *heard* of "a Society for the Diffusion of Useful Knowledge." Heard of it, but not personally acquainted with it. For, though he was careful not to miss a recitation, it is plain that he was not present at it, but was already like the man he mentions, who, "in some spring of his life, saunters abroad into the Great Fields of thought, goes to grass like a horse, and leaves all his harness behind in the stable. I would say to the Society for the Diffusion of Useful Knowledge, sometimes,—Go to grass." So many of us said most fervently, but not because we had attached ourselves to his shyness in order to saunter with him into the Great Fields of thought, where "a man's ignorance sometimes is not only useful, but beautiful."

But he passed for nothing, it is suspected, with most of us; for he was cold and unimpressible. The touch of his hand was moist and indifferent, as if he had taken up something when he saw your hand coming, and caught your grasp upon it. How the prominent, gray-blue eyes seemed to rove down the path, just in advance of his feet, as his grave Indian stride carried him down to University Hall! This down-looking habit was Chaucer's also, who walked as if a great deal of surmising went on between the earth and him. . . . But Chaucer's heart sent brisk blood to and fro beneath that modest look, and his poetry is more teeming with the nature of men and women than with that of the air and earth. Thoreau was nourished by its simplicity, but not fanned by its passion. He was colder, but more resolute, and would have gone to prison and starvation for the sake of his opinions, where Chaucer weakly compromised to preserve freedom and comfort. The vivid human life in the Elizabethan writers did not wake a corresponding genius in Thoreau: he seemed to be feeding only upon their raciness and Saxon vigor, upon the clearly phrased and unaffected sentiment. The rest of the leaf never bore the marks of any hunger.

He did not care for people; his classmates seemed very remote. This reverie hung always about him, and not so loosely as the odd garments which the pious household care furnished. Thought had not yet awakened his countenance; it was serene, but rather dull, rather plodding. The lips were not yet firm; there was almost a look of smug satisfaction lurking round their corners. It is plain now that he was preparing to hold his future views with great setness, and personal appreciation of their importance. The nose was prominent, but its curve fell forward without firmness over the upper lip; and we remember him as looking very much like some Egyptian sculptures of faces, large-featured, but brooding, immobile, fixed in a mystic egotism. Yet his eyes were sometimes searching, as if he had dropped, or expected to find, something. It was the look of Nature's own child learning to detect her wayside secrets; and those eyes have stocked his books with subtle traits of animate and inanimate creation which had escaped less patient observers. For he saw more upon the ground than anybody suspected to be there. His eyes slipped into every tuft of meadow or beach grass, and went winding in and out of the thickest undergrowth, like some slim, silent, cunning animal. They were amphibious besides, and slid under fishes' eggs and into their nests at the pond's bottom, to rifle all their contents. Mr. Emerson has noticed, that Thoreau could always find an Indian arrowhead in places that had been ploughed over and ransacked for years. "There is one," he would say, kicking it up with his foot. In fact, his eyes seldom left the ground, even in his most earnest conversation with you, if you can call earnest a tone and manner that was very confident, as of an opinion that had formed from granitic sediment, but also very level and unflushed with feeling. The Sphinx might have become passionate and exalted as soon.

In later years his chin and mouth grew firmer as his resolute and audacious opinions developed, the curves of the lips lost their flabbiness, the eyes twinkled with the latent humor of his criticisms of society. Still the countenance was unruffled: it seemed to lie deep, like a mountain tarn, with cool, still nature all around. There was not a line upon it expressive of ambition or discontent: the affectional emotions had never fretted at it. He went about, like a priest of Buddha who expects to arrive soon at the summit of a life of contemplation, where the divine absorbs the human. All his intellectual activity was of the spontaneous, open-air kind, which keeps the forehead smooth. His thoughts grew with all the rest of nature, and passively took their chance of summer and winter, pause and germination: no more forced than pine-cones; fragrant, but not perfumed, owing nothing to special efforts of art. His extremest and most grotesque opinion had never been under glass. It all grew like the bolls on forest-trees, and the deviations from stem-like or sweeping forms. No man was ever such a placid thinker. It was because his thinking was observation isolated from all the temptations of society, from the artificial exigencies of literature, from the conventional sequence. Its truthfulness was not logically attained, but insensibly imbibed, during wood-chopping, fishing, and scenting through the woods and fields. So that the smoothness and plumpness of a child were spread over his deepest places.

His simple life, so free from the vexations that belong to the most ordinary provision for the day, and from the wear and tear of habits helped his countenance to preserve this complacency. He had instincts, but no habits; and they wore him no more than they do the beaver and the blue-jay. Among them we include his rare intuitive sensibility for moral truth and for the fitness of things. For, although he lived so closely to the ground, he could still say, "My desire for knowledge is intermittent; but my desire to bathe my head in atmospheres unknown to my feet is perennial and constant. The highest that we can attain to it is not knowledge, but sympathy with intelligence." But this intuition came up, like grass in spring, with no effort that is traceable, or that registers itself anywhere except in the things grown. You would look in vain for the age of his thoughts upon his face.

Now, it is no wonder that he kept himself aloof from us in college; for he was already living on some Walden Pond, where he had run up a temporary shanty in the depths of his reserve. He built it better afterwards, but no nearer to men. Did anybody ever tempt him down to Snow's, with the offer of an unlimited molluscous entertainment? The naturalist was not yet enough awakened to lead him to ruin a midnight stomach for the sake of the constitution of an oyster. Who ever saw him sailing out of Willard's long entry upon that airy smack which students not intended for the pulpit launched from port-wine sangarees? We are confident that he never discovered the back-parlor aperture through which our finite thirst communicated with its spiritual source. So that his observing faculty must, after all, be charged with limitations. We say, *our* thirst, but would not be understood to include those who were destined for the ministry, as no clergyman in the embryonic state was ever known to visit Willard's. But Thoreau was always indisposed to call at the ordinary places for his spiritual refreshment; and he went farther than most persons when apparently he did not go so far. He soon discovered that all sectarian and denominational styles of thinking had their Willard within economical distance; but the respective taps did not suit his country palate. He was in his cups when he was out of doors; where his lips fastened to the far horizon, and he tossed off the whole costly vintage that mantled in the great circumference.

But he had no animal spirits for our sport or mischief. We cannot recollect what became of him during the scenes of the Dunkin Rebellion. He must have slipped off into some "cool retreat or mossy cell." We are half inclined to suppose that the tumult startled him into some metamorphose, that corresponded to a yearning in him of some natural kind, whereby he secured a temporary evasion till peace was restored. He may also, in this interim of qualified humanity, have established an understanding with the mute cunning of nature, which appeared afterwards in his surprising recognition of the ways of squirrels, birds, and fishes. It is certainly quite as possible that man should take off his mind, and drop into the medium of animal intelligence, as that Swedenborg, Dr. Channing, and other spirits of just men made perfect, should strip off the senses and conditions of their sphere, to come dabbling about in the atmosphere of earth among men's thoughts. However this may be, Thoreau disappeared while our young absurdity held its orgies, stripping shutters from the lower windows of the buildings, dismantling recitation rooms, greeting tutors and professors with a frenzied and groundless indignation which we symbolized by kindling the spoils of sacked premises upon the steps. It probably occurred to him that fools might rush in where angels were not in the habit of going. We recollect that he declined to accompany several fools of this description, who rushed late, all in a fine condition of contempt, with Corybantic gestures, into morning prayers,—a college exercise which we are confident was never attended by the angels. . . .

There was no conceit of superior tendencies and exclusive tastes which prevented him from coming into closer contact with individuals. But it was not shyness alone which restrained him, nor the reticence of an extremely modest temperament. For he was complacent; his reserve was always satisfactory to himself. Something in his still latent and brooding genius was sufficiently attractive to make his wit "home-keeping;" and it very early occurred to him, that he should not better his fortunes by familiarity with other minds. This complacency, which lay quite deep over his youthful features, was the key to that defect of sympathy which led to defects of expression, and to unbalanced statements of his thought. It had all the effect of the seclusion that some men inflict upon themselves, when from conceit or disappointment they restrict the compass of their life to islands in the great expanse, and become reduced at last, after nibbling every thing within the reach of their tether, to simple rumination, and incessant returns of the same cud to the tongue. This, and not listlessness, nor indolence, nor absolute incapacity for any professional pursuit, led him to the banks of Walden Pond, where his cottage, sheltering a self-reliant and homely life, seemed like something secreted by a quite natural and inevitable constitution. You might as well quarrel with the self-sufficiency of a perfect day of Nature, which makes no effort to conciliate, as with this primitive disposition of his. The critic need not feel bound to call it a vice of temper because it nourished faults. He should, on the contrary, accept it as he sees that it secured the rare and positive characteristics which make Thoreau's books so full of new life, of charms unborrowed from the resources of society, of suggestions lent by the invisible beauty to a temperate and cleanly soul. A greater deference to his neighborhood would have impaired the peculiar genius which we ought to delight to recognize as fresh from a divine inspiration, filled with possibilities like an untutored America, as it hints at improvement in its very defects, and is fortunately guarded by its own disability. It was perfectly satisfied with its own ungraciousness, because that was essential to its private business. Another genius might need to touch human life at many points; to feel the wholesome shocks; to draw off the subtile nourishment which the great mass generates and comprises; to take in the reward for parting with some effluence: but this would have been fatal to Thoreau. It would have cured his faults and weakened his genius. He would have gained friends within the world, and lost his friends behind it.

It is very plain, that, however much he may have suffered for want of human sympathy, and the correction of the manners of a fine circle, his complacency turned the pain to himself into opportunity for his thought. He could meditate well upon friendship; but he soon learned to do without friends. Occasionally, as in "Concord and Merrimac," . . . he seems to be yearning for intercourse with worthy and noble mates; but he is merely describing his own ideals. These peers whom he stands ready to love, to share his integrity with them, his sense of all beautiful and manly things, to suffer their heroic criticism, and to cure them with a surgery as prompt, are only the offspring of his solitary pen. He would care less to make an effort to discover and come to an understanding with such candidates for friendship after his deliberate description of them. After the trouble of conceiving them, they would not be worth the trouble of knowing. His imagination enjoyed itself so well, that it dreaded to be interrupted, perhaps to be deceived, by people pretending to be its counterparts. They excited his jealousy, as though they had come to survey and stake out his Walden privilege, with a view to an air-line railroad through his front door. He had long ago escaped from all this bustle and obtrusion: not only tricky and conventional people, shallow neighbors, impertinent with the success of their professions and handicrafts, mere talkers and jugglers, had been left outside the wood, but his superiors also; for they could never satisfy his requisitions at a moment's notice, and they were so human as to drop away sometimes from his inexorable thought. . . .

He came to destroy customs of living, not to fulfil them: at least, he is willing to make a personal example of the possibility of living without compliances that are more costly to the conscience than to the purse. The pleasantest family circle cannot tempt him to manifest regard for the American thriftiness that is so full of pretence. And his earliest temper is shown in extreme protest against the comforts and habits of the town. He would fain convince people, that, instead of living, they are merely implicated in a life-long struggle to save their furniture, pay rent for garrets littered with cast-off conveniences, and keep a best room for no eye on earth to see, no human presence to enjoy. He will escape to some place whence he can show how living can be reduced to its minimum; not reflecting, in his first contempt for our habits of self-embarrassment, that his example bids every head of a family take to the woods, there to solve life's problem by arresting life. But New-England enterprise does not affect him; its roads do not pierce nor bridge his complacent economy. The cost of civilization, in human feeling, in wasteful processes, and in hypocrisy, piques him into pronouncing it a disease.

There is no selfishness in this; he is not avoiding trouble, but hoping not to increase the trouble that already exists in the world. He must preserve the chastity of his imagination, if he dies of starvation; and will be a little pinched and bony, with a touch of tartness, rather than be dissolute. . . .

We cannot, therefore, subscribe to the regret that is expressed in the in- imitable biographical sketch, introductory to the volume of "Excursions:" the writer there says, "I so much regret the loss of his rare powers of ac- tion, that I cannot help counting it a fault in him that he had no ambition. Wanting this, instead of engineering for all America, he was the captain of a huckleberry party." But what if the berries that filled his pail were of a kind never picked before, from a stock not previously discovered in our pastures, staining his hands and pages with the blood that circulates be- hind the earth, that puts forth, indeed, the earth itself as a berry on the tree Igdrasil. That kind of engineering tunnels the darkness which we call the visible world, and lets us through into a more lively continent than this graded and turnpiked one. Thoreau was "born for great enterprise and for command," to civilize Nature with the highest intuitions of the mind, which show her simplicity to restless and artificial men; thus framing a treaty of amity and commerce by which new advantages for the finite are gathered from the infinite, and one system of law is extended over both spheres. His books are full of these unexpected coincidences, which reveal the regularity and beauty of creation: from a twig or a leaf, his adventurous spirit, "o'er-festooning every interval," swings across, and fastens the first rope of a bridge that shall become solid for a million feet. These hints of the divine intention, of the tolerance and impartiality that fill all animated forms with one kind spirit; this unerring scent that finds footsteps where no microscope could gather one, and refers all their stratagems to a single Presence, that barely escapes his impetuous instinct, and cannot cover up its tracks so fast as he pursues; this knowledge of the habits, graces, and shifts of all wild creatures, which humanizes them by the curious analo- gies it suggests, so that we adopt them into the family, and they pay their board by helping our perception of order and symmetry, as we find it in the succession of forest-trees, and in that of races, in the development of wild fruits and crabbed stocks, in the relations of fauna and flora, in the graces of spring days, till all of us, birds, men, beasts, and blossoms, seem to breathe in unison that One Intelligence, whose moment is the same yesterday, to-day, and for ever,—this was the enterprise of Thoreau; and all developments of his energy, or new command gained over his gifts, would have perfected, and not changed, the nature of his employment. It was the only way he had, or ever could acquire, for serving politics, society, and the religious life.

For no writer of the present day is more religious; that is to say, no one more profoundly penetrated with the redeeming power of simple integrity, and the spiritualizing effect of a personal consciousness of God. It is in the interest of holiness that he speaks slightingly of Scripture and its holy men. "Keep your Christ," he says; "but let me have my Buddha, and leave me alone with him." He catches up this Buddha for a chance defence against the conventional Christ of Democrats, slaveholders, sharpers in trade and in society, literal theologians, and over-pious laymen. . . .

He will be rightly understood only by reference to his books, and not to separate pages; for his whole mental disposition was religious. He is not content to make little portable statements, after the manner of sermonizers, who discharge themselves by clauses of their weekly accumulation of awe and hope, and then are laid up, like the gymnotus, for repairs. But every page is firmly built upon moral earnestness and regard for the unseen powers. He is a spiritual writer in the sense of worshipping the presence of infinite consistency and beauty; yet he always behaves as if his religion was "nothing to speak of." He often quarrels with the technicalities of church-goers, and is more petulant than he need be, lest you should suspect him of hypocrisy. After reading the earliest English translations of Eastern scriptures, as Colebrooke's, and perhaps some fragments in the French, he recommends them to the people, because his sense of justice is hurt at the exclusive and ignorant fetichism which is paid to the Old and New Testaments. He cannot have the notion of supplanting them; but he longs to have all men recognize the continuous inspiration of the Spirit through all climes and ages. He does not undertake to patronize the Bible, and says few good words for it; but his books are fountains of sincerity and moral sweetness, such as the Bible emphasizes, and they always worship "in spirit and in truth." . . .

Toward the close of his life, he was visited by one of those dealers in ready-made clothing, who advertise to get any soul prepared at a moment's notice for a sudden trip. Complete outfits, including "a change," and patent fire-proof, are furnished at the very bedside, or place of embarkation, of the most shiftless spirits. "Henry, have you made your peace with God?" To which our shop-dealer received the somewhat noticeable reply, "I have never quarrelled with him." We fancy the rapid and complete abdication of the cheap-clothing business in the presence of such forethought.

A friend of the family was very anxious to know how he stood affected towards Christ, and he told her that a snowstorm was more to him than Christ. So he got rid of these cankers that came round to infest his soul's blossoming time. Readers ought not to bring a lack of religion to the dealing with his answers.

His spiritual life was not deficient in soundness because it stood unrelated to conventional names and observances. Let it be known by the fruits of integrity, high-mindedness, and purity, which cluster on the pages of these volumes; by the cold and stern yet salutary ideals of behavior in all the human relations; by his sense of dependence upon the invisible life, and absolute surrender to its dictates. . . .

[John Weiss], "Thoreau," *Christian Examiner* 79 (July 1865): 96–105, 107–12.

[Remembrances of Thoreau in 1865]

Samuel Storrow Higginson (1842–1907) attended Franklin Sanborn's school when it opened in 1855 in Concord, where he met Thoreau two years later; he graduated from Harvard College in 1863. He was the nephew of literary critic and editor Thomas Wentworth Higginson, whose abolitionist sentiments he shared. As editor of the *Harvard Magazine,* Storrow Higginson published a tribute to Thoreau the month that he died. This article conveys Higginson's admiration for this "singular person who might be seen each day pacing through the long village street, with sturdy step and honest mien, now pausing to listen to some rich warble from the elms high overhead." To Higginson, as to several other young men and women in Concord, Thoreau was "Nature's child" (313, 317). During the Civil War, Higginson served as Chaplain for the Ninth Regiment of the U.S. Colored Infantry. After the war, he went to Argentina and opened a school in Buenos Aires; later he was appointed rector to the National College of Conception del Uruguay. Returning to Boston, he later worked as a publisher, as an editor for the *Boston Herald,* and as the Superintendent of Archives for Massachusetts. Eventually Higginson moved to Chicago, where he worked for Rand, McNally publishers. In this letter, written while stationed with his Union army unit in Brownsville, Texas, Higginson thanks Sophia Thoreau for the recent gift of Thoreau's *Letters to Various Persons,* published earlier that year. From the vantage of a soldier at the end of the Civil War, Higginson thoughtfully understands Thoreau's frustrated comments, in an April 1861 letter to Parker Pillsbury, about the outbreak of this military conflict.

To Sophia E. Thoreau, 9 October 1865

I am touched by the kindly remembrance which sends across these thousand leagues this exquisite expression of Henry Thoreau's great soul. It seems as if it came not by mail or express but rather on sympathizing winds like a still clear breath of morning-air, laden with the perfume of tansy & golden-rod and the faint delicious aroma of the purple or imperial aster.

[65]

I am aware as I read these deepest expressions of self—letters, of a defect in Thoreau's nature—as it seems to me—: the absence of social instinct. Yet none the less do his words so full of earnest *truth* and searching sincerity of language, thrill me with a pure delight, for I think he was of all men I ever knew the healthiest and his indifference to society & country & nationality arose not from cynicism or misanthropy, but from a positive respect of nature. Surely the closing letters would wound him who did not understand how, in Thoreau, politics became of necessity subordinated to spiritual thought, and his scorn of the war was not so much affected as a part of that very deficiency in his composition. It seemed as if Nature, weary with the accustomed routine had in a moment of darkness formed a Spirit which should rise above everything earthly & dwell in the pure atmosphere of Mr Thoreau—hills, stirred not by the clangor of "Society" but the sweet litany of the murmuring pines and the tender rustle of the night winds. He was, to me, like Shelley, unearthly, gifted with a poetic etherialized thought too pure for the world at large to comprehend, full of beauty and of truth, albeit too subjective for society. (Herein Shelley rises far above our friend for in the latter subjectivity predominated—in Shelley self was merged in the welfare of fellow-men.) Pardon me if I speak to you with candor. It were irreverent and unworthy so godlike a soul as Thoreau's to speak otherwise. And if I regret that in so spiritlike a nature the love of fellow-men *seems* at least, secondary to subjective contemplation, it is only that I love the radiance of his Truthfulness too much to dissimulate that I breathe my deepest thought to you.

But how sublime is the self analysis & philosophy of this soul! "Men cannot conceive of a state of things so fair that it cannot be realized" (p 44) "What can be expressed in words, can be expressed in life" (p 45) "If you would convince a man that he does wrong do right"—(p 46) *"When you knock, ask to see God—none of the servants,"* the passage concluding with "let the beautiful laws prevail" (p 57) "Do what you know you ought to do" (p 44) "We are not the less to aim at the summits, though the multitude does not ascend them" (p 139) *"Nature is goodness crystallized"* (p 194) and a hundred others, such sayings go right to the heart of him who receives truth and the clear sincerity with which they were spoken. These are immortal and perchance when years of ignoble stripe have passed away we shall rise to behold in one so good & pure nature's own philanthropist, loving men not through daily intercourse but the beautiful appeal of a pure life and a fragrant memory. Then we shall see that this indifference to the world was perhaps a virtue we cannot now understand and we shall love him more & more like as a child of Nature ("his happiness is like that of the woodchuck"). To me Beauty is the most exquisite expression of Divine Goodness. I bow before a purity like that of the wild-flowers, and cherish with tenderest emotion the memory of him with whose life is associated the sweetest season of my life. . . .

Storrow Higginson to Sophia Thoreau, 9 October 1865, Letter File 3a, H36; CAS D-2030e, Special Collections, Concord Free Public Library, Concord, MA.

From "Thoreau" (1866)

[Moncure Daniel Conway]

Virginia native Moncure Daniel Conway (1832–1907) was a Harvard-educated Unitarian minister, an abolitionist, and an author who came to admire Thoreau after spending several months in Concord while on summer break from college in 1853. In 1858, Conway married Ellen Dana, whom he met when serving as pastor of a Unitarian church in Cincinnati. His abolitionist and increasingly radical theological views led him to break with the American Unitarian church in the early 1860s; in 1864 the Conways moved to London, where Conway spent the second half of his life as minister at the Free Thought South Place Chapel. As did other second-generation Transcendentalists, Conway published reminiscences about the Concord writers, but he also authored full-length biographies of Emerson, Hawthorne, Thomas Paine, and Thomas Carlyle, in addition to several antislavery novels. In *Pine and Palm* (1887), Henry Thoreau appears as an abolitionist who dispels an angry mob's attack by quoting from the Bhagavad Gita.

Appearing first in the London-based *Fraser's,* Conway's article is one of the earliest reminiscences to strike a more objective rather than adulatory tone; Conway also offers helpful contextual background about the Transcendentalist era. His narration here of Thoreau and his family's aid in July 1853 to an unidentified male slave who had escaped from Virginia is also recounted in his two-volume *Autobiography Memories and Experiences* (1904). With lengthy excerpts from Thoreau's poetry, *Letters to Various Persons, A Week,* and *Walden,* this article also put before a largely unfamiliar British audience the details of Thoreau's life along with the scope of his writings. "Thoreau" was excerpted in several nineteenth-century British and American periodicals, including a condensed version in the *National Anti-Slavery Standard* on 23 June 1866.

IT IS NOW nearly four years since the inhabitants of the little town of Concord, Massachusetts, were gathered round the grave of one who, though a hermit, was dear to all of them, and who, as a naturalist and scholar, had received the homage of those literary men who have given to that town the celebrity of an American Weimar. . . .

I have met with but few in England who have seen any one of Thoreau's books, and have seen no public notice of any of them except in the *Saturday Review,* which contained one or two articles concerning some of them last year, in one of which their author was designated, not quite happily I think, as "an American Rousseau." The reasons for this absence of any general recognition of so rare a mind lay doubtless rather in the peculiarities of the man himself than in the blindness of the world. As there are essences of such delicate flavour that they can be preserved only by being kept covered, there are characters whose fine aromas are destroyed by exposure to the *popularis aura*—spirits that must sit at silent, solitary tasks, leaving the world to enter and admire when they have passed away. Thoreau was eminently one of these; and his writings were so physiognomical, so blended with his personality, that they seemed to show their author's aversion to publicity. He once told me with evident satisfaction that his first, and at that time his only book—which was printed, I think, about twenty years ago—was still on its publisher's shelf, with the exception of copies given by him to his friends. Like the pious Yógì of the East, so long motionless, whilst gazing on the sun, that knotty plants encircled his neck, and the cast snake-skin his loins, and the birds built their nests upon his shoulders, this seer and naturalist seemed by an equal consecration to have become a part of the field and forest amid which he dwelt; and he with his works, to read which is like walking through morning meadows, or amid the mystic wolds of nightingales, might naturally be undiscerned in the landscape by the great world thundering past in its train, even in an interval when the newspaper or the railway romance might be laid aside. . . .

He could make a boat, or a fence, or plant a garden, and when he needed money obtained it by doing some such piece of work. It is plain, however, that he had no "talent for wealth," and it was an early perception with him that a man's real life was generally sacrificed to obtaining the means of living; he was resolved to make his wealth consist in his having few wants. His natural skill in mensuration, however, and his intimate knowledge of the neighbourhood, rendered his services as a surveyor valuable to the farmers—of whom, for the most part, the town consists; and, leading him often to the fields and woods, this furnished to him an occupation so agreeable to his tastes, that he drifted into it as a profession. . . .

In the hand of the true priest of nature the most barren rod blossoms. Under Thoreau's touch the smallest, most ordinary facts attain a mystic significance. As he parches Indian corn by his fire, he is reminded that "there should always be some flowering and maturing of the fruits of nature in the cooking process." . . .

Although Thoreau lived personally apart from the world, it is interesting to observe how, in his action and his writings, the society around him is reflected, though somewhat inverted. At the time when he was making the week's voyage, which I have followed a little, New England was burgeoning forth, under the tropical breath of Transcendentalism, with strange and rare growths of new thoughts and essays at thought, much to the dismay of the Puritan Apostolic succession. The capital of that strange realm was at Concord, where Emerson, the mildest promoter of a reign of terror imaginable, and Margaret Fuller, and Hawthorne, and Elizabeth Peabody, and others, dwelt and worked as monarch and ministry of a new spiritual kingdom. It soon became plain that what these were endeavouring to put into literature, Thoreau was aiming to put into individual life; not consciously, perhaps, but because he must be the product of the intellectual as well as the physical elements surrounding him there at his first or his second birth. When the *Dial*—the quarterly magazine which represented the new movement—began its career in 1841 he was one of its contributors, and there were printed in it several of the papers which are now collected in the volume called *Excursions*. . . . But the Transcendental agitation was not more reflected in the secluded, wayward stream of Thoreau's life than the Socialistic movement which followed it, and was doubtless, its first offspring. When nearly every leading spirit of what were called "the New Views" went into the Brook Farm community—even Channing and Hawthorne, who were not distinctively Transcendentalists—Emerson remained at home to evolve Arcadias of pure thought, and Thoreau to reproduce Utopias of individual life. . . .

On a summer morning about fourteen years ago I went with Mr. Emerson and was introduced to Thoreau. I was then connected with Divinity College at Cambridge, and my new acquaintance was interested to know what we were studying there at the time. "Well, the Scriptures." "But *which*?" he asked, not without a certain quiet humour playing about his serious blue eye. It was evident that, as Morgana in the story marked all the doors so that the one ceased to be a sign, he had marked Persian and Hindu and other ethnical Scriptures with the reverential sign usually found on the Hebrew writings alone. . . . Out of courtesy to my introducer, doubtless, he asked me to go with him on the following day to visit some of the pleasant places around the village (in which I was as yet a stranger), and I gladly accepted the offer. When I went to the house next morning, I found them all (Thoreau was then living in his father's house) in a state of excitement by reason of the arrival of a fugitive negro from the South, who had come fainting to their door about daybreak and thrown himself on their mercy. . . . I sat and watched the singularly tender and lowly devotion of the scholar to the slave. He must be fed, his swollen feet bathed, and he must think of nothing but rest. Again and again this coolest and calmest of men drew near to the trembling negro, and bade him feel at home, and have no fear that any power should again wrong him. He could not walk that day, but must mount guard over the fugitive, for slave-hunters were not extinct in those days; and so I went away after a while, much impressed by many little traits that I had seen as they had appeared in this emergency, and not much disposed to cavil at their source, whether Bible or Bhaghavat.

A day or two later, however, I enjoyed my first walk with Thoreau, which was succeeded by many others. We started westward from the village, in which direction his favourite walks lay, for I then found out the way he had of connecting casual with universal things. He desired to order his morning walk after the movement of the planet. The sun is the grand western pioneer; he sets his gardens of Hesperides on the horizon every evening to lure the race; the race moves westward, as animals migrate, by instinct; therefore we are safe in going by Goose-pond to Baker's-farm. Of every square acre of ground, he contended, the western side was the wildest, and therefore the fittest for the seeker to explore. *Ex oriente lux ex occidente frux.* I now had leisure to observe carefully this man. He was short of stature, well built, and such a man as I have fancied Julius Caesar to have been. Every movement was full of courage and repose; the tones of his voice were those of Truth herself; and there was in his eye the pure bright blue of the New England sky, as there was sunshine in his flaxen hair. He had a particularly strong aquiline-Roman nose, which somehow reminded me of the prow of a ship. There was in his face and expression, with all its sincerity, a kind of intellectual furtiveness: no wild thing could escape him more than it could be harmed by him. The grey huntsman's suit which he wore enhanced this expression. . . . The cruellest weapons of attack, however, which this huntsman took with him were a spyglass for birds, a microscope for the game that would hide in smallness, and an old book in which to press plants. His powers of conversation were extraordinary. I remember being surprised and delighted at every step with revelations of laws and significant attributes in common things—as a relation between different kinds of grass and the geological characters beneath them, the variety and grouping of pine-needles and the effect of these differences on the sounds they yield when struck by the wind, and the shades, so to speak, of taste represented by grasses and common herbs when applied to the tongue. The acuteness of his senses was marvellous: no hound could scent better, and he could hear the most faint and distant sounds without even laying his ear to the ground like an Indian. As we penetrated farther and farther into the woods, he seemed to gain a certain transformation, and his face shone with a light that I had not seen in the village. He had a calendar of the plants and flowers of the neighbourhood, and would sometimes go around a quarter of a mile to visit some floral friend, whom he had not seen for a year, who would appear for that day only. We were too early for the *hibiscus,* a rare flower in New England, which I desired to see. He pointed out the spot by the river-side where alone it could be found, and said it would open about the following Monday and not stay long. I went on Tuesday evening and found myself a day too late—the petals were scattered on the ground. . . .

Thoreau was a good reader of books, and was fond of conversing about his favourites in this kind. "Books," he said, however, "can only reveal us to ourselves, and as often as they do us this service we lay them aside." He had studied carefully the old English chronicles, and Chaucer, Froissart, Spenser, and Beaumont and Fletcher. He recognised kindred spirits in George Herbert, Cowley, and Quarles—considering the latter an example of how a man may be a poet, yet not an artist. He explored the old books of voyages—Drake, Purchas, and many another and rarer—who assisted him much in his circumnavigations of Concord, which he thought equally important. The Oriental Bibles, which he read in the French and German editions, were his daily bread; and Homer and Aeschylus, from whom he made some excellent translations, were his luxuries. Of moderns he was much indebted to Wordsworth, Coleridge, and (though to a less extent) Carlyle and Goethe. He admired Ruskin, especially his *Modern Painters,* though he thought the author bigoted. In the *Seven Lamps of Architecture* he found with the good stuff "too much about art," as he said, "for me and the Hottentots. Our house is yet a hut." He enjoyed much reading the works of William Gilpin, his *Hints on Landscape Gardening; Tour of the River Wye;*

and a dozen others perhaps. He read also with care the works of Dr. Franklin. He had as a touchstone for authors their degree of ability to deal with supersensual facts and feelings with scientific precision and dignity. What he admired in Emerson was that he discerned the phenomena of thought and the functions of every idea as if they were *antennae* or *stamina*. To the young men and women who sought his advice as to their reading, he generally recommended intellectual biographies, or autobiographies if possible, as those of Goethe, Alfieri, Benvenuto Cellini, Dr. Franklin, De Quincey's Confessions, &c.

Yet one would soon learn in conversation with him that all these writers had in his estimation only put clever foot-notes here and there to the true volume he was reading. And here I may mention also his mental habit of regarding his neighbourhood as of cosmical importance. Mr. Emerson says that he returned *Kane's Arctic Voyage* to a friend with the remark that "most of the phenomena noted might be observed in Concord." He seemed a little envious of the Pole for the coincident sunrise and sunset, or five minutes' day after six months: a splendid fact which Annursnuc had never afforded him. He found red snow in one of his walks near Concord, and was hoping one day to find the *Victoria Regia*. He reported to Emerson somewhat triumphantly that the foreign *savans* had failed to discriminate a particular botanical variety. . . . He would not read the newspapers which demanded his attention most impertinently for Europe or Washington instead of Walden Pond. One of his beatitudes ran—"Blessed are the young, for they do not read the President's Message." Of friends who read to him of the Crimean War he asks, "Pray, to be serious, where is Sevastopol? Who is Menchikoff;" and goes on to meditate on the white oak in his stove. His motto being thus—*Ne quid quoesiveris extra te Concordiamque,* he did not, as he was well able to do, explore the great West; nevertheless he visited Cape Cod and wrote a curious and valuable work on its ancient and its natural history; also Canada, concerning which he wrote a valuable paper not included in the published volumes. He visited also the mountains of Maine and New Hampshire.

Though shy of general society, Thoreau was a hero among children, and the captain of their excursions. He was the *sine quâ non* of the Concord huckleberry-party, which is in that region something of an institution. To have Thoreau along with them was to be sure of finding acres of bushes laden with the delicious fruit. On these occasions his talk with the children was as a part of the spirit and circumstance which go to make up what is called in Yankee phrase "a good time." A child stumbles and falls, losing his carefully gathered store of berries; Thoreau kneels beside the weeping unfortunate, and explains to him and to the group that Nature has made these little provisions for next year's crop. If there were no obstacles, and little boys did not fall occasionally, how would berries be scattered and planted? and what would become of huckleberryings? He will then arrange that he who has thus suffered for the general good shall have the first chance at the next pasture.

Mr. Emerson relates that one day, when he was about to deliver the lecture at the Concord Lyceum, Thoreau remarked to him, that whatever succeeded with the audience was bad. Mr. E. replied—"Who would not like to write something which all can read, like *Robinson Crusoe*? and who does not see with regret that his page is not solid with a right materialistic treatment, which delights everybody?" Henry objected, of course, and vaunted the better treatment which reached only a few persons. But at supper a young girl, understanding that he was to lecture at the Lyceum, sharply asked him "whether his lecture would be a nice interesting story, such as she wished to hear, or whether it was one of those old philosophical things that she did not care about." Henry turned to her (says Emerson) and bethought himself, and, I saw, was trying to believe that he had matter that might fit her and her brother, who were to sit up and go to the lecture, if it was a good one for them.

Sometimes I have gone with Thoreau and his young comrades for an expedition on the river, to gather, it may be, water-lilies. Upon such excursions his resources for our entertainment were inexhaustible. He would tell stories of the Indians who once dwelt thereabout until the children almost looked to see a red man skulking with his arrow on shore; and every plant or flower on the bank or in the water, and every fish, turtle, frog, lizard, about us was transformed by the wand of his knowledge, from the low form into which the spell of our ignorance had reduced it, into a mystic beauty. One of his surprises was to thrust his hand softly into the water, and as softly raise up before our astonished eyes a large bright fish, which lay as contentedly in his hand as if they were old acquaintances! If the fish had also dropped a penny from its mouth, it could not have been a more miraculous proceeding to us. The entire crew bared their arms and tried to get hold of a fish, but only the captain succeeded. We could not get his secret from him then, for it was to surprise and delight many another merry boat-full; but later I have read in his account of the bream, or ruff (*pomotis vulgaris*) of that river, that "it is a simple and inoffensive fish, whose nests are visible all along the shore, hollowed in the sand, over which it is steadily poised through the summer hours on waving fin." . . . I do not doubt but that it was this and other intimacies of Thoreau with various animals that suggested to his friend and neighbour Mr. Hawthorne the character of Donatello in the tale of *Transformation*. . . .

But it seems that the elves of wood and water were alluring him from the earth. The seeds of consumption were prematurely developed, perhaps by his life of exposure; but the distress and appeals of friends and relatives could not, to the last, overcome the fascinations of Nature, and persuade him to remain within doors. He was sent at length to the more gentle climate of the Mississippi; but it was of no avail, and he soon returned home to die. . . .

[Moncure Daniel Conway], "Thoreau," *Fraser's Magazine for Town and Country* 73 (April 1866): 447–48, 452–53, 460–65.

From "Literary Frondeurs" (1866)

Eugene Benson

> Artist and literary critic Eugene Benson (1839–1908) published widely, in-
> cluding influential articles in the *Atlantic Monthly, Galaxy, Round Table,* and
> *Putnam's.* A vocal critic of postbellum American society, particularly corrupt
> business practices, Benson provides in the excerpt below, a similarly spir-
> ited defense of Thoreau against the attack by James Russell Lowell published
> the year before in the *North American Review.* According to Robert Scholnick,
> "Benson looked back to the American Romantics for a strategy, a vision, to
> enable modern man to maintain and develop personal identity in a threaten-
> ing world" (246). Benson defines a *frondeur* as "one who assails, criticises, or
> mocks established facts or appearances. . . . He affronts, outrages, defies, or
> rails at something which time or custom has made respectable." Benson sees
> himself in this role as he defends fellow frondeur Henry Thoreau.

THE TWO MOST perfect types of the literary frondeur in this country were
Edgar A. Poe and Henry D. Thoreau—the first a man of letters with the artistic or literary spirit, the second a man of letters without the artistic spirit,
but so thoroughly emancipated and so sincere that his writings have the
beauty of truth if not the truth of beauty. Poe disturbed the tranquil self-
satisfaction of a great many excellent men and meritorious writers; Thoreau affronted every literary man in the country by the practical teaching
of his life, and the straightforward expression of his aversion to clergymen,
towns, cities, newspapers, and, in a word, civilization. His voluntary isolation cost him grace and sweetness. . . .

Hawthorne . . . was too much of an artist to be a frondeur. . . . Mrs. [Eliza-
beth] Stoddard might be a frondeur; she has the instincts of a frondeur, but
she has not the *abandon* of a frondeur, and she hesitates on "the dangerous
edge of things." . . . I do not reproach Lowell that he criticised Thoreau,
for when Lowell criticises he instructs and entertains us; I reproach him
that he stood among the self-righteous crowd of Thoreau's detractors, that
is, among tradesmen, presiding officers, lecturers, mill-owners, and spoke

their thought about Thoreau; interpolated *their* Poor-Richard philosophy of life with the purer text of his own literary appreciation of Thoreau. As Lowell is more of an artist than Thoreau, and was disturbed by Thoreau's want of sweetness, and grace, and suavity, I can understand and welcome his criticism; but as he is a man of letters, quick to resent the tyranny of American Philistines, and a lover of the most indigenous growth we have yet to show in our native literature, I mourn that he allowed himself to act as prosecutor for the Boston public; and I can only acknowledge that, as literary Attorney-General for the State, his arraignment and prosecution of Thoreau before the North American tribunal was an ingenious and brilliant effort; and after it, I have no doubt but that the kid glove literary and clerical mob of the country were ready to cry out, Release Barabbas but crucify Thoreau, for he has mocked our gods and he has been indifferent to our high priests. . . . We want literary frondeurs to destroy our self-satisfaction. We must be made restless—placed beyond the flattering sounds of our material prosperity; we must live better; we must be more artistic, less mechanical. We are taking great trouble, with mills and stock-boards. . . .

We need frondeurs. They prevent stagnation; they frighten the sheep, but they save them from the wolf. The rank and file of society have always been as sheep, and they have followed the "bell-wether." . . .

Eugene Benson, "Literary Frondeurs," *Galaxy* 2 (1 September 1866): 79–82.

From the "Editor's Easy Chair"
(1869, 1874, and 1878)

[George William Curtis]

Author, critic, and editor George William Curtis (1824–1892) first met Thoreau in the mid-1840s, when he lived and worked with the family of Concord farmer Edmund Hosmer. In the summer of 1845, he and Hosmer were among those who helped raise the frame for Thoreau's cabin at Walden Pond. Curtis served as editor of *Putnam's Monthly Magazine* from 1852 to 1857; from 1853 to 1892, he contributed a regular column, the "Editor's Easy Chair" to *Harper's New Monthly Magazine.* During his editorship of *Putnam's,* Curtis omitted what he considered objectionable material (e.g., negative portrayals of Catholic priests) from Thoreau's "An Excursion to Canada," which Thoreau had submitted to him at Horace Greeley's recommendation. The first three installments of the projected five-part article appeared in *Putnam's* in January, February, and March 1853, but on learning of the excisions, Thoreau asked Curtis to discontinue the series. When Greeley defended Curtis's editorial scalpel, Thoreau responded that since he "was born to be a pantheist," he could not help but "do the deeds of one" (*Correspondence,* 294). Despite this altercation and a similar one over "Cape Cod" in 1855, several "Editor's Easy Chair" columns from the 1860s through the 1880s reflect Curtis's high regard for Thoreau, in contrast to the permanent breach left by Thoreau's editorial fracas with James Russell Lowell in 1858. Two months after Thoreau's death, Curtis paid homage to Thoreau as "a man of singular rectitude, independence, and sagacity" ("Editor's Easy Chair," [July 1862], 270).

February 1869

The last time that this Easy Chair saw that noble and remarkable man, Henry Thoreau, he came quietly into the study of a famous scholar to get a volume of Pliny's letters. Expecting to see no one, and accustomed to attend without distraction to the business in hand, he was as quietly going out, when the host spoke to him, and without surprise, and with a cool, erect courtesy, Thoreau greeted his friends. He seated himself, maintaining the same habitual erect posture, which made it seem impossible that he could ever lounge or slouch, and which made Hawthorne speak of him as "cast iron," and immediately began to talk in the strain so familiar to his friends. It was a staccato style of speech, every word coming separately and distinctly, as if preserving the same cool isolation in the sentence that the speaker did in society; but the words were singularly apt and choice, and Thoreau had always something to say. His knowledge was original. He was a Fine-ear and a Sharp-eye in the woods and fields; and he added to his knowledge the wisdom of the most ancient times and of the best literature. His manner and matter both reproved trifling, but in the most impersonal manner. It was like the reproof of the statue of a god. There seemed never to be any loosening of the intellectual tension, and a call from Thoreau in the highest sense "meant business."

On the morning of which we are speaking the talk fell upon the Indians, with whom he had a sympathy which was unprecedented, and of whose life and ways and nature he apparently had an instinctive knowledge. In the slightly contemptuous inference against civilization which his remarks left, rather than in any positively scornful tone, there was something which rather humorously suggested the man who spoke lightly of the equator, but with the difference that there would have been if the light speaking had left a horrible suspicion of that excellent circle. For Thoreau so ingeniously traced our debts to the aborigines that the claims of civilization for what is really essential palpably dwindled. He dropped all manner of curious and delightful information as he went on, and it was sad to see in the hollow cheek and the large, unnaturally lustrous eye the signs of the disease that very soon removed him from among us. . . .

His talk of the Indians gave an impression entirely unlike that of the Cooper novel and the red man of the theatre. It was untouched by romance or sentimentality. They appeared a grave, manly race, intimately familiar with nature, with a lofty scorn of feebleness. The sylvan shade and the leafy realm and Arden and pastoral poetry were wholly wanting in the picture he drew, quite as much as the theory that they are vermin to be exterminated as fast as possible. He said that the pioneers of civilization, as it is called, among them are purveyors of every kind of mischief. We graft the sound native stock with a sour fruit, then denounce it bitterly and cut it down. What was most admirable in Daniel Boone was his Indian nature and sympathy; and the least admirable part was his hold, such as it was, upon civilization. He seemed to imply that if Boone could only have succeeded in becoming an Indian altogether, it would have been a truly memorable triumph. Thoreau acknowledged that the Indian was not only doomed, but, as he gravely said, damned, because his enemies were his historians; and he could only say, "Ah, if we lions had painted the picture!" . . .

July 1874

Henry Thoreau cherished a secret conviction that they [Indians] were very much superior to their Saxon successors in America, and insisted that most of our improvements were merely a painful increase of resultless vexation, and that the finer and nobler qualities of human character are no more evident in us than in the red men. But Thoreau loved a paradox, and sometimes confounded civilization with its abuses and diseases. He had a natural sympathy with the Indian, for he had a love of wild nature, nature untouched by art—the primeval forest, the solitary stream, the haunt of the beaver and the fox—and he had a curious knowledge of the aspects of the daily life of the woods and fields, the habits of animals and plants. The Easy Chair remembers a weird night with Thoreau in his boat upon the Concord River, the Musketaquid, in whose neighborhood he found arrow-heads and Indian relics that eluded all other eyes, and seemed to have kept themselves patiently for him. The object of the excursion was to watch the night life of the stream. An iron crate was built out from the bow of the boat and filled with the dead roots of old pine-trees—fat pine—and when this was kindled the blaze threw a broad glare for some distance upon the water, shutting out every thing else, and slowly drifting with the stream we could see clearly every thing below us. We hung seemingly suspended in air over fish and grass and sand, floating imperceptibly upon the current. Thoreau's acute observation, his intimate knowledge, his respect for the Indian, and his much-modified admiration of his own race and time were all very evident.

But this is wandering. To speak of the Indian, however, is to think of Thoreau. . . .

March 1878

A man who was very little known while he lived, but who, since his death, is constantly more famous, and whose name is very sure to survive among those of the most original Americans, is Henry Thoreau. He lived and died in Concord, Massachusetts, seldom leaving home, and never for long absences. Thirty years ago he was well known to every body in the town, but few probably thought that the eccentric and independent man would, with the Revolutionary battle, and the genius of Emerson and Hawthorne, shed lustre upon the quiet village. To many of his old neighbors he was simply a queer and incomprehensible character, full of odd whimseys, going cheerfully to jail rather than pay taxes, and living alone in a hut by a pond near the village. To many others, men of education and literary taste, who had known him at college, and who knew his writings, he was merely an extravagant imitator of Emerson, copying his tone of thought, his style, and even his personal manner and expression. This class was more impatient of him than his neighbors, and was secretly inclined to think of him, in plain speech, only as a lazy humbug.

Yet, in fact, Thoreau was one of the group of remarkable men that appeared in New England during the last generation, all of whom were by no means the children of transcendentalism, but whose combined names largely compose the chief glory of our literature. Thoreau graduated forty years ago at Harvard, without special distinction, and then engaged in making lead pencils with his father. But his chief interest and occupation were the observation of nature and literary study, and in 1842, we think it was, he published in the *Dial* a paper on the natural history of Massachusetts, in the form of a review of a recent official report upon the subject, which showed as close and exquisite an eye as that of White of Selborne, with a sturdy thought and humor and originality beyond that of the good English curate. That paper alone showed that Thoreau was strictly himself and not an imitator, and throughout, although whenever he spoke of public affairs it was in a tone of sympathy with the prevailing sentiment of New England, it was also in a perfectly independent, courageous, and individual manner.

Thoreau has been already the subject of many articles, and even books, the latest of which is "a study," by Mr. H. A. Page, an Englishman, but it is not easy to give a proper account of him. His figure, as we said, was familiar in the village. He was a man of the ordinary height, always very plainly dressed, but without any oddity of costume. His habitual gait was rapid; and whether or not his known fondness for Indians affected the observer, his movement seemed not unlike that of an Indian. His features were large, the nose very prominent, and his complexion fair. He was not shy, and was always ready to talk; but he was serious, although wholly without melancholy, and had no small-talk or twaddle. The personal impression that he made was that of entire composure and self-possession, with a frosty grave cheerfulness, earnest, without affectation of devotion—a man with a serene perpetual consciousness of the richness and beauty of life and nature. He seemed to need no relaxation of mind or body, sat upright in his chair, and although with entire appreciation of humor, he made no jokes. It was the impression of this inflexibility, a rigidity without intention, which was inevitably but unconsciously a rebuke of frivolity, this constant but natural tension at concert-pitch, which made Hawthorne half impatiently call him "that cast-iron man." He was not indignant with conventional forms, he was merely unconscious of any force in them; yet he never offended good-breeding. He evidently thought that civilization had so loaded life with artificial embarrassments that its freshness and vigor and enjoyment were lost, and the simplicity of the Indian and the easy satisfaction of his few wants seemed to him to offer to the educated man the opportunity of the real knowledge and pleasure that elaborate civilization made impracticable.

Yet there was not a touch of cynicism in his nature. He could not be disappointed or imbittered. Swift would have been as strange to him as Rochester. The disembarrassment or the attempted disembarrassment of his life from the usages of society was instinctive. He made no fuss about it. He did not self-consciously and ostentatiously protest. To pay taxes was to support an unnecessary and cumbrous machinery, which, among other absurd and unjust things, undertook to return innocent persons to slavery. To get money to contribute to this unworthy purpose, time and labor must be spent that might be devoted to some useful end, to the acquisition of knowledge, to peaceful contemplation, and he therefore declined to do any thing so ridiculous. The officers naturally enforced the law, and he went cheerfully to jail, and staid there until a neighbor procured his release. If he had been asked how society could hold together if nobody should pay taxes, he would certainly have answered that he did not know, and still less did he know that it was desirable society should hold together for the purpose of doing injustice. But there would be no heat, no personal feeling of any kind, in the discussion, and he would unquestionably have mounted the scaffold with the same composure and good humor that he went to jail.

Thoreau's true life was in the observation and the suggestion of nature, and of these his books are the record. His distinction among observers is that while he had the eye of the naturalist, he had the mind of the poet. He had a healthy and refreshing delight in every detail of the spectacle of nature, and no less an exquisite perception of its infinite symbolism and correspondence. His eye and his mind are simultaneously busy. There is no such comprehensive observation as his recorded in literature, united with a style so racy, so incisive, and so pictorial. His individuality was so supreme, his attention to his own business was so perfect, and his account of it so complete and satisfactory, that a late writer in the *World* describes him as before all an artist, and laughs at Mr. Page for finding him to be a reformer or a modern St. Francis of Assisi, and wonders at Mr. Emerson for wishing that he should have been other than he was. And, indeed, we do not see how Thoreau could have been spared from his work any more than Hawthorne from his. His books are as unique in literature as Hawthorne's, and they are all robust and hearty and healthy. There is no touch of sentimentality. His genius was sweet and clear, and Thoreau was a noble and characteristic product of modern America. He was only forty-four years old when he died, just at the beginning of the war in 1861.[1]

Note

1. Curtis errs here; Thoreau died on 6 May 1862.

[George William Curtis], "Editor's Easy Chair," *Harper's Monthly* 38 (February 1869): 415; 49 (July 1874): 284; 56 (March 1878): 624–25.

From *Thoreau: The Poet-Naturalist* (1873)

William Ellery Channing

Poet William Ellery Channing (1817–1901) has been characterized as "the man (outside the Thoreau family) with whom [Thoreau] was closest" (Hudspeth, 34). As his nearly constant outdoor companion, Channing almost certainly shared a greater number of hours alone with Thoreau than did any other member of his intimate circle. Ironically, Channing's statement that Thoreau "had no tolerance for 'loafers,' bar-room idlers, and men who 'have nothing to do'" describes how many in Concord regarded Channing, and at times, Thoreau himself. In 1841, Channing married Ellen Fuller, the younger sister of Transcendentalist author and women's rights advocate Margaret Fuller. Over the course of a difficult marriage—aggravated by Channing's flirtatious behavior with other women, most notably Caroline Sturgis, and his poor conduct as both husband and father—the Channings had five children. Ellen died shortly after giving birth to their last child, in 1856.

Although Thoreau complained that Channing influenced him "to certain licences of speech—i.e., to reckless & sweeping expressions of which I am wont to regret that I have used," he generally tolerated these shortcomings as well as overlooking his friend's more serious episodes of familial irresponsibility. No figure populates Thoreau's journal commentary more regularly than Channing (*PEJ*, 8:39). Yet Thoreau refers to Channing as "the real Simon Pure," while Channing venerated Thoreau with an effusive regard that he described at length in 1858 to their mutual friend Daniel Ricketson: "He is so noble and admirable a man, that I wonder he was not long since canonized, or raised up among men as an elder or a guide. But he is too good for a supereminent position, which he dwarfs by the majesty of his genius. Let you and I in our dying moments lack not one thought and one feeling if not many more for this admirable man, who has not only instructed us by his excellent writings, but has also led us forward, to do and to dare, by the example of a brave and generous life" (*Correspondence*, 413; qtd. in Ricketson, 207). In May 1862, Channing claimed that "half the world died for me when I lost Mr. Thoreau. None of it looks the same as when I looked at it with him" (qtd. in Harding, *Days*, 466).

> *The Poet-Naturalist*, the first biography of Thoreau, reflects Channing's de-
> tailed knowledge and respect for Thoreau as student, scholar, and author.
> Channing was the custodian of Thoreau's journals for several years follow-
> ing his friend's death; his familiarity with them is evident in his patched-
> together narrative, which includes lengthy excerpts from the journals as
> well as interspersed chapters of imagined outdoor dialogues between Tho-
> reau and Channing. In Channing's poetic, sympathetic portrayal, Thoreau
> emerges as a fully realized human being, mourned greatly by this friend but
> not overtly idealized.

THINGS MADE A deep and ineffaceable impression on his mind. He had no
trace of that want of memory which besets some amiable beings. . . . Sometimes, where the matter was important, he carried with him a string of
leading questions, carefully written, which he had the ability to get as skill-
fully answered,—though, if there was a theory to maintain, with a possible
overlapping to his side of the argument. Ever on the search for knowledge,
he lived to get information; and as I am so far like Alfieri that I have almost
no curiosity, I once said to him how surprised I was at the persistence of
this trait in him. "What else is there in life?" was his reply. He did not end,
in this search, with the farmers, nor the broadcloth world; he knew another
class of men, who hang on the outskirts of society,—those who love "grog"
and never to be seen abroad without a fish-pole or a gun in their hands;
with elfish locks, and of a community with nature not to be surpassed.
They lived more out of doors than he did, and faced more mud and water
without flinching,—sitting all day in the puddles, like frogs, with a line in
the river, catching pouts, or wading mid-leg in marshes, to shoot wood-
cock. . . . I never knew him to go by this class without the due conversation;
but I observed that he had no tolerance for "loafers," bar-room idlers, and
men who "have nothing to do." The fishermen and hunters he knew and
enjoyed were experienced in birds and beasts and fishes, and from them
he loved to draw their facts. They had a sort of Indian or gypsy life, and he
loved to get this life even at second hand. He had sufficient innocence for
both sides in these interviews.

He was a natural Stoic, not taught from Epictetus nor the trail of Indians. Not only made he no complaint, but in him was no background of complaint, as in some, where a lifelong tragedy dances in polished fetters. He *enjoyed* what sadness he could find. He would be as melancholy as he could and rejoice with fate. "Who knows but he is dead already?" . . .

He was one of those who keep so much of the boy in them that he could never pass a berry without picking it. For huckleberries, wild strawberries, chestnuts, acorns, and wild apples he had a snatch of veneration almost superstitious. I being gifted with a lesser degree of this edible religion, frequently had to leave him in the rear, picking his berry, while I sat looking at the landscape, or admiring my berry-loving lad; nor was I less pleased to see him sometimes cutting off a square of birch-bark, out of which, in five minutes, he would construct a safe and handsome basket for his prize. The same simplicity and mechanical skill has often saved us from a severe drenching in those sudden thunder-storms so common to this climate. With his trusty knife (of which he always carried two,—one specially, with a short, strong, stubbed blade), before the shower could overhaul us, and in a very few minutes, he would make a very good shelter. Taking the lower limbs of an oak for his rafters, and instantly casting on a supply of long birches, with their butt-ends over the oak-boughs for cross-pieces,—over these must be thatched all the bushes and branches contiguous, thus keeping us absolutely dry in a deluge. He thought it could also be done by simply cutting a big strip of bark, with a hole for the "noddle." . . .

Thoreau says that he knew he loved some things, and could *fall back* on them. . . . His interest in swamps and bogs was familiar: it grew out of his love for the wild. He thought that he enjoyed himself in Gowing's Swamp, where the hairy huckleberry grows, equal to a domain secured to him and reaching to the South Sea; and, for a moment, experienced there the same sensation as if he were alone in a bog in Rupert's Land, thus, also, saved the trouble of going there. . . .

The high moral impulse never deserted him, and he resolved early (1851) "to read no book, take no walk, undertake no enterprise, but such as he could endure to give an account of to himself; and live thus deliberately for the most part." In our estimate of his character, the moral qualities form the basis: for himself, rigidly enjoined; if in another, he could overlook delinquency. . . .

A notice of him would be incomplete which did not refer to his fine social qualities. He served his friends sincerely and practically. In his own home he was one of those characters who may be called household treasures: always on the spot with skilful eye and hand to raise the best melons in the garden, plant the orchard with the choicest trees, act as extempore mechanic; fond of the pets, the sister's flowers, or sacred Tabby. Kittens were his favorites,—he would play with them by the half-hour. Some have fancied because he moved to Walden he left his family. He bivouacked there, and really lived at home, where he went every day.

It is needless to dwell on the genial and hospital entertainer he always was. His readers came many miles to see him, attracted by his writings. Those who could not come sent their letters. Those who came when they could no more see him, as strangers on a pilgrimage, seemed as if they had been his intimates, so warm and cordial was the sympathy they received from his letters. If he did the duties that lay nearest and satisfied those in his immediate circle, certainly he did a good work; and whatever the impressions from the theoretical part of his writings, when the matter is probed to the bottom, good sense and good feeling will be detected in it. A great comfort in him, he was eminently reliable. No whim of coldness, no absorption of his time by public or private business, deprived those to whom he belonged of his kindness and affection. He was at the mercy of no caprice: of a firm will and uncompromising sternness in his moral nature, he carried the same qualities into his relation with others, and gave them the best he had, without stint. He loved firmly, acted up to his love, was a believer in it, took pleasure and satisfaction in abiding by it. . . .

The living, actual friendship and affection which makes time a reality, no one knew better. . . . He did not wish for a set of cheap friends to eat up his time; was rich enough to go without a train of poor relations. . . . In the best and practical sense, no one had more friends or was better loved. . . . He was ready to *accommodate* those who differed from him with his opinion; and never too much convinced by opposition. To those in need of information—to the farmer-botanist naming the new flower, the boy with his puzzle of birds or roads, or the young woman seeking for books—he was always ready to give what he had.

Literally, his views of friendship were high and noble. Those who loved him never had the least reason to regret it. He made no useless professions, never asked one of those questions which destroy all relation; but he was on the spot at the time, and had so much of human life in his keeping, to the

[87]

last, that he could spare a breathing place for a friend. When I said that a change had come over the dream of life, and that solitude began to peer out curiously from the dells and wood-roads, he whispered, with his foot on the step of the other world, "It is better some things should end." . . .

No matter where he might have lived, or in what circumstance, he would have been a writer: he was made for this by all his tendencies of mind and temperament; a writer because a thinker, and even a philosopher, a lover of wisdom. No bribe could have drawn him from his native fields, where his ambition was—a very honorable one—to fairly represent himself in his works, accomplishing as perfectly as lay in his power what he conceived his business. More society would have impaired his designs; and a story from a fisher or hunter was better to him than an evening of triviality in shining parlors where he was misunderstood. . . .

The excellence of his books and style is identical with the excellence of his private life. He wished to write living books that spoke of out-of-door things, as if written by an out-of-door man. . . . In this he was an artist. . . . He observed nature; but who would have known or heard of that except through his literary effort? He observed nature, yet not for the sake of nature, but of man. . . .

Before he set out on a foot journey, he collected every information as to the routes and the place to which he was going, through the maps and guide-books. For Massachusetts he had the large State map divided in portions convenient, and carried in a cover such parts as he wanted: he deemed this map, for his purposes, excellent. Once he made for himself a knapsack, with partitions for his books and papers,—india-rubber cloth, strong and large and spaced (the common knapsacks being unspaced). The partitions were made of stout book-paper. His route being known, he made a list of all he should carry,—the sewing materials never forgotten (as he was a vigorous walker, and did not stick at a hedge more than an English racer), the pounds of bread, the sugar, salt, and tea carefully decided on. After trying the merit of cocoa, coffee, water, and the like, tea was put down as the felicity of a walking "*travail*,"—tea plenty, strong, with enough sugar, made in a tin pint cup; thus it may be said the walker will be refreshed and grow intimate with tea-leaves. With him the botany must go too, and the book for pressing flowers (an old "Primo Flauto" of his father's), and the guide-book, spy-glass, and measuring-tape. Every one who has carried a pack up a mountain knows how every fresh ounce tells. He would run up the steepest place as swiftly as if he were on smooth land, and his breath never failed. He commended every party to carry "a junk of heavy cake" with plums in it, having found by long experience that after toil it was a capital refreshment. . . .

Thoreau considered his profession to be literature, and his business the building up of books out of the right material,—books which should impress the reader as being alive. As he loved not dead birds, so neither loved he dead books; he had no care for scattered fragments of literature. His aim was to bring his life into the shape of good and substantial literary expression; and to this end he armed himself with all the aids and appliances usual to literature. . . .

He was by no means one of those crochety persons who believe, because they set up Plato or Goethe or Shakespeare as the absolute necessities of literary worship, that all other students must so make idols of them. I never knew him say a good word for Plato, and I fear he had never finished Shakespeare. His was a very uncompleted reading; there being with him a pressure of engrossing flowers, birds, snow-storms, swamps, and seasons. He had no favorites among the French or Germans and I do not recall a modern writer except Carlyle and Ruskin whom he valued much. . . . For novels, stories, and such matters, he was devoid of all curiosity; and for the works of Dickens had a hearty contempt. . . .

He loved the world and could not pass a berry, nor fail to ask his question, I fear—leading. Men who had seen the partridge drum, caught the largest pickerel, and eaten the most swamp apples, did him service; and he long frequented one who, if not a sinner, was no saint,—Goodwin the gunner. The Farmer who could find him a hawk's egg or give him a fisher's foot, he would wear in his heart of hearts, whether called Jacob Farmer or not. . . .

He wished so to live as to derive his satisfactions and inspirations from the commonest events, every-day phenomena; so that what his senses hourly perceived, his daily walk, the conversation of his neighbors, might inspire him; and he wished to dream of no heaven but that which lay about him. . . .

His mental appearance at times almost betrayed irritability; his words were like quills on "the fretful porcupine." . . . Yet, truly, the worship of beauty, of the fine things in nature, of all good and friendly pursuits, was his staple; he enjoyed common people; he relished strong, acrid characters. . . .

When with temperaments radically opposed to his, he drew in the head of his pugnacity like that portion of one of his beloved turtles, and could hiss and snap with any ancient of them all. . . . His advice to a drunkard as the wisest plan for him to reform, "You had better cut your throat,"—that was his idea of moral suasion. . . .

No man had a better unfinished life. His anticipations were vastly rich: more reading was to be done over Shakespeare and the Bible; more choice apple-trees to be set in uncounted springs,—for his chief principle was faith in all things, thoughts, and times, and he expected, as he said, "to live for forty years." . . .

Truth, audacity, force, were among Thoreau's mental characteristics, devoted to humble uses. His thoughts burned like flame, so earnest was his conviction. He was transported infinitely beyond the regions of self when pursuing his objects, single-hearted, doing one thing at a time and doing that in the best way! . . .

His love of wildness was real. Whatever sport it was of Nature, this child of an old civilization, this Norman boy with the blue eyes and brown hair, held the Indian's creed, and believed in the essential worth and integrity of plant and animal. This was a religion to him; to us, mythical. He spoke from a deeper conviction than ordinary, which enforced on him that sphere and rule of life he kept. So far an anchorite, a recluse, as never to seek popular ends, he was yet gifted with the ability and courage to be a captain of men. Heroism he possessed in its highest sense,—the will to use his means to his ends, and these the best. Inexplicable he was, if spontaneous action and free genius are not transparent: as they cannot be to those who put aside the principles of being, as understood by himself, and adopt an estimate that confines all men to one spiteful code,—their own.

As to his results,—possibly the future may determine that our village life, unknown and unnoticed, without name and influence in the present, was essential and vital, as were the realities he affected, the immutable truths he taught,—learned in the school of Nature. Endowed with unusual power and sagacity, if he did not shine in public councils, or lead the State, he yet defended the right, and was not the idle spectator of wrong and oppression. He showed that the private man can be a church and state and law unto himself. In a possible New England he may stand for the type of coming men, who shall invent new forms and truer modes of mortal society. . . .

William Ellery Channing, *Thoreau: The Poet-Naturalist with Memorial Verses,* new ed., enl. (Boston: Charles E. Goodspeed, 1902), 10–13, 15, 16, 24–25, 30–31, 38–39, 41–42, 49, 58, 68, 118, 327–28, 329, 333, 341–42.

From "Henry David Thoreau: The 'Poet-Naturalist' of Concord" (1874)

Louise Chandler Moulton

Author and poet Louise Chandler Moulton (1835–1908) was married to Boston publisher William U. Moulton. Her earliest stories appeared in the weekly *True Flag*, based in Boston; her literary output from 1859 onward includes several volumes of stories and collections of verse, including *This, That and the Other* (1854), *Juno Clifford* (1855), *My Third Book* (1859), *Bed-time Stories, Firelight Stories* (1883), and *Stories Told at Twilight* (1890). In the 1870s Moulton contributed regularly to the *New York Tribune*, and later to the *Boston Herald;* she became well known as the host of one of Boston's most popular literary salons. This review of William Ellery Channing's biography offers a thought-provoking assessment of Transcendentalism and Thoreau, whom she admires especially for his dignity and his morality. Apparently, however, Moulton and Thoreau never met.

THERE IS SCARCELY, in the history of American literature, so unique and individual a figure as Thoreau, after we have excepted Emerson and Hawthorne. And yet when one has read Channing's *Thoreau*—to which volume I would here acknowledge my indebtedness for most of the few facts I shall give you concerning the "Poet-Naturalist"—one seems rather to know of what manner of man he was, than much that he did. He was a creature of contradictions, in whom our complex human nature was more complex than usual. He loved solitude, and yet he delighted in companionship. To some woes he was as stolid and unsympathetic as an Indian. He had small pity for headaches or heartaches; and yet upon other occasions he could be tender as a woman. He resented, yet would not refute, a false accusation. He had a spiritual dignity which was almost arrogance, and which made him feel that no man's opinion was so important to him as his own. He was satisfied with the simplest attire, and yet was most fastidious as to the "cut" of his garments; which he said must be shaped to suit *him* as he was to wear them. Every one of his attributes was many-sided; and it is matter of curious interest to know what factors of descent, of culture, of occupation, of station in life, went to the making up of this character, so singular and so strong. . . .

His next work was to build himself a small house close by the shore of Walden Pond, in Concord—a little shelter, where he could sleep or meditate. It had no lock on the door, or curtain to the window—it belonged to nature almost as much as to him. It has been remarked, sneeringly, that while Thoreau thus lived in hermitage, he never forgot his daily way to his mother's pantry. The truth was he never meant to forget it. His purpose was not at all to sever himself from his home, to which he was strongly attached, but to have an extra lodgment, so exclusively his own that he could retire there and be secure against interruption—at home with the solitude, the deep stillness, which he often said he found more suggestive than any company. He had a curious mechanical skill; and out of scanty bits of driftwood from his native stream he made himself chests and bookcases and cabinets. He bound his own books. Also, he was a good practical surveyor, and used by this profession to supply his few personal wants. He was very accurate in his measurements, and much sought as an adjustor of landmarks. Thus he came to see the inside of all the farmers' houses, and of their heads and hearts, also. To listen to gossip was a delight to him, because thus he could study characters; and he boasted that he could sit out the oldest frequenter of the bar-room, because he was alive from top to toe with curiosity. This curiosity concerned itself only incidentally with the affairs of his neighbors—it was awake in all directions. It sought out the haunts of the flowers, and the secrets of the birds. When he returned from a journey, he emptied his pack of shells, and seeds, and plants, and a score of similar treasures. He was always ready to share his discoveries and experiences with others—to "take one or twenty into partnership."

Thoreau was by nature a Stoic. He not only did not complain—he did not feel like complaining. He accepted any melancholy mood as a luxury, as one enjoys minor music. He voyaged about his river in December, when the drops froze on the oar, as cheerily as in June; and called the icicles "toys of immortal water, alive even to the superficies." His interest in swamps and bogs was keen—he loved everything that was wild. He must have been, unconsciously perhaps, an evolutionist. All growing things were alive to him. He hated to hurt a flower, and he wrote of his walks:

"Kings unborn shall walk with me;
And the poor grass shall plot and plan.
What it will do when it is man."

While, as I said, he was indifferent to the headaches and small megrims of his friends, great things moved him greatly. He was made ill by the John Brown tragedy; and the war of the Rebellion depressed him fearfully—he used to say he could never get well while it lasted.

His high moral purpose never deserted him. Early in life he resolved "to read no book, take no walk, undertake no enterprise, but such as he could endure to give an account of to himself." His moral qualities were the very foundation of his character, on which all the rest was built. Truth, he said, before all things—integrity above all—purity in all, even the faintest thought. A man who lived thus was certainly a religious soul; but he had no creed unless it were one so catholic as to embrace the world. He could sympathize with all religions, warm himself at every altar-fire. A friend once described to me a conversation to which she listened, in Concord, in Thoreau's time. A more orthodox person than it was usual to meet in those transcendental gatherings chanced to be of the party; and the talk turned on the tendencies of modern thought. "It seems to me we are going backward to Paganism," said the orthodox guest. Thoreau looked at her with his keen eyes. "Say rather *forward* to Paganism, madam," he said, with a solemn bow. He believed that we could not worship too much. "I would fain," he wrote, "improve every opportunity to wonder and worship, as a sunflower welcomes the light." "God could not be unkind to me if he should try," was a quaint expression of his faith. Again he said, "Nothing is so much to be feared as fear."

He declined all polite shams. He was not fond of visiting; but when invited he would never say it was not convenient, or not in his power, or he regretted, but always the unmitigated truth—"I do not want to go." Yet he had friends whose houses he frequented, and whom he loved with a steadfast affection. To the place of his birth he was as constant as the most faithful of lovers. He never lived much elsewhere, but he made various journeys; and neither Staten Island, or the White Hills, or New Bedford seemed anything worth even comparing to the hills and meadows of Concord. He found among these woods and fields unlimited material for his work as a naturalist; and continual delight for his perceptions as a poet. The river was his great blessing. On it he boated, in season and out of season; and whenever he chose he would put into shore to examine an animal or a plant, or get a wider view. The study of the river-plants never ended; the birds and the insects wooed him to the shores; fish and musquash, sun and wind, were all interesting. Next to Concord he liked Cape Cod, where he did his stint of walking, and the old Cods took him for a peddler with his pack. . . .

A list of his works can be found in any catalogue; I will not dwell upon them. They are full of flavor and originality—they must always command the best readers or none; but, after all, the man Thoreau was greater and more original than any of his works. He was a close reader of the best literature. He used to say to young students, *"Begin with the best—start with that and never deviate."*

As an honorary member, Thoreau belonged to the Boston Society of Natural History, to which body he left his collections of plants, Indian tools, and the like. Often in his life he sent them some wonder which he found, and he found more wonders than any other man. He had a firm faith that everything, tropic or polar, could be discovered in Concord, if one only looked long enough for it. "First," he said, "the idea or image of a plant occupies my thoughts, and at length I surely see it, though it may seem as foreign to this locality as Hudson's Bay is." He had caught woodchucks by chasing them; but he failed in this experiment on a fox, catching, instead, a bronchial cold that did him great harm. He used to examine the squirrels' nests in the trees; and he climbed, successively, four pines after hawks' nests, and was much elated by the feat. Once he gathered the brilliant flowers of the white pine from the very top of the tallest tree; but such imprudent exertions strained him, and gradually impaired his health. Turtles were his pride and consolation. He piloted a snapping turtle, big enough to have carried the naturalist himself on its back, from his house to the river; and would sometimes hatch a batch of these Herculean monsters in his yard. The wood tortoise was another favorite of his. He wrote: "It is more glorious to live in Concord because the jay is so splendidly painted." His poetry was full of his subtle sympathy with wild nature. But, like all true poets, he dimly discerned the something beyond which forever eluded him. . . .

They laid his mortal ashes in the burying-ground at Concord; but the strong, free soul was gone—whither? He said once, on being asked his ideas concerning the future life, that he thought he should not go away from Concord. Who knows the locality of the Father's many mansions; or whether the "Poet-Naturalist" of Concord may not still float on the sweet waters, smell the pine's fragrance, and look in the shy eyes of bird and beast, there in the old haunts he loved so well? We do not see him, any more than we see the wind that fans our cheek; but he and the wind were kin. He was part of the dawn and the sunshine, and to the world he loved he can hardly be alien now.

Louise Chandler Moulton, "Henry David Thoreau: The 'Poet-Naturalist' of Concord," *Christian Union* 9 (4 March 1874): 173.

From "Our Poet-Naturalist" (1877)

JAMES T. FIELDS

> Influential publisher and editor James T. Fields (1817–1881) was a partner in the Boston publishing firm Ticknor and Fields, which brought out Thoreau's *Walden* in 1854. Thanks to Fields's active promotion, advance notices of *Walden* appeared in most of America's leading periodical and news outlets. As editor of the *Atlantic Monthly*, Fields also published "Walking," "Autumnal Tints," and "Wild Apples" in the months immediately following Thoreau's death. Later that year, Ticknor and Fields also brought out a second edition of *Walden*. Fields's appreciation of Thoreau was genuine and warm. As he remarked of Thoreau's visits, "I like to see him come in . . . he always smells of the pine woods" (102).

THERE ARE FEW writers who have died and left more interesting books behind them than Henry Thoreau. What more delightful reading can there be than his *Life in the Woods,* his *Excursions in Field and Forest,* his *Week on the Concord and Merrimac Rivers,* his *Yankee in Canada,* and his adventures in the *Maine Woods* and on *Cape Cod?* These books never fail to bring their own enchantment with them, and I do not wonder at the eulogies bestowed upon them by such rare judges as Emerson, Curtis, Alcott, and Channing. In Summer and Winter, by the fireside or in the open air, they are sweet and invigorating companions, and they can be read over and over again with profit and pleasure. When you walk beside Thoreau you get nature at first hand, and no mere hearsay reports of shipwrecks, mountains, rivers, and animals. The birds knew him by heart, and all forest and meadow people were his intimates. You can *learn* from Thoreau many things you can be taught nowhere else; and so he is always a nutritious author, to young people especially.

Like Agassiz, he was a *teacher* in the best sense of that much-abused office. An hour's silent talk from him is a real boon, and the more you get out of him the richer you will become.

Originality is a patent quality with *him.* Many modern works on natural history are made as apothecaries make a new mixture, by pouring out of several vessels into a new bottle; but Thoreau went into the open laboratories of nature and gathered what he offers with his own hands. He was one of the sharpest observers who ever lived, and whenever he went abroad among the scenes he loved to study, his eyes were never absent from his face. He took nothing for granted, and what he could not see he would never report. "Accuracy or silence," was his motto. He had a hunger and thirst for the truth in matters of information, and rested only at the fountain-head when he was hunting for a fact, believing with Charles Kingsley, that it is better to *know* one thing than to know *about* a thousand things. He believed that God was always *educating* man, and he wished to avail himself of the situation. . . .

I remember he once described to me, on that very road, a favorite cow which he had the care of thirty years before, and if she had been his own grandmother he could not have employed tenderer phrases about her. In youth his eyes and ears were ever on the alert, seeing and hearing what was going on in that delightful region where his first years were passed. It was his great good luck to be born in the country, and to have his ideas nurtured in the pure air of such a rural life as the one he came up in. . . .

He had lived so much under the open heavens that somehow he always seemed a part of outdoors. I used to think I could tell when he was in Boston by a kind of pine-tree and apple-tree odor that preceded him, and accordingly counted on a call that day from him. Sydney Smith said that a certain London cockney, when he visited the country, made all the region round about smell like Piccadilly. When Thoreau came to Boston from Concord he brought a rural fragrance with him from his native fields into our streets and lanes. Spicy odors of black birch, hickory buds, and pennyroyal lingered about his garments and made his presence welcome and sweet.

In his way, Thoreau was a wide reader, but his books were not those commonly chosen; the quotations in his published works show his quaint and careful excursions among authors. Dr. Donne, Samuel Daniel, Charles Cotton, Isaac Walton, Michael Drayton, were among his admired writers. Familiar with the classics, he made translations from Homer, Pindar, Pliny, and many other wise men of antiquity, but his teachers were the woods, the rivers, and the skies, and his communion with them was unceasing. His journals, if they are ever published, will give him a place among the keenest observers who have ever lived, and it is to be hoped some editor will be found competent to prepare them for the Press. He was the poet-naturalist of America, and our literature will never be complete without his truthful records of so many years of patient observations. The works he has printed and left for our perusal teach self-reliance, courage, and love of the country. He believed that only in nature can pure health be found, and endeavored all his life to prove the doctrine he taught. "I would keep," he says, "some book of natural history always by me as a sort of elixir, the reading of which should restore the tone of the system." And that is just what his own writings are eminently capable of doing. A fresh, invigorating breeze is always stirring through his pages, and the reader gets the benefit of it wherever he chances to turn the leaf. . . .

James T. Fields, "Our Poet-Naturalist," *Baldwin's Monthly* 14, no. 4 (April 1877): 1.

["Warrington" and Henry Thoreau] (1877)

[HARRIET HANSON ROBINSON]

Newspaper editor and political columnist William Stevens Robinson (1818–1876) was a Concord native, school classmate, and boyhood friend of Thoreau. In 1839, he became editor of the Concord *Yeoman's Gazette,* which he renamed the *Republican.* In 1848, Robinson married Lowell Mill textile worker Harriet Jane Hanson (1825–1911), who contributed to the mill's employee-run newsletter, the *Lowell Offering.* The Robinsons lived in Concord for a few years in the 1850s, renting from the Thoreaus their former home outside of town. During these years Harriet joined the female antislavery society and became friends with Sophia and Cynthia Thoreau. She frequently encountered Henry Thoreau when he handled maintenance tasks at their home.

As editor of the *Lowell American* in the early 1850s, and, commencing in 1856, as the columnist "Warrington" in the *Springfield Republican,* William Robinson often noted Thoreau's writings. Although complimentary of the merits of *Walden,* his obituary of Henry Thoreau in the *Republican* praised John Thoreau Jr., whom Robinson had preferred over the "cynical and egotistical and satirical" Henry (qtd. in Scharnhorst, *Annotated Bibliography,* 62). Harriet Robinson's memoir of her husband and compilation of his "Warrington" columns also includes Harriet's own recollections of Henry Thoreau, beginning with the fact that alongside her husband, he was the only other "widely known" local author to have been born in Concord.

THERE WERE FREQUENT opportunities of seeing Henry Thoreau, as he often came with his father to work on the land belonging to the house in which Mr. Robinson lived, or, as the children said, to "paint the handles of the trees." His meditative figure was often seen walking across the sunny meadows, with some live specimen of a "species" dangling from his hand, while (to use his own expression) "the sun on his back seemed like a gentle herdsman driving him home at evening." He sometimes called on Mr. Robinson. He was a great talker, sitting with his head bent over, and carrying on the "conversation" all by himself. On one occasion we had a visitor who had written several town histories, and was learned in Indian matters. Thoreau called while he was there; and, the conversation soon turning to Indian affairs, Thoreau talked our friend dumb in a very short time. His book ("Walden, a Life in the Woods") was published in 1854, and drew many visitors to the little hut by the shore of the pond where the philosopher had lived on three cents a day, planted his beans, and written his immortal pages. The fact of his living so cheaply was much discussed in Concord, more even than the quality of his writings; and it was suspected by his incredulous townspeople that the "cupboard" of this disciple of Pythagoras was often replenished from his mother's larder. Said Mr. Robinson in his "Warrington" Letters,—

> It is fortunate for literature that Thoreau lived, and built his house on the shores of Walden Pond, when he did. If his birth had been postponed twenty years, we should never have had his most delightful book, and one of the most delightful of all American books. "Walden" is as good of its kind as any thing in American or English literature. It is, on the whole, the best book ever written in Concord. He hated, *or affected to hate,* all crowds, and said the pleasantest place in Boston was the Fitchburg Railroad Dépôt, because it was the road home. What would he say if he could see Walden Pond as it is now, on whose banks he built his little house, and lived, raising beans on his farm, and charming the fishes with his flute? or, rather, what would he write and print, if pen and ink and the press were open to him? for I will not assume that he cannot see and talk as well as ever. The pond, six months ago, was more solitary than Sleepy-hollow Cemetery, where his body rests with Hawthorne, and others not so famous. Now the cemetery has the advantage of the pond; for the railroad trains frequently stop at the pond, and land their great picnic-parties, who, for the time being, make it the busiest part of the town. Thoreau professed to find his most entertaining company in the morning; for then nobody ever came to see him: and Mr. Emerson said of Walden Pond, that it was an excellent place for parties, especially parties of one."

Mr. Robinson thought Thoreau's poem "Sympathy" an evidence of true genius. . . .

"Warrington" Pen Portraits: A Collection of Personal and Political Reminiscences from 1848 to 1876 from the Writings of William S. Robinson, ed. Mrs. W. S. [Harriet Hanson] Robinson (Boston: Mrs. W. S. Robinson, 1877), 67–68.

[Reminiscences of Thoreau] (1878, 1881, and 1882)

Joseph Hosmer Jr.

Concord native Joseph Hosmer Jr. (1814–1886) was the older brother of Horace Hosmer and a close friend of Henry Thoreau's brother, John. Hosmer helped his father on the family's farm in Concord, which he sold in 1857 before moving to Chicago. In several reminiscences published in Concord newspapers in the 1870s and 1880s, Hosmer attempted to set the record straight about the Thoreau he had known and obviously admired, a man who "stood a living protest against the frivolities, fashions, humbugs, and pretences, of the social, political and religious age in which he lived" (qtd. in Hendrick, 135–36). Leonard N. Neufeldt observes that Hosmer's version of "Thoreau . . . is shrewd, calculating, individualistic, quietly obstinate, perennially hopeful, and morally impeccable. . . . [as is] compatible with his own sense of what it means to be a product, indeed an epitome, of a Concord he liked to remember, a Concord unlike the one he had felt constrained to leave" (98).

"An Hour with Thoreau," 22 August 1878

As a ladies' man and a dandy, Thoreau would not be deemed a success, but as a student of nature in its most subtle windings, he had few equals living or dead. He possessed a character and lived a life peculiar to himself, and when out of his sphere, was commonplace enough, but in nature's undiscovered realm was the most interesting of men.

It was his delight to study the habits of and become intimately acquainted with the lower animals, and they in turn seemed to understand and appreciate him.

He would sit motionless for hours, and let the mice crawl over him and eat cheese out of his hand (and not scream; think of that girls).

The fish and the mud turtles were the subjects of his patient study. The mud turtles he told me were the largest wild animals in Massachusetts, he having discovered and secured one in Fair Haven Bay that weighed nearly one hundred pounds.

On one of his accustomed rambles he came where I was at work near the river, and hearing a well known sound that is heard in the low land along the banks of the Assabet, a sound as of a bird, yet somewhat like the notes of a tree-toad, only more bird like, he entered into conversation about it.

The noise alluded to always excited wonder especially with the older people, they believing it to be some kind of a bird, as nothing but a bird can sing so sweetly, yet on going where the sound came from, nothing could be discovered. It made its appearance in the last of summer and disappeared in the early autumn.

It was the received opinion of the people fifty years ago that the swallows dove into the water and burrowed in the mud during the winter, and as they were first and last seen over the ponds and streams, and hence the mysterious sounds were supposed to emanate from some kind of a bird.

Thoreau said it was a frog and he thought he could show it to me. He described it as apparently a green leaf, and when near it would point in the direction with the stick he held in his hand. After giving me minute directions how to proceed and to do in all things as he did, we started in the direction of the object we had in view, which was some eight or ten rods distant. When it sang we hastened on and just before the last note was uttered, we stopped till it began again and then on as before. When we were within a few rods of it, we dropped on our hands and knees, and worked up to it stealthily, but only when it sang. At last we were rewarded with a full view of it some twelve feet distant. It rose slowly, inflated itself and uttered its little song. It had planned a retreat in case of a surprise, and directly under the leaf it had a hole running down to the water and when we approached it disappeared.

Thus was solved by the sagacity of Thoreau, what had been heretofore a wonder and a mystery.

"In Praise of Concord Town," 24 November 1881

Fair Haven Cliffs, one of the favorite resorts of the Thoreau's, must be seen to be known and appreciated. The Concord river, with its serpentine figure pushing its way to the ocean; the Monadnoc and Wachusett in the distance, together with Lake Walden in full view on the east, presents the same appearance to us that they did in our boyhood, and to remind us that, while we are changing and passing, they are not! Nothing can surpass this sublime picture of beauty and loveliness.

I rode up the boiling spring, (minus the boil) on Fair Haven Hill, recently, and then took the path that Thoreau had often trod, over the top, down the "devil's stairway," over rocks, down its craggy sides, now sliding, now hanging by a twig that was anchored firmly to its side on to the bottom of the cliffs. I then followed westwards through brush and bramble to the river. The descent is not difficult, but the ascent is quite another thing. It was the same old way that, in my boy days, in company with John and Henry Thoreau, we wandered one bright spring day in a year that has so long since past that it now seems dim and shadowy. Many recollections were pleasing, but I often found my eyes wet with tears.

The ramble gave me a vivid reminder of one of Henry's exploits in after years, when he covered himself with brush and leaves one autumn night and awaited developments. After he had snugly prepared himself for the night's watch, he remained quiet. In the course of a few hours he heard the tread of an animal about his couch or hiding place. It was dark and prevented him from seeing what it was. Presently it began to poke its way in, when he with one punch of his cane revealed the fact that a skunk had come to say good evening to him, (in the skunk's own way.) Foxes he often saw and heard.

"Reminiscences of Thoreau," 1 September 1882

Thoreau was an enigma to all of us. No one could place him. His reticence and shyness, together with his rambling over the fields, waters and woodlands, by night and day, was uncommon and mysterious to his townspeople, to say the least. His field of operations was hidden and unknown to all. He studied the mysteries of nature's laws, with an earnest pleasure if not with brilliant results.

When he trundled his wheelbarrow down to the river's bank just at dusk, freighted with pitch-pine knots for an all night float on the "bosom" of his Concord, one of his neighbors would sometimes say, "I wonder how many gold dollars Thoreau expects to find on the bottom of the river?" and another "thought he would eventually become insane."

Thoreau was no egotist and he did not tell us all he knew, but like a skilful general, kept his reserves well in hand. Many persons may have seen at about this season of the year (Sept. 1st.), a yellowish colored water grass in the Concord and Assabet rivers. It is to be found on the sandy bottom at "Hubbard's," and "Uncle Ben Hosmer's" fishing places, (that were) on the Concord. It grows entirely under the water, and the current gives to it a serpentine motion. It had always been a fruitful theme and a study to us as to how it came there, and how it renewed itself from year to year. It had no flower and no seed that we could discover, but it annually came and disappeared from altogether unknown causes to us. One day as Thoreau was perambulating the intervals on the Assabet, I asked him concerning this grass, if it was not a spontaneous production of nature? He said that it had a flower of a very delicate pinkish white, not larger than a pea; that it blossomed in the night and closed before sunrise in a fair day, so sensitive are the petals to the light. The grass was (and is now probably), very plenty on the bottom of the Assabet, from the railroad bridge near Derby's, to the stone bridge east of the prison.

It is nearly twenty years since we laid away in Sleepy Hollow the machine, or body, that represented the will power, or spirit of the person that we called H. D. Thoreau. When shut up in jail for non-payment of taxes, he said that H. D. Thoreau was out on the street all the same attending to his business, only the body that had done nothing was confined in prison walls.

Whatever relates to him, or that tends to reveal him as he was, is eagerly caught up and read by the public. His fame increases as the years roll away and the body becomes dust. He had many peculiar and absurd ideas, viewed from our standpoint, but the following apostrophe to the Concord Lyceum will be read and admired by all men hundreds of years hence as today, for the philosophical truths enunciated, the poetic beauty of expression, and its pure naturalness.

Joseph Hosmer Jr., *Concord Freeman,* "An Hour with Thoreau," 22 August 1878; "In Praise of Concord Town," 24 November 1881; and "Reminiscences of Thoreau," 1 September 1882.

From "Thoreau" (1879)

Thomas Wentworth Higginson

In a life that spanned nearly a century, Thomas Wentworth Higginson (1823–1911) was a Unitarian minister, an editor, an author, a literary critic, an abolitionist, a women's rights activist, a colonel who commanded the first unit comprised of freed slaves during the Civil War, and a friend and coeditor of poet Emily Dickinson. Meeting Thoreau in the early 1850s, Higginson found him "more human and polite than I supposed . . . a little bronzed spare man. . . . [who] surveys land, both mathematically and meditatively; lays out house-lots in Haverhill and in the moon. He talks sententiously and originally" (qtd. in Mary Thacher Higginson, 98). The two men shared a commitment to antislavery and a love of the outdoors, both of which brought them together often during the 1850s. Like others, Higginson found much to praise and just its theology to blame in *A Week*, "the only thoroughly outdoor book I have ever seen . . . fascinating beyond compare to any one who knows Nature, though the religion and philosophy are of the wildest" (*Letters and Journals*, 105). In 1854, Higginson enthused equally about *Walden* and "Slavery in Massachusetts," a speech in which Thoreau extolled the heroism of Higginson and other abolitionists for attempting to rescue incarcerated slave Anthony Burns from his Boston jail cell in May 1854.

After Thoreau died, as others memorialized his seriousness of purpose and noble character, Higginson called attention, rather, to Thoreau's charm and humor, qualities he claimed had tangibly influenced the antebellum literary climate. In several studies, Higginson argues for Thoreau's originality and importance as an author, particularly defending him against the severe censure of James Russell Lowell, criticism that Higginson especially blamed for Thoreau's lack of renown in England (*Carlyle's Laugh*, 70). Higginson viewed Horace Greeley's indefatigable efforts on behalf of Thoreau's writings as evidence that "much of the sunshine at that period came also to many from Thoreau himself, whose talk and letters, like his books, were full of delicate humor; and who gave to outdoor hours such an atmosphere of serene delight as made one feel that a wood thrush was always soliloquizing somewhere in the background. Walks with him were singularly unlike those taken with Alcott, for instance. . . . Thoreau brought his outward observations indoors"

(*Part of a Man's Life*, 23). Lawrence Buell believes that "what clearly drew Higginson to Thoreau and what especially kept him there was the image of Thoreau the perceiver of beautiful unexpected microscopic truths about the flora and fauna of his own backyard." Interestingly, although Higginson admired Thoreau's antislavery activism and his uncategorical homage to John Brown, Buell also notes that "Thoreau the dissenter . . . is not what he chiefly talked about when he talked about Thoreau in public" ("Henry Thoreau Enters the American Canon," 45; *Environmental Imagination*, 357).

THERE IS NO FAME more permanent than that which begins its growth after the death of an author, and such is the fame of Thoreau. Before his death he had published but two books, *A Week on the Concord and Merrimack Rivers,* and *Walden.* Since his death four more have been printed, besides a volume of his letters, and two biographies. One of these last appeared within a year or two in England, where he was, up to the time of his death, absolutely unknown. Such things are not accidental or the result of whim, and they prove the literary fame of Thoreau to be secure. Indeed, it has already survived two of the greatest dangers that can beset reputation—a brilliant satirist for a critic, and an injudicious friend for a biographer.

Both admirer and censor—both Channing in his memoir, and Lowell in his well-known criticism—injure the memory of Thoreau in the same way, by bringing his eccentricities into undue prominence, and placing too little stress on the vigor, the good sense, the clear perceptions of the man. I have myself walked, talked, and corresponded with him, and can testify that the impression given by both these writers is far removed from that personally made by Thoreau himself. While tinged here and there, like most New England thinkers of his time, with the manner of Emerson, he was yet, as a companion, essentially sincere, wholesome, and enjoyable. Though more or less of a humorist, nursing his own whims, and capable of being tiresome when they came uppermost, he was easily led away from them to the vast domains of literature and nature, and then poured forth endless streams of the most interesting talk. He taxed the patience of his companions, but not more so on the whole than is done by many other eminent talkers, when launched upon their favorite themes.

It is hard for one who thus knew him to be quite patient with Lowell in what seems almost wanton misrepresentation. Lowell applies to Thoreau the word "indolent;" but you might as well speak of the indolence of a self-regulating thermometer; it does not go about noisily, yet it never knows an idle moment. Lowell says that Thoreau "looked with utter contempt on the august drama of destiny, of which his country was the scene, and on which the curtain had already risen" . . . but was it Thoreau or Lowell who found a voice when the curtain fell, after the first act of that drama, upon the scaffold of John Brown? Lowell accuses him of "a seclusion which keeps him in the public eye," and finds something "delightfully absurd" in his addressing six volumes under such circumstances to the public, when the critic knows very well that four of these volumes were made up by friends from his manuscripts, or from stray papers in newspapers and magazines. Lowell assumes throughout the popular attitude, which he himself did much to create or strengthen, that Thoreau hated civilization, and affected to believe only in the wilderness; whereas the latter defined his own position on this point with exceeding clearness, and made it essentially the same with that avowed by his critic. . . .

Seen in the light of such eminently sensible remarks as these, it will by and by be discovered that Thoreau's whole attitude has been uselessly and almost cruelly distorted. Lowell says that "his shanty-life was a mere impossibility, so far as his own conception of it goes, as an entire independency of mankind. The tub of Diogenes had a sounder bottom." . . . But what a man of straw is this that Lowell is constructing! What is this "shanty-life"? A young man living in a country town, having a passion for the minute observation of nature, and a love for Greek and Oriental reading, takes it into his head to build himself a study, not in the garden or the orchard, but in the woods, a mile from any other house, by the side of a lake. Happening to be poor, and to live in a time when social experiments are in vogue at Brook Farm and elsewhere, he takes a whimsical satisfaction in seeing how cheaply he can build his hut and support himself by the labor of his hands. He is not really banished from the world, nor does he seek or profess banishment; indeed, his hut is not two miles from his mother's door, and he goes to the village every day or two, by his own showing, to hear the news. . . . In this half-seclusion he spends two peaceful years, varied by an occasional excursion into the deeper wilderness at a distance. He earns an honest living by gardening and land surveying, makes more close and delicate observations on nature than any other American has ever made, and writes the only book yet written in America, to my thinking, that bears an annual perusal. Can it be really true that this is a life so wasted, so unpardonable?

The artist LaFarge built himself a studio as bare as Thoreau's, and almost as lonely, among the Paradise Rocks, near Newport, and used to retreat from the fashionable summer world to that safe seclusion. Lowell himself has celebrated in immortal verse the self-withdrawal of Prof. Gould, who would lock himself into his Albany observatory, and leave his indignant trustees to "admire the key-hole's contour grand" from without. Is the naturalist's work so much inferior to the artist's? Are the stars of thought so much less important than those of space, that LaFarge and Gould are to be praised for their self-devotion, and yet Thoreau is to be held up to all coming time as selfish? For my own part, with *Walden* in my hands, I wish that every other author in America might try the experiment of two years in a "shanty."

Let me not seem to do injustice to Lowell, who closes his paper on Thoreau with a generous tribute that does much to redeem its beginning. The truth is, that Thoreau shared the noble protest of what is called the "transcendental" period against conventionalism and worldliness, and naturally shared some of its extreme attitudes; but he did not, like some of his contemporaries, make his whims an excuse for mere selfishness, and his home-life, always the best test, was thoroughly affectionate and faithful. His life-long celibacy was due, if I have been correctly informed, to an early act of lofty self-abnegation toward his own brother, whose love had taken the same direction with his own. Thoreau's personal fortitude amid the privations and limitations of his own life was nothing less than heroic. There is nothing finer in literary history than his description, in his unpublished diary, of receiving from his publishers the unsold copies—nearly the whole edition—of his *Week on the Concord and Merrimack Rivers,* and of his carrying the melancholy burden up-stairs on his shoulders to his study. "I am now the owner," he writes (I quote from memory), "of a library of nine hundred volumes, seven hundred of which I wrote myself. . . ."

It will always be an interesting question how far Thoreau's peculiar genius might have been modified or enriched by society or travel. . . . A larger experience might have liberalized some of his judgments, and softened some of his verdicts. He was not as just to men as to woodchucks; and his "simplify, I say, simplify," might well have been relaxed a little for mankind, in view of the boundless affluence of external nature. The magnificent world of art, too, would have reached and touched his profound nature, could he have had the opportunity. Emerson speaks of "the raptures of a citizen arrived at his first meadow;" but the precise shade of emotion evoked in a pure, deep, ascetic soul like Thoreau's, by the first sight of a cathedral, would have been worth going far to observe.

The impression that Thoreau was but a minor Emerson will in time pass away, like the early classification of Emerson as a second-hand Carlyle. All three were the children of their time, and had its family likeness; but Thoreau had the *lumen siccum*, or "dry light," beyond either of the others, indeed beyond all men of his day. His temperament was like his native air in winter—clear, frosty, inexpressibly pure and bracing. His power of literary appreciation was something marvelous, and his books might well be read for their quotations, like the sermons of Jeremy Taylor. His daring imagination ventured on the delineation of just those objects in nature which seem most defiant of description, as smoke, mist, haze; and his three poems on these themes have an exquisite felicity of structure such as nothing this side of the Greek anthology can equal. The literary value of the classic languages was never better exemplified than in their influence on his training. They were real "humanities" to him, linking him with the great memories of the race, and with high intellectual standards, so that he could never, like some of his imitators, treat literary art as a thing unmanly and trivial. His selection of points in praising his favorite books shows this discrimination. He delights to speak of "the elaborate beauty and finish, and the lifelong literary labors of the ancients . . . works as refined, as solidly done, and as beautiful almost as the morning itself." . . . I remember how that fine old classical scholar, the late John Glen King, of Salem, used to delight in Thoreau as being "the only man who thoroughly loved both Nature and Greek."

Thoreau died at forty-four, without having achieved fame or fortune. It is common to speak of his life as a failure, but to me it seems, with all its drawbacks, to have been a great and eminent success. Taking into view only the common appetite of authors for immortality, his seems to me already a sure and enviable place. Time is rapidly melting away the dross from his writings, and exhibiting their gold. But his standard was higher than the mere desire for fame, and he has told it plainly. . . .

T. W. Higginson, "Short Studies of American Authors. III. —Thoreau," *Literary World* (24 May 1879): 169–70.

[Appraisals of Thoreau] (1888)

WALT WHITMAN

America's "good grey poet," Walt Whitman (1819–1892), met Thoreau only once, in the company of Bronson Alcott and Sarah Tyndale, when they paid him a visit in November 1856 in the home he shared with his mother and siblings in Brooklyn. Both Thoreau's journal entry at this time and subsequent letter to H. G. O. Blake about Whitman reflect an earnest approval of and curiosity about this controversial author. "He has spoken more truth than any American or modern that I know. I have found his poem exhilirating encouraging" (*Correspondence*, 445), Thoreau confided to Blake. Over the years, according to Horace Traubel's accounts of multiple conversations, Whitman's primary grievance against Thoreau rested on what Whitman regarded as a "disdain, contempt, for average human beings: for the masses of men" (Traubel, 1:285). As conveyed below in Traubel's recollections, Whitman observed late in life that Thoreau "had reservations" about him; yet more than twenty years before, Thoreau had already addressed this concern: Whitman "said that I misapprehended him. I am not quite sure that I do" (*Correspondence*, 441).

26 May 1888

Thoreau's great fault was disdain—disdain for men (for Tom, Dick and Harry): inability to appreciate the average life—even the exceptional life: it seemed to me a want of imagination. He couldn't put his life into any other life—realize why one man was so and another man was not so: was impatient with other people on the street and so forth. We had a hot discussion about it—it was a bitter difference: it was rather a surprise to me to meet in Thoreau such a very aggravated case of superciliousness. It was egotistic—not taking that word in its worst sense. . . . We could not agree at all in our estimate of men—of the men we meet here, there, everywhere—the concrete man. Thoreau had an abstraction about man—a right abstraction: there we agreed. We had our quarrel only on this ground. Yet he was a man you would have to like—an interesting man, simple conclusive. . . ."

[111]

24 December 1888

[When asked] "if it was quite certain that Emerson will size up in history ultimately bigger than Thoreau?" . . . W[hitman] took his glasses off his nose and said: "Tom, I'm not dead sure on that point either way: my prejudices, if I may call them that, are all with Emerson: but Thoreau was a surprising fellow—he is not easily grasped—is elusive: yet he is one of the native forces—stands for a fact, a movement, an upheaval: Thoreau belongs to America, to the transcendental, to the protesters: then he is an outdoor man: all outdoor men everything else being equal appeal to me. Thoreau was not so precious, tender, a personality as Emerson: but he was a force— he looms up bigger and bigger: his dying does not seem to have hurt him a bit: every year has added to his fame. One thing about Thoreau keeps him very near to me: I refer to his lawlessness—his dissent—his going his own absolute road let hell blaze all it chooses."

27 December 1888

"Henry was not all for me—he had his reservations: he held back some: he accepted me—my book—as on the whole something to be reckoned with: he allowed that I was formidable: said so to me much in that way: over in Brooklyn: why, that very first visit: 'Whitman, do you have any idea that you are rather bigger and outside the average—may perhaps have immense significance?' That's what he said: I did not answer. He also said: 'There is much in you to which I cannot accommodate myself: the defect may be mine: but the objections are there.'"

Horace Traubel, *With Walt Whitman in Camden,* vol. 1 (New York: D. Appleton, 1908); vol. 3 (New York: Mitchell Kennerley, 1914) 1:212–13; 3:374–75, 403.

"Henry D. Thoreau: A Disquisition" (1879)

Prescott Keyes

Prescott Keyes (1858–1943) was the son of Concord lawyer John Shepard Keyes and Martha Prescott Keyes. He graduated from Harvard in 1879 and returned to Concord, where in 1881 he married Alice Reynolds, and became a lawyer, district judge, bank president, head of an insurance company, and a trustee of the Concord Free Public Library. Although never delivered, this "Disquisition" on Thoreau was to have been part of Keyes's Harvard commencement program. As Walter Harding has noted, it is especially appealing as a contrasting study with his father's typically scornful views of Henry Thoreau, whom the senior Keyes belittled as a "queer mixture of sense & nonsense he got off in his Emersonian style," "the poet naturalist without much claim to either title" (Harding, "John Shepard Keyes," 3). Prescott Keyes could not have disagreed more.

DAVID HENRY THOREAU was born in Concord in 1817. His father was a lead-pencil maker and he himself worked at that trade until he was sent to Harvard at the age of 17. While in college he gained but little from his instructors or their text-books; he spent his time rummaging about in the dusty corners of the College library.

After graduating in 1837 he had to decide to what he should devote his life; which of the many paths that lay opening out before him he should choose. He turned aside from the accustomed paths and chose the by-path of a simple, sincere life, devoted to literature, to the study of Nature, to the development of what he felt to be highest and best in his own character—in short, to the art of living well. He refused to allow *his* life to be frittered away by detail, or its cares and labors to prevent his plucking its finer fruits. Most men are attracted to society; Thoreau to solitude, to Nature. Most men work in organized bodies; Thoreau did his life-work alone. Individuality is the key-note of his whole career.

He foresaw that he might be subjected to ridicule and that he would lose much in a worldly point of view, but believing in the great principle that a man should do that work in life for which he has an earnest enthusiasm, and feeling his own enthusiasm and deep love for Nature, he decided that his life ought to be spent with his mistress and not toiling and moiling in the busy world.

After teaching school for a year or two and making some more lead-pencils, he slowly drifted into the occupation of surveying the farms about Concord. This furnished him an honest, independent, though meagre support; it brought him into close contact with the farmers whose characters he studied with interest; "it led him continually into new and secluded grounds, and helped his studies of Nature," for while he surveyed the land for the farmer, he surveyed the landscape for himself.

His endless walks made up a great part of his life. Thoreau really understood the art of taking walks—of "sauntering through the woods and over the hills & fields." He left the world with its cares far behind him and walked, a free man, through the realm of Nature. He made himself thoroughly familiar with every nook and corner of the country round about his native village. He knew every animal and its habits, every plant from the mighty oak to the tiny moss that grows at its foot. The partridge had shown him her nest and the squirrel where the chestnuts and acorns lay hidden for the winter. He had seen the sun set and seen it rise again from the top of all the hills. He had rowed upon the river, by night and by day, from its source to its mouth, had bathed in its waters and slept on its banks.

To give a wider range to these rambles he went several times to Cape Cod, the Maine Woods and the White Mountains. But as even these excursions did not satisfy his longing to live close to Nature, he built himself a hut on the shore of Walden Pond in Concord. Here he lived for two years—years which he counted as better worth living than any others of his whole life. His sojourn at Walden was no affectation, nor was it a sour shutting himself out from his fellow-men. It was a deep draught from the fountain head of Nature's spring, giving him new life and placing him in a new relation to society. This "bachelor of thought and Nature," went to Walden to try a simple experiment in plain living and high thinking, "to meet face to face the essential facts of life and learn of them what they had to teach."

But what did Thoreau do for the good of society in his life free as it was from the narrowing and confining work of the world?

In estimating the life-work of such a man it must be remembered that more than all others it is the reformer who influences the permanent progress of a nation; that the destiny of a race is marked out by the leading minds of that race; that the great moving forces in this world's history have always been, and still are, truths perceived by individual men and pointed out by them to the multitudes. How much more noble is it to lead than to follow! and how much more lasting is the leader's work!

Thoreau told his country men in plain terms that they were running wild after the "almighty dollar," while neglecting their higher and truly essential nature; to use Mill's words, "that the life of the whole of one sex was devoted to dollar-hunting and of the other to breeding dollar-hunters." Thoreau taught them that true wealth lay in making their wants few—in reducing their denominator; that to live a true life—to get at the very meat of life—required but few of the so-called "means" of living; that the accident of poverty or riches was of but little moment. He once said:—"I am constantly reminded that if I had bestowed on me the wealth of Croesus, my aims must be still the same and my means essentially the same."

Thoreau showed that Mother Nature is after all the best of nurses as well for the soul as for the body, soothing, refreshing, and exhilarating; that "solitude in the presence of Nature is the proper cradle of all lofty thoughts and aspirations"; that Nature breathes into the character of man simplicity and sincerity: the false and the artificial quail in her awful presence. His own character was as pure as the crystal waters of his Walden. As an example of a just, sincere, stainless man, his name deserves the respect of coming generations. He hated sham with a bitter hatred and liked better to talk with children or the plain woodchopper than with men-of-the-world.

> For no trivial bridge of words,
> Or arch of boldest span,
> Can leap the moat that girds
> The sincere man.

Uncompromising in spirit, he could brook no make-shifts, could never give up the right or the just to the expedient. His scorn of pretence and hypocrisy shook to the foundation many a custom dear to society; his attack was not politic, but fierce and direct; he did not stop to count the cost but went straight to his end with a firmness of purpose not to be shaken. For instance, he never lost an opportunity to express his contempt for the Nation's halting policy in regard to slavery and the Fugitive Slave law. From the beginning he openly counciled resistance and himself helped many a slave toward Canada. Just after his friend, Captain John Brown, was taken prisoner at Harper's Ferry, when even the most reckless Abolitionists faltered and held back, Thoreau came bravely forward to speak the first words of public approval and eulogy of that hero whose name has been sung these twenty years in every Northern home. It was the first, as it was the strongest, wave of the returning tide.

His books are the simple record of his life and thoughts, a sort of diary of his rambles; and yet they teach a morality as high and pure as the scriptures of any language,—a morality that appeals to that element in man's nature which unites him with his Creator. They contain here and there touches of real poetry such as would do honor to Wordsworth, and many a beautiful and poetic thought crystallized into sentences equal to any in the language. Lowell says "there is no writing that is comparable in degree with Thoreau's where it is best, where it runs limpid and smooth and broadening as it runs, a mirror for whatever is grand and lovely in both worlds."

Thoreau's was a life full of brave ideas and hopes inspired by Nature herself; but alas! a life cut short in its prime with its brightest promises still unfulfilled. . . .

Prescott Keyes, "Henry D. Thoreau: A Disquisition," Vault A35, H. D. Thoreau Unit 3, Special Collections, Concord Free Public Library, Concord, MA.

From "A New Estimate of Thoreau" (1880)

William Sloane Kennedy

William Sloane Kennedy (1850–1929) grew up in Oxford, Ohio and graduated from Yale University in 1875. He began a career in journalism in 1879 at
the *Philadelphia American* and later worked for the *Boston Evening Transcript*.
Kennedy was a prolific writer, authoring biographies of Henry Wadsworth
Longfellow and John Greenleaf Whittier as well as his own poetry and nature
essays. He was a staunch defender of Walt Whitman and authored *Reminiscences of Walt Whitman* (1896), *Walt Whitman's Diary in Canada* (1904), and
The Fight of a Book for the World (1926). His thoughtful evaluation of Thoreau's life and work valorizes the examples of a solitary life and an impassioned individual who "was the richest man in all the wide Americas."

TO APPROACH OUR TASK: Here is a certain phenomenon called Thoreau; the
first thing to do is to account for him, to uncover the long filamental roots
that run out from his life, far back into the past, and out on every side into
the fabric of contemporary society. That society is a little too modest in its
rejection of Thoreau. He is one of its fruits; let it then except him, and fairly
and candidly try to explain him. Without doubt, the result of the examination will be far more honorable to him than was supposed, and at the same
time productive of wholesome effects upon society, in leading it to see itself
in new and startling aspects.

Thoreau, the solitaire, is no new phenomenon, although he happened
to be so in America. A practical, money-getting nation, naturally looked
with some perplexity upon the advent in its midst of a pure and solitary
mystic who looked with indifference, if not with contempt, upon the precious wealth which most of them spend their lives in accumulating. They
thought him a fool, of diseased mind. But the story of such lives as his may
be read in the literatures of all the olden countries of the globe. He takes
his place with the great throng of sensitive geniuses, whom the hard blows
of the world have always driven to nature and to books. The possession of

rarer mental powers than the mass of men have, has always driven the pos-sessor into some degree of solitude, and always will. . . .

The spell of illusion seems to be so woven over the minds of many, that they are unable to distinguish between the unhealthy and morbid dreamer, and the real prophet of a higher life among them, such as Thoreau was among his countrymen. It is such men as he who compel us to recognize the fact that society, as it is now constituted, is not altogether lovely in itself, but is all blotched and tainted with imperfections.

If Thoreau had done nothing more than point out the unloveliness of so-ciety in many of its aspects, without any attempt to better it himself, his life would have been of as little value as it is by many supposed to have been. But nothing could be farther from the truth than such a view of his life and work. No truer patriot, no truer man has ever breathed the air of this new world. By his fine Spartan life he taught us how to live. The influence of his rugged energy, his fine idealism, the purity and honesty, and manli-ness of his life, shall for generations breathe through the literature and the life of America like a strengthening ocean breeze, adding tone, toughness, elasticity, and richest Attic sparkle to the thought of men. His influence is almost wholly hygienic and sanative to those who know how to read him,—avoiding his hobbies, and passing by his too morbid dislike of men. Why is it that the lives of such men as Alcott and Thoreau excite such warm oppo-sition in some quarters? Is it not partly because there are many who keenly feel the rebuke which such lives imply? It does not do to be too good in this world; it excites envy. Then there is often a curious and not very laudable feeling of irritation at seeing something successfully accomplished, which people had voted well nigh impossible. The problem of the reconcilement of labor and culture, is one of these, and it has been worked out in Con-cord, Massachusetts. . . .

What is wonderful in Thoreau's case is, that he accomplished so much. What we want in order to save society from moral rottenness is, fifty thou-sand Henry Thoreaus in the class of farmers and mechanics. If in every generation there were even five hundred men in a nation, who, starting with next to no capital, could roll up such a fortune as he did in culture, manli-ness, and purity and sweetness of character, and dying, leave behind them such fragrant memories and such pregnant and stimulating writings, then would it be madness to ever despair of the future of Democracy.

To the fellow-citizens of Thoreau I would say: Let us cherish the memory of this saintliest of men. He is one of our saviours, if we would but see it. Fitting it were to strew our costliest flowers as a votive offering upon the grave of one of the truest, manliest hearts that ever beat, to plant around the now neglected spot that holds his dust the wild, rich weeds and plants he loved so passing well, and to inscribe, perhaps, upon his monument such words as these: "Here lies one whose only crime it was to be too pure and stainless in his life, and to love too well the meadows, woods and streams."

If in the years to come the lovers of Henry Thoreau in this country, are not counted by tens of thousands, (as they are now by hundreds) then might we well be tempted to think meanly of our America. Alas! shall men forever continue to run after every charlatan who can dazzle their eyes with cunning mask and bedizened coat, and pass unheeded by the great and genuine souls in their midst? If to be great means to always speak the truth, to be faithful in friendship, industrious, frugal, patriotic, dauntless in moral courage, cultured, a teacher of men, and an enthusiastic scientific student, if it means this, then was he of whom we are speaking a great man. He was not only great, this plain-dressed, plain-speaking, plain-souled Thoreau, but he was the richest man in all the wide Americas. For when he came to maturity of years, he was presented by a certain enchanter, with a pass-key to a far-stretching, sunlit garden called Nature, which contains the larger part of the real wealth of the world. A ticket to this garden is for life, and is really a deed in fee-simple of the whole estate. Thoreau was the happy possessor of one of these deeds.

His patriotism was deep and strong—knit into the very fibre of his being. He was patriotic in his own way, however. He loved not so much the people in the abstract and philanthropic sense, as he did individual friends. He was in love with the brown soil, the azure sky, the clouds, the honest rocks, the artless flowers and shrubs in their charming and unconscious beauty; trees, rivers, lakes and hills—all these he loved with a passionateness such as no other American, with whom we are acquainted, ever felt. He loved nature, and he loved good men; he prized above all, liberty and justice. If the testimony of his friends to the warmth and tenderness of his affection were not more than sufficient to prove his love of men, his Anti-Slavery papers would put it beyond doubt. It is touching and pathetic to read of the kind of terror, the paralysis of mind and the gloom which came over him at the time of the enforcement of the Fugitive Slave Law by the delivering up of Anthony Burns on the part of the Massachusetts civil officers. He said he could not enjoy nature as before. Life seemed worth much less to him in Massachusetts than formerly. No more terrible indignation was ever put into words than we find in his patriotic papers. His sentences cut like a knife; they draw blood. His feelings are at a white heat, but his words are as quiet and measured as if he were speaking upon an indifferent theme. His hearers and readers at that time must have writhed under the steady fusillade of his scorching sarcasms and bitter reproaches.

There are sentences in these Anti-Slavery papers which deserve to be engraved in gold and set in diamonds, to be hung up in every court of justice in America. . . .

On the theme of Friendship, Thoreau (in his *Week*), has said some of the most subtle things that have ever been uttered. These, taken in connection with his *Letters,* show how rich and pure his affections were—only they tell us that his friendships were for idealized persons, rather than for the actual persons themselves in all the grossness and imperfection of the flesh.

Thoreau's finely-strung and vibrant nature led him to shun as much as possible the gross real. He yearned to live wholly in the ideal. He fled from the jangle and jar of clashing interests. Far up along the azure cliffs of life he moved, breathing an atmosphere not respirable by the mass of men. His life was pure and simple as that of the Alpine herdsman, and he drank from the streams of truth and joy, whose sources lie above the clouds. . . .

Those who refuse to believe that Thoreau cherished warm and humanitarian sympathies beneath his stoical exterior, will, of course, see in his passion for the wild in nature, nothing but confirmation of their conviction that he had only a cold and repellant disposition. A deep and permanent love of the wild is something so rare, that most people are inclined to regard it as an uncanny thing, and as triumphant proof of a soured and disappointed nature. But it is nothing of the kind. In and of itself, if it is not carried to excess, it is one of the chief sources of freshness and originality. In all rural poetry it is the indispensable condition of success. . . . Thoreau's praise of the wild, as contrasted with the tame and factitious, was undoubtedly extreme. It was his nature to always attempt to see what could be said upon the unpopular or opposite side of any question. This arose, I think, not so much from a love of singularity, or from obstinacy, as from a love of strict justice, and a desire to help the weaker side. He was always for the under dog in the fight. It must be continually borne in mind that his exaggeration of solitude and the wild, as sources of happiness, was made with deliberate purpose. He says in his paper on walking, that he wishes to make an extreme statement, if so he may make an emphatic one, for "there are enough champions of civilization." I regard this passage as the key to Thoreau's whole life conduct. His circumstances, and his taste as a naturalist having led him to the forests and the fields, and to Spartan simplicity of life, he saw that the sources of enjoyment to be found there were, to a great extent, unknown to his countrymen; that the pernicious habit of all classes of crowding into great cities in search of happiness, is the cause of untold amounts of vice and misery. And so he gradually came to feel that his mission to men was to recall them to the simple pleasures of rural life. He did this work, and did it well. His books have restored to sane and healthy views of life many a despondent soul. They are not to be devoured all at once, in a month, or in three months. They must be read in parts, in the warm days of Summer and Autumn, in the open fields, in the mountain camp, or by the sea. You are to resort to them for their bracing and restorative effects upon the *ennuyé* and *blasé* mind, just as you resort to mountain, field, or sea for invigorating air and sunshine. . . .

His religion was a cheerful and reverent mysticism. His attitude in respect of the details of the infinite life was one of suspended judgment, as that of every man ought to be. With the imbecilities and pretences of conventional religion he clashed, as, again, every true man must. In his sparring with the Church, he struck out from the shoulder, hit hard, and hit in the face like a man. There is no shilly-shallying; no shuffling. No quarter is given, and none is asked. The truth must out. Hypocrisy, Christian casuistry and sophistry, cant and the thousand vices which they breed, are sources of pain to every knightly and heroic soul; he at least will fight his fight with them, come what may, and in battle against them flash in their eyes the lightnings of his ethereal-tempered sword of truth. . . . he was really one of the purest of Christians, one whom Christ would have loved with all the warmth of his lofty and kindred soul. . . .

The desire of some of Mr. Thoreau's friends to relieve him from the unpopularity which his stern reproofs of society have given him, to tame his magnificent wildness, and represent him as a good and regular citizen (only a little eccentric)—this desire of his friends, I say, springs from the most laudable motives, but still is based, it seems to me, upon an error as to the real facts in the case, an error as to the real value and significance of his life and work. As to the facts—one could quote from his books hundreds of passages to prove how irksome the mass of men were to him, and what intense delight he took in finding places about Concord, in the Maine woods, and elsewhere, where the work of man had not caused that deformity in the landscape which so often attends his footsteps, especially in a new country. . . .

William Sloane Kennedy, "A New Estimate of Thoreau," *Penn Monthly* 11 (October 1880): 795–803, 805, 807.

From "Thoreau's Wildness" (1881)

JOHN BURROUGHS

> Prolific nature writer John Burroughs (1837–1921) never met Thoreau and did not visit Concord until years after Thoreau's death. Yet in several articles over a span of two decades, from the 1870s to the 1890s, he alternately honors and condemns Thoreau, repeatedly stressing two criteria that he admires: Thoreau's sympathy for John Brown and Thoreau as an aboriginal man, "the wildest civilized man this country has produced" ("Henry D. Thoreau," 371). Burroughs portrays Thoreau in convicted and personal characterizations that are impossibly specific for someone he had never met: "He was a man devoid of compassion, devoid of sympathy, devoid of generosity, devoid of patriotism, as these words are usually understood" (369).
>
> In reviews that usually favored Burroughs, he was often considered a descendant of Thoreau, as in this comparison in *Scribner's:* "The writer with whom Burroughs is perpetually compared with is Thoreau. The latter is more minute; perhaps he was more original. But to-day the style of Burroughs is more charming than that of the recluse of Walden Pond" ("John Burroughs's 'Pepacton,'" 634). Those who had known Thoreau, however, were less complimentary to Burroughs. Thomas Wentworth Higginson, for example, contended that Thoreau "put his observations always on the level of literature, while Mr. Burroughs, for instance, remains more upon the level of journalism" (*Carlyle's Laugh,* 71). Burroughs's concluding speculation, that Thoreau's life was a perpetual search for the unattainable, recurs in many of his publications.

DOUBTLESS THE WILDEST MAN New England has turned out since the red aborigines vacated her territory was Henry Thoreau—a man in whom the Indian reappeared on the plane of taste and morals. One is tempted to apply to him his own lines on "Elisha Dugan," as it is very certain they fit himself much more closely than they ever did his neighbor. . . . His whole life was a search for the wild, not only in nature, but in literature, in life, in morals. The shyest and most elusive thoughts and impressions were the ones that fascinated him most, not only in his own mind but in the minds of others. His startling paradoxes are only one form his wildness took. He cared little for science except as it escaped the rules and technicalities and put him on the trail of the ideal, the transcendental. Thoreau was of French extraction, and every drop of his blood seems to have turned toward the aboriginal, as the French blood has so often done in other ways in this country. He for the most part despised the white man, but his enthusiasm kindled at the mention of the Indian. He envied the Indian; he coveted his knowledge, his arts, his wood craft. He attributed to the Indian a more "practical and vital science" than was contained in the books. . . .

His genius itself is arrow-like and typical of the wild weapon he so loved—hard, flinty, fine-grained, penetrating, winged—a flying shaft, bringing down its game with marvelous sureness. His literary art was to let fly with a kind of quick inspiration, and though his arrows sometimes go wide, yet it is always a pleasure to watch their aerial course. Indeed, Thoreau was a kind of Emersonian or transcendental red man going about with a pocket glass and an herbarium instead of with a bow and tomahawk. He appears to have been as stoical and indifferent and unsympathetic as a veritable Indian; and how he hunted—without trap or gun, and fished without hook or snare! Everywhere the wild drew him. He liked the telegraph because it was a kind of aeolian harp; the wind blowing upon it made wild sweet music; he liked the railroad through his native town because it was the wildest road he knew of; it only made deep cuts into and through the hills. . . .

Thoreau hesitated to call himself a naturalist. That was too tame; he would perhaps have been content to have been an Indian naturalist. . . . Indeed, what Thoreau was finally after in nature was something ulterior to science, something ulterior to poetry, something ulterior to philosophy; it was that vague something which he calls "the higher law," and which eludes all direct statement. He went to Nature as to an oracle, and though he sometimes, indeed very often, questioned her as a naturalist and a poet, yet there was always another question in his mind. He ransacked the country about Concord in all seasons and weathers, and at all times of the day and night; he delved into the ground, he probed the swamps, he searched the waters, he dug into woodchuck holes, into muskrats' dens, into the retreats of the mice and squirrels; he saw every bird, heard every sound, found every wild flower, and brought home many a fresh bit of natural history; but he was always searching for something he did not find.

John Burroughs, "Thoreau's Wildness," *Critic* 1 (26 March 1881): 74–75.

"Introductory Note" to *Early Spring in Massachusetts* (1881)

H. G. O. Blake

Harrison Gray Otis Blake (1816–1898) graduated from Harvard College in 1835 and Harvard Divinity School in 1838. By the time he met Thoreau in the mid-1840s, he had left the Unitarian ministry and was an educator and private tutor in Worcester, Massachusetts. Blake and Thoreau began corresponding in 1848 after Blake, seeking "a spiritual teacher," recognized Thoreau "as a man uniquely fitted for the task," according to Bradley Dean (11). In his edition of their correspondence, *Letters to a Spiritual Seeker* (2004), Dean argues for the importance of this relationship to the maturation of Thoreau's own thinking as well as to the expansion of his readership within a circle of Blake's Worcester acquaintances (22–23). As Thoreau described to Blake in 1857, "I am much indebted to you because you look so steadily at the better side, or rather the true center of me (for our true center may and perhaps oftenest does lie entirely aside from us, and we are in fact eccentric,). . . . You speak as if the image or idea which I see were reflected from me to you, and I see it again reflected from you to me" (*Correspondence*, 298–99).

When Sophia Thoreau died in 1876, Blake inherited nearly forty manuscript notebooks of Thoreau's journals, from which he published excerpts from 1881 to 1892. His "Introductory Note" prefaces the first of these volumes. Here Blake presents Thoreau's character and unique genius as intellectual curiosities rather than an accumulation of facts about his life. As do many of Thoreau's friends and admirers, Blake responds to Waldo Emerson's charge that Thoreau lacked ambition, explaining Thoreau's "ambition [as] far higher than the ordinary." This defense would not have surprised Emerson, who had once explained to James T. Fields that "when he [Blake] was connected with theological matters . . . 'he believed wholly in me at that time, but one day he met Thoreau and he never came to my house afterwards'" (qtd. in Howe, 89–90). In contrast to other Thoreau friends, such as Daniel Ricketson, Blake accepted Thoreau as he was—standoffish at times, demonstrably touched by Blake's letters at others. As Blake explained: "Geniality, versatility, personal familiarity are, of course, agreeable in those about us, and seem necessary in human intercourse, but I did not miss them in Thoreau, who was . . . such an effectual witness to what is highest and most precious in life" (qtd. in Salt, 145).

Blake's publication of several volumes of Thoreau's journal extracts, arranged seasonally, created a resurgence of both general interest in and critical attention to Thoreau's writing, leading to "a popularity they had never enjoyed before" (Harding and Meyer, 206). Importantly, Blake revitalized Thoreau's significance as an author: "These writings abounding in what is of deepest concern to us all, uttered with a strength of conviction to which his whole life bore witness, make it plain that Thoreau had chosen the right path for himself as few men do, that in no other way could he have served humanity so well. . . . In Thoreau's writings we see the end for which he lived" (Blake, "Thoreau"). Yet Blake's arbitrary method of presentation also manipulated and distorted the journals' context and, as Robert Sattelmeyer points out, "imposed an artificial structure" on their subject matter, in addition to the fact that Blake was a careless editor who defaced and often obliterated Thoreau's text by heavily marking the manuscript leaves and by losing at least one journal notebook ("General Introduction," 583). Sattelmeyer further contends that "despite Blake's desire to portray the philosophical side . . . the seasonal books maintained and advanced the popular estimation of Thoreau as a progenitor of American natural history writing, a Yankee version of Gilbert White whose Selborne was Concord, Massachusetts" (584).

More than any other correspondent, Blake clearly inspired Thoreau to heights of exuberance and insight. As he prodded him in December 1856: "Blake! Blake! Are you awake? Are you aware what an ever-glorious morning this is? What long expected never to be repeated opportunity is now offered to get life and knowledge?

For my part I am trying to wake up,—to wring slumber out of my pores;— For, generally, I take events as unconcernedly as a fence post,—absorb wet and cold like it, and am pleasantly tickled with lichens slowly spreading over me. Could I not be content then to be a cedar post, which lasts 25 years?" (*Correspondence*, 443). More than thirty years later, Blake remained a grateful friend, declaring decades after Thoreau's death, "I could hardly say more than I have said, that he is the most interesting person I have known" (qtd. in Mason, "Harrison G. O. Blake" 93).

THOREAU SEEMS deliberately to have chosen nature rather than man for his companion, though he knew well the higher value of man. . . . Still, in ordinary society, he found it so difficult to reach essential humanity through the civilized and conventional, that he turned to nature, who was ever ready to meet his highest mood. From the haunts of business and the common intercourse of men he went into the woods and fields as from a solitary desert into society. He might have said with another,—he did virtually say,—"If we go solitary to streams and mountains, it is to meet man there where he is more than ever man."

But while I have sought in these selections to represent the progressive life of nature, I have also been careful to give Thoreau's thoughts, because though his personality is in a striking degree single, he being ever the same man in his conversation, letters, books, and the details of his life, though his observation is imbedded in his philosophy ("how to observe is how to behave," etc.), yet if any distinction may be made, his thoughts or philosophy seem to me incomparably the more interesting and important. He declined from the first to live for the common prizes of society, for wealth or even what is called a competence, for professional, social, political, or even literary success; and this not from a want of ambition or a purpose, but from an ambition far higher than the ordinary, which fully possessed him,—an ambition to obey his purest instincts, to follow implicitly the finest intimations of his genius, to secure thus the fullest and freest life of which he was capable. He chose to lay emphasis on his relations to nature and the universe rather than on those he bore to the ant-hill of society, not to be merely another wheel in the social machine. He felt that the present is only one among the possible forms of civilization, and so preferred not to commit himself to it. Herein lies the secret of that love of the wild which was so prominent a trait in his character.

It is evident that the main object of society now is to provide for our material wants, and still more and more luxuriously for them, while the higher wants of our nature are made secondary, put off for some Sunday service and future leisure. A great lesson of Thoreau's life is that all this must be reversed, that whatever relates to the supply of inferior wants must be simplified, in order that the higher life may be enriched, though he desired no servile imitation of his own methods, for perhaps the highest lesson of all to be learnt from him is that the only way of salvation lies in the strictest fidelity to one's own genius.

A late English reviewer, who shows in many respects a very just appreciation of Thoreau, charges him with *doing* little beyond writing a few books, as if that might not be a great thing; but a life so steadily directed from the first toward the highest ends, gaining as the fruits of its fidelity such a harvest of sanity, strength, and tranquillity, and that wealth of thought which has been well called "the only conceivable prosperity," accompanied, too, as it naturally was, with the earnest and effective desire to communicate itself to others,—such a life is the worthiest deed a man can perform, the purest benefit he can confer upon his fellows, compared with which all special acts of service or philanthropy are trivial.

H. G. O. Blake, "Introductory Note," *Early Spring in Massachusetts from the Journal of Henry D. Thoreau,* ed. H. G. O. Blake (Boston: Houghton, Mifflin, 1881), iv–vii.

From *Henry D. Thoreau* (1882)

F. B. SANBORN

At Waldo Emerson's suggestion, Franklin Benjamin Sanborn (1831–1917) opened a school in Concord with his sister, Sarah Sanborn, after he graduated from Harvard College in 1855. He lived here with her, and later with his second wife, Louisa Leavitt, for the rest of his life. On moving to Concord, Sanborn rented a home across the street from the Thoreaus, with whom he took his meals, resuming his acquaintance with Henry, whom he had met briefly earlier that year. In addition to running his school, during the antebellum years Sanborn served as Secretary of Massachusetts's Free Kansas Committee, in which position he raised money and supplies to support abolitionists' military and settlement efforts in the western territories of Kansas and Nebraska. With Thomas Wentworth Higginson, Samuel Gridley Howe, Theodore Parker, Gerrit Smith, and George Luther Stearns, Sanborn was one of the "Secret Six" conspirators who supported John Brown's radical abolitionism, including the eventual raid on the federal arsenal at Harpers Ferry, Virginia. It was through Sanborn that Thoreau and Brown met in March 1857, during the first of Brown's two visits to Concord.

After the Civil War, in which despite his militant antislavery politics he did not participate, Sanborn edited the *Boston Commonwealth* and the *Journal of Social Science;* he also contributed frequently to the *Springfield Republican.* In 1865, he founded the American Social Science Association and also served on the boards of several charitable organizations. He lectured widely, including often at the Concord School of Philosophy, which Louisa May Alcott had organized for her father in 1879, and which, through readings and lectures, kept alive the Transcendentalist spirit in Concord. Throughout his life, Sanborn published dozens of articles and books about famous men he had known, including biographies of Samuel Gridley Howe, John Brown, Nathaniel Hawthorne, Bronson Alcott, and Waldo Emerson, in addition to Thoreau. In the words of Robert Burkholder, he was "an indefatigable chronicler of the social, political, and literary currents that swirled around him" (255). Sanborn's editorial work on these and other figures, however, is notoriously sloppy.

Sanborn wrote three biographies of Thoreau. The first, excerpted here, was the third volume to appear in Houghton, Mifflin's *American Men of Letters* series, and was undertaken to capitalize on Thoreau's increasing stature by the 1880s. The next two, *The Personality of Thoreau* (1901) and *Life of Henry David Thoreau* (1917), include lengthy excerpts from Thoreau's early and college essays as well as extensive biographical details about his ancestors. Reviews of *Henry D. Thoreau* were mixed, with many judging that Sanborn had "exaggerate[d] the importance of his subject" (qtd. in Scharnhorst, *Annotated Bibliography*, 228). Regardless of its critics, however, the book renewed attention to Thoreau as a literary figure in an important new series edited by Gilded Age favorite Charles Dudley Warner.

IT HAS BEEN A common delusion, not yet quite faded away, that the chief Transcendentalists were but echoes of each other,—that Emerson imitated Carlyle, Thoreau and Alcott imitated Emerson, and so on to the end of the chapter. No doubt that the atmosphere of each of these men affected the others, nor that they shared a common impulse communicated by what Matthew Arnold likes to call the *Zeitgeist,*—the ever-felt spirit of the time. . . . Thoreau brought to his intellectual tasks an originality as marked as Emerson's, if not so brilliant and star-like—a patience far greater than his, and a proud independence that makes him the most solitary of modern thinkers. I have been struck by these qualities in reading his yet unknown first essays in authorship, the juvenile papers he wrote while in college, from the age of seventeen to that of twenty, before Emerson had published anything except his first little volume, "Nature," and while Thoreau, like other young men, was reading Johnson and Goldsmith, Addison and the earlier English classics, from Milton backward to Chaucer. . . .

My own acquaintance with Thoreau did not begin with our common hostility to slavery, which afterwards brought us most closely together, but sprang from the accident of my editing for a few weeks the "Harvard Magazine," a college monthly, in 1854–55, in which appeared a long review of "Walden" and the "Week." In acknowledgment of this review, which was laudatory and made many quotations from his two volumes, Thoreau, whom I had never seen, called at my room in Holworthy Hall, Cambridge, in January, 1855, and left there in my absence, a copy of the "Week" with a message implying it was for the writer of the magazine article. It so happened that I was in the College Library when Thoreau was calling on me, and when he came, directly after, to the Library, some one present pointed him out to me as the author of "Walden." I was then a senior in college, and soon to go on my winter vacation; in course of which I wrote to Thoreau from my native town, as follows:—

> We who at Cambridge look toward Concord as a sort of Mecca for our pilgrimages, are glad to see that your last book finds such favor with the public. It has made its way where your name has rarely been heard before, and the inquiry, "Who is Mr. Thoreau?" proves that the book has in part done its work. For my own part, I thank you for the new light it shows me the aspects of Nature in, and for the marvelous beauty of your descriptions. At the same time, if any one should ask me what I think of your philosophy, I should be apt to answer that it is not worth a straw. Whenever again you visit Cambridge, be assured, sir, that it would give me much pleasure to see you at my room. . . .

Some six weeks after its date, I went to live in Concord, and happened to take rooms in Mr. Channing's house, just across the way from Thoreau's. I met him more than once in March, 1855, but he did not call on my sister and me until the 11th of April, when I made the following brief note of his appearance:—

> To-night we had a call from Mr. Thoreau, who came at eight and stayed till ten. He talked about Latin and Greek—which he thought ought to be studied—and about other things. In his tones and gestures he seemed to me to imitate Emerson, so that it was annoying to listen to him, though he said many good things. He looks like Emerson, too,—coarser, but with something of that serenity and sagacity which E. has. Thoreau looks eminently *sagacious*—like a sort of wise, wild beast. He dresses plainly, wears a beard in his throat, and has a brown complexion. . . .

Notwithstanding the slow admiration that these trivial comments indicated, our friendship grew apace, and for two years or more I dined with him almost daily, and often joined in his walks and river voyages, or swam with him in some of our numerous Concord waters. In 1857 I introduced John Brown to him, then a guest at my house; and in 1859, the evening before Brown's last birthday, we listened together to the old captain's last speech in the Concord Town Hall. The events of that year and the next brought us closely together, and I found him the stanchest of friends. . . .

Thoreau's business in life was observation, thought, and writing, to which last, reading was essential. He read much, but studied more; nor was his reading that indiscriminate, miscellaneous perusal of everything printed, which has become the vice of this age. He read books of travel, scientific books, authors of original merit, but few newspapers, of which he had a very poor opinion. . . .

His method in writing was peculiarly his own, though it bore some external resemblance to that of his friends, Emerson and Alcott. Like them he early began to keep a journal, which became both diary and commonplace book. But while they noted down the thoughts which occurred to them, without premeditation or consecutive arrangement, Thoreau made studies and observations for his journal as carefully and habitually as he noted the angles and distances in surveying a Concord farm. In all his daily walks and distant journeys, he took notes on the spot of what occurred to him, and these, often very brief and symbolic, he carefully wrote out, as soon as he could get time, in his diary, not classified by topics, but just as they had come to him. To these he added his daily meditations, sometimes expressed in verse, especially in the years between 1837 and 1850, but generally in close and pertinent prose. Many details are found in his diaries, but not such as are common in the diaries of other men,—not trivial but significant details. From these daily entries he made up his essays, his lectures, and his volumes; all being slowly, and with much deliberation and revision, brought into the form in which he gave them to the public. After that he scarcely changed them at all; they had received the last imprint of his mind, and he allowed them to stand and speak for themselves. But before printing, they underwent constant change, by addition, erasure, transposition, correction, and combination. A given lecture might be two years, or twenty years in preparation; or it might be, like his defense of John Brown, copied with little change from the pages of his diary for the fortnight previous. But that was an exceptional case; and Thoreau was stirred and quickened by the campaign and capture of Brown, as perhaps he had never been before. . . .

The fact that Thoreau noted down his thoughts by night as well as by day, appear also from an entry in one of his journals, where he is describing the coming on of day, as witnessed by him at the close of a September night in Concord. "Some bird flies over," he writes, "making a noise like the barking of a puppy (it was a cuckoo). It is yet so dark that I have dropped my pencil and cannot find it." No writer of modern times, in fact, was so much awake and abroad at night, or has described better the phenomena of darkness and of moonlight. . . .

F. B. Sanborn, *Henry D. Thoreau* (Boston: Houghton, Mifflin, 1882), 148–49, 195–99, 300–4.

From "Henry D. Thoreau" (1886)

H. S. Salt

> Author Henry Stephens Salt (1851–1939) was an animal rights activist and a British Fabian and campaigner for social reform. His *Life of Henry D. Thoreau* (1890) was the first comprehensive assessment of Thoreau from the English literary establishment. Salt also authored biographies on Percy Bysshe Shelley, Richard Jefferies, James Thomson, and Thomas De Quincey. The article that follows first appeared in Britain but was published in America in the *Critic* in two installments in 1886–7. Salt had become enamored of Thoreau's political and moral writings; he determined to right what he considered the several wrongs of Thoreau's contemporary reputation, namely that he had been a hermit and a misanthrope. Thanks to Salt's efforts, Thoreau began to attract a "cult following" among English "social progressives" in the 1880s (Scharnhorst, *Case Study*, 37).

WE ARE NOT SURPRISED to find that Thoreau's doctrines obtained but little recognition during his lifetime; he was regarded with profound respect by a few select friends, Emerson among the number; but to the many he appeared merely eccentric and quixotic, his sojourn at Walden gaining him the reputation of a hermit and misanthrope. Even now, nearly a quarter of a century after his death, he is not known as he deserves to be either in America or this country; most readers ignore or misunderstand him; and it is left to a small but increasing number of admirers to do justice to one of the most remarkable and original characters that America has yet produced. Thoreau was pre-eminently the apostle of "plain living and high thinking"; and to those who are indifferent to this doctrine he must ever appeal in vain; on the other hand, those who have realized the blessings of a simple and healthful life can never feel sufficient gratitude or admiration for such a book as "Walden," which is rightly regarded as the masterpiece of Thoreau's genius. . . .

It has been remarked by some critics, who take an unfavourable view of Thoreau's philosophy, that his life was strikingly devoid of those wide ex-

periences and opportunities of studying mankind, which alone can justify
an individual in arraigning, as Thoreau did, the whole system of modern
society. It should be remembered, however, that he possessed that keen
native wisdom and practical insight, which, combined with fearless self-
inspection, are often a better form of education than the more approved
methods. Like all other enthusiasts, Thoreau sometimes taught a half-truth
rather than a whole one; but that does not alter the fact that his teaching
was true as far as it went. In his life-protest against the luxury and self-
indulgence which he saw everywhere around him, he no doubt occasionally over-stated his own case, and ignored some objections which might
reasonably have been raised against his doctrines; but in the main his conclusions are generally sound and unimpeachable. Self-taught, time-saving,
and laconic, he struck by a sort of unerring instinct at the very root of the
question which he chanced to be discussing, not pausing to weigh objections, or allowing any difficulties to divert him from his aim. We may now
proceed to consider the chief features of his philosophy.

Thoreau has been called a Stoic; and there is undoubtedly much in his
philosophy that is akin to the spirit of ancient Stoicism. With him, as with
Epictetus, conformity to nature is the basis of his teaching, and he has been
finely called by Emerson the "Bachelor of Nature," a term which might well
have been applied to many of the old Greek and Roman Stoics. It is a remarkable fact that there is rarely any mention of love in his writings, but
friendship, as with the Stoics, is a common theme, this subject being treated
of at considerable length in the "Week." His main point of similarity, however, to the Stoic philosophers is to be found in his ceaseless protest against
all kinds of luxury and superfluous comforts. Like Socrates, he could truly
say, on seeing the abundance of other people's possessions, "How many
things are there that I do *not* desire!" and every page of "Walden" bears
testimony to the sincerity of this feeling. The keynote of the book is the
sentiment expressed in Goldsmith's words, "Man wants but little here
below," with the difference that Thoreau did not merely *talk* of Arcadian
simplicity, in the manner that was so common with literary men a century
ago, but carried his theories into practical effect. . . . Freedom from artificial wants, and a life in harmony with nature, are again and again insisted
upon by Thoreau as the basis of all true happiness; and these he certainly
pursued with unfaltering consistency through his own singular career. In
this sense he was a true Stoic philosopher. But there are also important

differences. Thoreau was free from that coldness of heart which was too often a characteristic of the Stoics of old, and was animated by a far wider and nobler spirit of humanity. It is true that there was a certain reserve in his manner which made his acquaintances a little afraid of him, and caused one of his friends to remark, "I *love* Henry, but I cannot *like* him." But this existed only in his manner; in heart he was at all times thoroughly kindly and sympathetic. . . . His enthusiastic admiration for the heroes of the anti-slavery agitation was a proof that he was quite free from the coldness of a merely theoretic Stoicism; indeed he has a just claim to be considered one of the leaders of the great humanitarian movement of this century, his sympathy with the lower animals being one of the most extraordinary features of his character. He had been influenced far too deeply by the teaching of Channing, Emerson, and the transcendental school, to permit of his being classed as a mere cynic or misanthrope.

"Simplify, simplify," was the cry that was for ever on Thoreau's lips, in his life-protest against the increasing luxury and extravagance and hypoc-risy of the age. The lesson taught us by "Walden" is that there are two ways of becoming rich; one—the method usually adopted—by conforming to the conventional laws of society, and amassing sufficient money to enable one to purchase all the "comforts" of which men think they have need; the other—a simpler and more expeditious process—by limiting one's desires to those things which are really necessary; in Thoreau's own words, "A man is rich in proportion to the number of things which he can afford to let alone." It is habit only which makes us regard as necessary a great part of the equipments of civilized life, and an experience such as that of Thoreau during his sojourn at Walden goes to prove that we might be healthier and happier if we could bring ourselves to dispense with many of our superflu-ous and artificial wants, and thus substitute a manly independence for our present childish dependence on the labour of others. Thoreau was not a foolish champion of savage and barbarous isolation against the appliances and improvements of civilized society; it is not denied by him that on the whole the civilized state is far preferable to the savage condition; but he shows that in some ways the increase of artificial wants, and of skill in sup-plying them, has proved a curse rather than a blessing to the human race, and he points out an easy and perfectly practicable way out of this diffi-culty. Every one may add to his own riches, and may lessen his own labour, and that of others, in the treadmill of competitive existence, by the simple expedient of living less artificially. There are few indeed who, if they go to the root of the matter, and cast aside the prejudices of custom and convention, will not discover that they could be equally happy—nay, far happier, without much of what is now most expensive in their houses, in the way of furniture, clothing, and diet. Thoreau discovered by his own experiment, that by working about six weeks in the year, he could meet all the expenses of living, and have free for study the whole of his winters as well as most of his summers, a discovery which may throw considerable light on the solution of certain social problems in our own country. Even if we allow an ample margin for the peculiarity of his case, and the favourable conditions under which he made his experiment, the conclusion seems to be unavoidable that the burden of labour which falls on the majority of the human race is not only very unfairly distributed, but in itself unnecessarily heavy.

Thoreau cannot be called a Socialist; he was rather an Individualist of the most uncompromising type. One of his most striking characteristics was his strong contempt for the orthodox social virtues of "charity" and "philanthropy," which lead men—so he thought—to attempt a cheap method of improving their fellow-creatures without any real sacrifice or reform on their own side. In no part of "Walden" is the writing more vigorous and trenchant than when Thoreau is discussing the "philanthropic enterprises" in which some of his fellow-townsmen reproachfully invited him to join. "Doing good," he declares, is one of the professions that are full; and if he knew for a certainty that a man was coming to his house with the design of doing him good, he should run for his life, for he would rather suffer evil the natural way. So too with charity. . . .

There is one aspect of Thoreau's teaching which is scarcely mentioned by his biographers, though it is of considerable importance in forming a just estimate of his character; I refer to his humanitarian views. His hatred of war is very strongly expressed in those passages where he condemns the iniquitous attack which the United States were then making on Mexico; war, he says, is "a damnable business;" since those concerned in it, "soldiers, colonel, captain, corporal, powder-monkeys, and all," are in reality peaceably inclined, and are forced to fight against their common sense and consciences.

Of his detestation of the system of slavery I shall have occasion to speak farther on. But Thoreau went much farther than this; his humanity was shown not only in his relations to men, but also in his dealings with the lower animals. Emerson tells us that, though a naturalist, Thoreau used neither trap nor gun—a fact which must have been independently noticed by all readers of "Walden" or the diaries. It was his habit to eat no flesh; though with characteristic frankness he confesses to having once slaughtered and devoured a woodchuck which ravaged his bean-field. . . .

Thoreau's retirement to Walden has naturally led many people to consider him as a sort of modern hermit, and the attraction he exercised over the inhabitants of the woods and waters was only one of many points of resemblance. There was the same recognition of the universal brotherhood of men, the same scorn of the selfish luxury and childish amusements of society, and the same impatience of the farce which men call "politics," the same desire of self-concentration and undisturbed thought. Thoreau also possessed, in a marked degree, that power of suddenly and strongly influencing those who conversed with him, which was so characteristic of the hermits. Young men who visited him were often converted in a moment to the belief "that this was the man they were in search of, the man of men, who could tell them all they should do." But it would be a grievous wrong to Thoreau to allow this comparison, a just one up to a certain point, to be drawn out beyond its fair limits. He was something more than a solitary. He had higher aims than the anchorites of old. He went to the woods, as he himself has told us, because he wished "to live deliberately, to front only the essential facts of life." So far he was like the hermits of the East. But it was only a two-years' sojourn, not a life-visit that he made to Walden; his object was not merely to retire, but to fit himself for a more perfect life. He left the woods "for as good reason as he went there," feeling that he had several more lives to live, and could not spare more time for that one. Even while he lived at Walden he visited his family and friends at Concord every two or three days; indeed, one of his biographers asserts that he "bivouacked" at Walden rather than actually lived there, though this is hardly the impression conveyed by Thoreau himself or other authorities. Very different also was Thoreau in his complete freedom from the morbid asceticism and unhealthy habit of body which too often distinguished the hermits. His frugality was deliberate and rational, based on the belief that the truest health and happiness must be sought in wise and unvarying moderation; but there was no trace of any unreasoning asceticism; his object being to vivify, not mortify, the flesh. His nature was essentially simple and vigorous; he records in his diary that he thought bathing one of the necessaries of life, and wonders what kind of religion could be that of a certain New England farmer, who told him he had not had a bath for fifteen years. Now we read of St. Antony—and the same is told of most other hermits—that he never washed his body with water, and could not endure even to wet his feet; dirtiness therefore must be considered a *sine quâ non* in the character of a true hermit, and this would entirely disqualify Thoreau for being ranked in that class. It is at once pleasanter and more correct, if we must make any comparisons at all, to compare him to the philosopher Epictetus, who lived in the vicinity of Rome in a little hut which had not so much as a door, his only attendant being an old servant-maid, and his property consisting of little more than an earthen lamp. Thoreau had the advantage over the Stoic in having no servant-maid at Walden; but as he indulged himself in a door, we may fairly set one luxury against the other, and the two philosophers may be classed on the whole as equally praiseworthy examples of a consistent simplicity and hardihood.

Thoreau's diaries afford much delightful reading, and give us a good insight into his character and mode of life. They abound in notes of his observations on Natural History, with here and there some poetical thought or moral reflection attached; sometimes there is an account of a voyage up the Assabet River, or a walking tour to Monadnock, or some other neighbouring mountain. These diaries have lately been edited by Mr. H. G. O. Blake, a friend of Thoreau, who has arranged them according to seasons, not years, various passages written in different years being grouped together under the same day of the month, thus giving a more connected picture of the climate under which Thoreau lived, and the scenes in which he took such delight.

Thoreau's poems are certainly the least successful part of his work. They were published in various American magazines, and he is fond of interpolating parts of them in his books. Some selections from them may be found in Page's "Life of Thoreau." But it must be confessed that though Thoreau had a truly poetical mind, and though he may justly be styled the "Poet-Naturalist," he had not that power of expression in verse which is a necessary attribute of the true poet. Prose-poet let us call him, as we call De Quincey or Ruskin, or Hawthorne; but poet in the ordinary sense he was not. He was a clear-headed, fearless thinker, whose force of native shrewdness and penetration led him to test the value of all that is regarded as indispensable in artificial life, and to reject much of it as unsound; he was gifted also with an enthusiastic love of nature, and with literary powers, which, if not of a wide and extensive range, were peculiarly appropriate—in an almost unrivalled degree—to the performance of that life-duty which he set before him as his ideal. He was in the truest sense an original writer; his work is absolutely unique. "Walden" alone is sufficient to win him a place among the immortals, for it is incomparable alike in matter and in style, and deserves to be a sacred book in the library of every cultured and thoughtful man. Never was there written a book more simple, more manly, more beautiful, more pure; it is, as Thoreau himself describes the pond from which it derives its name, "a gem of the first water which Concord wears in her coronet." Concord is indeed rich in literary associations and reminiscences of great men. Emerson—Hawthorne—Thoreau; these are mighty names, a trinity of illustrious writers, almost sufficient in themselves to represent a national literature. It is not the least of Thoreau's honours that he has won a place in this literary brotherhood; but perhaps his greatest claim to immortality will be found in the fact that there is a natural affinity and fellowship between his genius and that of Walt Whitman, the great poet-prophet of the large-hearted democracy that is to be. . . .

Certain it is that of all philosophers, whether in the old world or the new, few have read the mysteries of this immaterial heaven and its starry intimations more truthfully and faithfully than Thoreau.

H. S. Salt, "Henry D. Thoreau," *Temple Bar* 78 (November 1886): 369–73, 375–76, 380–83.

[Conversations on Concord] (1892 and 1893)

Edward Sherman Hoar

Edward Sherman Hoar (1823–1893) was the brother of George, Rockwood, and Elizabeth Hoar. He accompanied Thoreau on an excursion to the Maine woods in July–August 1857, and to the White Mountains of New Hampshire in July 1858. Without a doubt, however, his most infamous connection to Thoreau occurred on 30 April 1844—when as a result of carelessly cooking fish the two men accidentally started a fire in Concord in the woods overlooking Fairhaven Bay. The fire destroyed over eight hundred acres largely owned by the Hubbard and Wheeler families. The fact that Edward Hoar's father, Samuel Hoar, was a wealthy and prominent citizen whose financial position, fortunately, meant that he could settle with these families saved Thoreau from the severe humiliation and financial stress of such a disaster. Like his friend Edward Emerson, Edward Hoar responded profoundly to Thoreau: "With Thoreau's life something went out of Concord woods and fields and river that will never return. He so loved Nature, delighted in her every aspect and seemed to infuse himself into her" (qtd. in Edward Emerson, *Henry Thoreau as Remembered by a Young Friend*, 118). To those who accused Thoreau of being antisocial, Hoar explained his bearing as "a sort of inherited petulance, that covered a sensitive and affectionate nature easily wounded by the scornful criticism" (qtd. in Harding, "Edward Hoar," 7). In conversations recorded in the early 1890s with educator and naturalist Edmund Sandford Burgess (1855–1928), Hoar reflects on his friendship with Thoreau and others in Concord as well as the wider Transcendentalist circle.

To Edward S. Burgess, 30 December [18]92

I have just finished reading Thoreau's Winter. There is not so much natural history in it as in some other volumes, not so much as there is of matter addressed to man's moral nature.

I have greatly regretted that I did not know Thoreau better. . . .

I was shown that side of his nature to the full, the natural history side, the minute observer. But there were other sides to him, and I was wholly unaware then of the moral side that appears so strongly in his books. He did not show that in our walks. Thoreau was intensely a moralist, to him everything was valuable according as it appealed to the moral sentiment and he would lose no opportunity to enforce a moral sentiment. Nor would he lose any opportunity for observing nature even if it was to get up in dark night and watch for hours the lightening around a rotten log in Maine. He was ready to open that side of himself to any one who would pay the price. But that meant, to go with him in his walk; to walk long and far; to have wet feet, and go so for hours; to pull a boat all day; to come home late at night after many miles. If you would do that with him he would take you with him. If you flunked at anything he had no more use for you.

Thoreau was of a very fine-grained family. He knew he had not long to live and he determined to make the most of it. How to observe and acquire knowledge and secure the true objects of life without much expenditure of money was his great study. He would not wait as most men, to acquire a competence, before settling down to realize the ends of life. He would show how they could be secured without money; or with very little. This was the secret of his Walden Pond. . . .

I could have become a good ornithologist. When I was young I was a good shot, could hit a bird on the wing at 200 yards. But when I became acquainted with Henry Thoreau he persuaded me out of it. He would never shoot a bird; and I think his method greatly preferable to that of Mr John Burroughs. Thoreau would lie and watch the movements of a bird for hours, and so get the knowledge he wanted. He used to say that if you shot the bird you got only a dead bird anyway; you could make out a few parts in anatomy or plumage, just such as Dr. Coue's work is; but you couldn't see how the bird lives and acts. Since then I have never shot a bird. . . .

To Edward Sandford Burgess, 4 January [18]93

Henry was very affectionate; he had a great deal of sympathy that people did not know; during his last illness he received a great deal of attention and people were constantly coming and sending him flowers. He came to feel very differently toward people, and said if he had known he wouldn't have been so offish. He had got into his head before that *people* didn't mean what they said. . . .

Edward Sherman Hoar to Edward Sandford Burgess, 30 December [18]92 and 4 January [18]93, Vault A45, Burgess Unit 1, Special Collections, Concord Free Public Library, Concord, MA. Ampersands in the original source have been silently emended to "and" in this piece.

From "Thoreau" (1889)

OCTAVIUS BROOKS FROTHINGHAM

Octavius Brooks Frothingham (1822–1895) was a Unitarian minister and an author with nearly twenty books about the Transcendentalist movement to his credit, in addition to biographies or memoirs on William Henry Channing, George Ripley, and Theodore Parker. As his theology and antislavery sentiments grew increasingly radical, he moved often—serving as a minister in Salem, Massachusetts, in New Jersey, and in New York. In 1867, Frothingham became the first president of the National Free Religious Association. Although he barely mentions Thoreau in his important work, *Transcendentalism in New England* (1876), this sketch provides an appreciative overview, published in a popular reference work, of Thoreau's increasing importance as a literary figure toward the end of the nineteenth century.

CITIES HE DISLIKED; civilization he did not believe in. Nature was his passion, and the wilder it was the more he loved it. He was a fine scholar, especially in Greek, translated two of the tragedies of Aeschylus, was intimate with the Greek anthology, and knew Pindar, Simonides, and all the great lyric poets. In English poetry he preferred Milton to Shakespeare, and was more familiar with the writers of the 17th century than with modern men. He was no mean poet himself; in fact, he possessed the essential quality of the poet—a soaring imagination. He possessed an eye and an ear for beauty, and had he been gifted with the power of musical expression, would have been distinguished. No complete collection of his pieces has ever been made or could be, but fragments are exquisite. Emerson said that his poem on "Smoke" surpassed any by Simonides. That Thoreau was a man of aspiration, a pure idealist, reverent, spiritual, is plain from his intimacy with Bronson Alcott and Emerson. . . . His religion was that of the transcendentalists. The element of negation in it was large, and in his case conspicuous and acrid. . . . His doctrine was that of individualism. Therein he differed from Emerson, who was sympathetic and began at the divine end. Thoreau began with the ground and reasoned up. He saw beauty in ashes. . . . He aimed at becoming elemental and spontaneous. He wrote hymns to the night quite in the pagan fashion. His very aptitudes brought him in contact with the earth. His aspect suggested a faun, one who was in the secret of the wilderness. . . . He built a hut on the shore of Walden pond in 1845, and lived there, with occasional absences, about two years and a half. He built on Emerson's land, though he had wished to build elsewhere. The house had no lock to the door, no curtain to the window. It belonged to nature as much as to man, and to all men as much as to any one. When Thoreau left it, it was bought by a Scotch gardener, who carried it off a little way and used it as a cottage. Then a farmer bought it, moved it still farther away, and converted it into a tool-house. A pile of stones marks the site of Thoreau's hut. He went into the woods, not because he wished to avoid his fellow-men, as a misanthrope, but because he wanted to confront Nature, to deal with her at first hand, to lead his own life, to meet primitive conditions; and having done this, he abandoned the enterprise, recommending no one to try it who had not "a pretty good supply of internal sunshine." . . . At Walden he labored, studied, meditated, edited his first book, the "Week," and gauged his genius. He redeemed and consecrated the spot. The refusal to pay taxes, and his consequent imprisonment, were due to a more specific cause—namely, his dissent from the theory of human government and from the practice of the American state, which supported slavery. He stood simply and plainly on the rights and duty of the individual. The act was heroic as he performed it, and, when read by the light of his philosophy, was consistent. Thoreau was anything but sour, surly, or morose. He could sing, and even dance, on occasion. He was sweet with children; fond of kittens; a sunbeam at home; the best of brothers, gentle, patient, helpful. Those he loved he gave his heart to, and if they were few it was perhaps because his affections were not as expansive as they were deep. But he showed little emotion, having learned, like the Indian, to control his feelings. He cultivated stoicism. He had the pride as well as the conceit of egotism, and while the latter gave most offence to those who did not know him well, the former was the real cause of his conduct. Thoreau had no zeal of authorship, yet he wrote a great deal, and left a mass of manuscripts, mostly in prose, for he produced very few verses after he was thirty years old. . . .

Octavius Brooks Frothingham, "Thoreau," *Appleton's Cyclopaedia of American Biography*, vol. 6, ed. James Grant Wilson and John Fiske (New York: D. Appleton, 1889), 100–1.

From "Glimpses of Force:
Thoreau and Alcott" (1891)

ROSE HAWTHORNE LATHROP

Rose Hawthorne Lathrop (1851–1926) was the youngest of Sophia Peabody and Nathaniel Hawthorne's three children. She spent the first decade of her life in England and Europe, during her father's term as Consul to Liverpool and as the family subsequently traveled abroad. In 1871, Rose Hawthorne married George Parsons Lathrop; both converted to Catholicism in 1891. After the two separated in 1895, Rose Lathrop devoted her life to serving the ill and indigent, founding St. Rose's Free Home for Incurable Cancer and Rosary Hill Home in Hawthorne, New York. In 1898, she became a nun and took the name Mother Mary Alphonsa; she later founded the Dominican Sisters of Hawthorne. Lathrop wrote stories and a book of poetry, *Along the Shore*, in 1888, in addition to a reminiscence of her father, *Memories of Hawthorne*, published in 1897. This sketch imparts her childhood and adolescent memories of Thoreau, whom she knew in the last two years of his life after her family had returned to Concord in 1860.

I WAS ABOUT 9 years old and coming sternly to realize that I had been transferred from English homelikeness to American sandbanks, when, a little above the garden path, I beheld two enormous eyes not far from each other. They moved toward me. I melted away. Thoreau had come to call at the house.

The horrible effect of the great eyes, grey as autumn pools lit by a rift in the clouds, upon a mind pining for luxurious verdure and gem-like blue heavens, created a thirst in me for the dreadful. I hung about the garden (it was a grim failure of a garden) until the strange being, native to harsh America, should again emerge for departure. Stationed in a more retired spot I watched for him, and by and by he came. I noticed with transfixed pulses that he strode, clothed in exaggerated dignity, with long steps, placing one foot exactly before the other according to the Indian fashion, which in Thoreau's case was a downright marvel, since his feet seemed interminable. I next became conscious of a vaguely large nose that finally curved to his chin, and then I realized that this being was looking at me—the huge eyes at a slight oblique angle; and he passed so close to me, in consequence of a roguish turn of the path, that I found his grey-brown irises were bordered by heavy dark lines, like a wild animal's. For years this vision really distressed me in remembrance, and appeared to have a harmonious connection with my bitter lot in being an exile from British daisies and robins. And yet the time came when both Thoreau and America were revealed to me!

The first thing which Thoreau did to soften my heart toward him was to fall desperately ill. My mother sent him our sweet old musicbox, which softly dreamed forth its tunes, and he enjoyed its gentle strains as he lay perishing. I had heard a great deal of his poetic nature and instructive genius, and when he died it seemed as if an anemone, more lovely than any other, had been carried from the borders of a wood, and dropped, fading, in its depths. I never crossed a hill or a field in Concord, or gathered a cardinal-flower or any other rare bloom, without thinking of Thoreau as a companion of delicacy, though also a brother of the Indian. However, I never quite forgave him the steady stare of those unhuman eyes when I was a disheartened child. And I think I was right, for I do not doubt that his peculiar step, the stride adopted, was a sign of affectation; and that his intense gaze was the result of an abnormal self-consciousness. As a child the superficial faults which I noticed stood for the man himself; but to-day I judge that of all affectations that ever were, perhaps his of a new outward bearing and manner of thought, to distinguish him severely from futile mortals, was the least culpable. He had so much provocation on his side! He longed to herald the fact that he was not one of the triflers, even at the risk of resembling a savage. Walden woods rustled the name of Thoreau whenever I walked in them; and the lovely pond looked always so beautiful as amply to excuse his odd retirement to its margin. Not a theory, so much as the enchantment of Walden, was the cause of his living for so long principally on his mother's bread. He thought he fed upon almost anything else not alienated from nature; but we, who are free from the intoxicating love of air and branches, we who stay calmly at home and eat strange food, know that but for Mrs. Thoreau's loaves of bread, faithfully supplied, Philosophy and Superiority would have held a council of war and have capitulated to smiling Conventionality.

A little cairn of shabby stones upon the pond's brink, added to by every thoughtful visitor, commemorated Thoreau's stay there. It may be very fitting to do one's best in his honor from the material nearest at hand; but such a cairn seems to some of us like a childish notion and casts a humorous ray upon the hero of it, making the regret sadder and longer that so fair a soul should have masqueraded at all as one set apart from his fellow men, and should have taken a queer flight into the neighborly, uncriticising solitude of Walden woods. Standing beside the cairn, it perhaps seems to the visitor that the people who snap their fingers at the route of their race, and swerve aside to better themselves intellectually, were the sport of great forces in moments of relaxation; while the despised herd—the race—looks at these seceders with a large tolerance from the vantage ground of co-operative work. But glancing off over Walden's beautiful dark stillness, crossed here and there with lines of light, one believes with all one's heart that the few men who see largely and think reverently away from the daily shams to the vast realities, are guides to the Eternal City. They may be quaint, but they are honest and unwearying, and their mission is divine. Thoreau! The very word has come to mean for me—notwithstanding his half humorous angers—force at peace; wisdom forgiving. . . .

Rose Hawthorne Lathrop, "Glimpses of Force: Thoreau and Alcott," *Sunday Inter Ocean* 20 (5 July 1891): 26.

From "Henry David Thoreau" (1891)

JULIAN HAWTHORNE AND LEONARD LEMMON

> Julian Hawthorne (1846–1934), son of Nathaniel and Sophia, was an author, an editor, and a literary critic who knew Thoreau for only a few years during Hawthorne's childhood but who capitalized on their "relationship" in several published studies in the late nineteenth and early twentieth centuries. Gary Scharnhorst has recently shown that, depending on Thoreau's stature at the time, the tenor of these evaluations changed substantially ("'The Most Dismal Fraud of the New England Transcendental Group': Julian Hawthorne on Thoreau," 125). The following selection from the textbook Hawthorne coauthored with Leonard Lemmon presents a more balanced, less personal assessment. Surprisingly, the ten-volume *Literature of All Nations and All Ages*, of which Julian Hawthorne was chief editor in 1900, contains no selection from Thoreau's writings.

[THOREAU] WAS ODD, in all senses of the term. He was bilious in constitution and in temper, with a disposition somewhat prone to suspicion and jealousy, and defiant, rather than truly independent, in spirit. He had a searching, watchful, unconciliating eye, a long, stealthy tread and an alert but not graceful figure. His heart was neither warm nor large, and he certainly did not share that "enthusiasm for humanity" which was the fashionable profession in his day. His habits were solitary and unsocial; yet secretly he was highly sensitive to the opinion of his fellow-men, and would perhaps have mingled more freely with them, but for a perception that there was no vehement demand for his company. The art of pleasing was not innate in him, and he was too proud to cultivate it. Rather than have it appear that society could do without him, he resolved to make haste and banish society; for a couple of years he actually lived alone in a hut built by himself, on the shores of Walden Pond, near Concord: all his life he kept out of people's way,—you were more apt to see his disappearing coat-tails than his face,—and he was most at ease in his walks through the woods and fields surrounding Concord, and on his exploring tramps to Canada, to Maine, to

Cape Cod and along the Merrimac River. Thus thrown back upon himself, his egotism and self-consciousness could not but become emphasized: and since he might not shine in society, he determined to be king in the wilderness. He asserted, and perhaps brought himself to believe, that all that was worthy in this world lay within the compass of a walk from his own doorstep; and we might add that he came to regard the owner of that doorstep as the centre of all this world's worth. Existing in space, as it were, with nothing to measure himself by, he seemed to himself colossal.

Had Thoreau been nothing more than has been indicated, the world would not have been likely to hear of him. But there was more in him than this, and more still was added by education and by the influence of certain of his contemporaries, and of their opinions. His father was able to send him to school and to Harvard College: after graduating he taught school, and finally learned surveying. This trade, and a little money that he had, sufficed to support one of habits so economical as his. He was endowed with some imagination, and it partly found expression in poetry—moralized descriptions of nature, a little rough in form, and anything but ardent in feeling, but individual and masculine. Several of these poems, written soon after Thoreau left college, were published in "The Dial," and also some essays on the natural history of Massachusetts. Emerson was the medium of this early literary recognition, and his contact with the odd and whimsical young man who had so few intimates inevitably had an effect upon Thoreau's development, both literary and philosophical. He did not want to imitate anybody, and he did his best to digest Emerson, so that his own work and cast of thought should not betray the contagion. Measurably, but not completely, he succeeded. His writings are thinly overspread with Thoreau, but here and there the coating has worn off, and the Emersonian basis shows through. It is quite open to question whether this has not done the writings more harm than good. The nectar and ambrosia of Emerson does not assimilate kindly with Thoreau's harsh and rather acrid substance. Thoreau was a humorist,—in the old, not in the new sense,—and it is indispensable to the prosperity of the humorist that he be himself. He was no optimist, and he cared nothing for the welfare of mankind, or the progress of civilization. When, therefore, he ornaments his records of the facts of nature with interpretations of their moral and spiritual significance, we feel a sense of incongruity. The interpretations have not the air of developing spontaneously from the interior of the writer's thought; they are deliberately fitted on from the outside, and the marks of juncture smoothed off. On the other hand, it did come naturally to Thoreau to fall into a vein of talking about natural objects—plants, animals and meteorology—as if they were human creatures, and to credit them with likes, dislikes, thoughts and personalities. When he does this, he is entertaining and attractive, and it is a pity he did not develop a vein so proper to him, rather than snatch with his earthly hands at the Empyrean.

His poems of observation were good, and, like a pointer-dog, he could fix his gaze upon an object for a long time at a stretch. Nevertheless, he cannot be considered an especially objective writer. He reverts continually to himself, and examines his own attitude and impressions in regard to the thing even more solicitously than the thing itself. The poet in him helps the naturalist, but the philosopher sophisticates him. Now and then, in the midst of the pathless woods, we are aware of a queer bookish flavor in the air. The literary artist arranges his little scene, pleasing in its way, and well done; only it was not just the kind of pleasure we were looking for. Other and greater artists can do that better: what we want of Thoreau is his own peculiar service, and nothing else.

In truth, he was not free from affectations; he was radically provincial; and often (as children complain of one another) he was "disagreeable." But he had deep and true thoughts, he was of pure and upright life and he made a real and lasting impression. He deserves the reputation that he has with the average reader, though not the violent panegyrics of his thick-and-thin admirers. He assumed the stoicism and some of the habits of the Indian, and his physical senses were approximately as acute as theirs; but he was really a civilized man who never found a home in civilization. One leaves him with a feeling of unmixed kindliness; and in his "Walden," his "Week on the Concord and Merrimac," his "Cape Cod" and other books, will be found many passages worthy of preservation, which only he could have written.

Julian Hawthorne and Leonard Lemmon, *American Literature: A Text-Book for the Use of Schools and Colleges* (Boston: D. C. Heath, 1891), 146–48.

From "Reminiscences of Thoreau" (1893)

[Horace R. Hosmer]

As a young boy, Horace R. Hosmer (1830–1894) attended John and Henry Thoreau's Concord school. He later lived in nearby Acton, Massachusetts, and worked in various jobs—store clerk, pencil maker and salesman, handyman, and farmer. Interviewed at length late in life by Dr. Samuel A. Jones, a Thoreau enthusiast from Michigan, the irascible Hosmer provided some of the most picturesque accounts of many antebellum Concord figures, particularly Thoreau, whom he regarded highly but always critically.

13 April 1893

More than forty years ago half a dozen boys were on the east bank of the Assabet river taking a sun bath after their swim in the stream. They were talking about the conical heaps of stones in the river, and wishing that they knew what build them. There were about as many theories as there were boys, and no conclusion had been arrived at, when one of the boys said "here comes Henry Thoreau, let us ask him." So when he came near, one of the boys asked him "what made those heaps of stones in the river." "I asked a Penobscot Indian that question," said Thoreau, "and he said 'the musquash did,' but I told him that I was a better Indian than he, for I knew and he did not," and with that reply he walked off. John —— said, "that is just like him, he never will tell a fellow anything unless it is in his lectures, darn his old lectures about chipmunks and Injuns, I wont go to hear him," and the unanimous conclusion of the boys was, that when they got left again, another man would do it. The boys could not understand Thoreau, and he did not understand boys, and both were losers by it.

While looking over Thoreau's "Autumn" lately, the writer was reminded of the time when Thoreau and the writer's father spent some two or three weeks running anew the boundary lines in Sudbury woods. I think it was in 1851, and there were grave disputes, and law suits seemed probable but after a while these two men were selected to fix the bounds. The real trouble was owing to the variation of the compass, the old lines having been run some 200 years before; but Thoreau understood his business thoroughly and settled the boundary question so that peace was declared. Thoreau's companion was an old lumberman and woodchopper and a close observer of natural objects; but he said that Thoreau was the best man he had ever known in the woods. He would climb a tree like a squirrel, knew every plant and shrub and really seemed to have been born in the forest. Thoreau asked many questions; one of them was, "Do you know where there is a white grape, which grows on high land, which bears every year and is of superior quality?" "Yes," was the reply. "It is a little north of Deacon Dakins' rye field and when the grapes are ripe if you are not on the windward side your nose will tell you where they are." Thoreau laughed and appeared satisfied.

About this time Thoreau went to a party in Concord, and he says in his journal or diary, that he would rather eat crackers and cheese with his old companion in the woods.

It is a great mistake to suppose that Thoreau was a solitary student of natural history in Concord and vicinity at that time. He was better equipped for his work, and could record his observations and discoveries better than his fellow students and this was enough to make him famous in later years. . . .

20 April 1893

Thoreau often visited the west part of Concord, passing along the east bank of the Assabet river from Derby's bridge up the stream, along the high banks which overlook the river to the land formerly owned by Timothy Shehan, and from there to the Ministerial swamp and vicinity where he first found the climbing fern. The writer saw him the day he found the rare plant while returning home with his prize. I never saw such a pleased, happy look on his face as he had that day. He took off his hat, in the crown of which the fern was coiled up, and showed me the dainty, graceful glory of the swamp. He said it had never been seen before in the New England states, outside of the botanical gardens in Cambridge, and he volunteered the information that it grew in a swamp between the place we were on and Sudbury.

Soon after, perhaps two weeks, two men who said they came from Cambridge came to me and asked where the climbing fern grew. I did not tell them for many reasons, perhaps the best one was that which Thoreau gave while speaking of the pink lilies which grew on the Cape. In reply to my question whether he had seen the pink lilies which grew in Hayward's pond in Westvale, he said he had never seen them there or on the Concord rivers, but there was a place on the Cape, a sort of creek, where they had grown unnoticed by the inhabitants until Theodore Parker saw them one summer and gathered them, and "after that," said Thoreau, "the bumpkins grubbed them up root and branch, and almost exterminated them." ...

Let the young men and women of Concord who have a love for the study of botany and natural history not be afraid to glean after Thoreau, for he said "that he had much to report on this subject." Two ladies who spent a part of the last summer in Acton found many rare plants and flowers, and introduced the Acton people to their own near neighbors. Last year there were large bunches of the beautiful bloodroot flowers gathered the 14th of April. The yellow violets grow in North Acton, the white "huckleberry" grows in several places, the beaked hazel is abundant on the northern slopes of Nagog hill, and late in November the air in the woods is heavy with the odor of the witch hazel which puts forth and blossoms like love and generosity in some human beings only just before the winter of death.

"Crayon" [Horace Hosmer], *Concord Enterprise,* "Reminiscences of Thoreau," "Reminiscences of Thoreau II," 13 and 20 April 1893.

From "Memories of Thoreau" (1897)

ANONYMOUS

> This anonymously authored article contains the recollections of Calvin Greene (1817–1898), of Rochester, Michigan, who responded warmly to *Walden* and wrote Thoreau in 1856 to request a copy of *A Week*, which Thoreau sent to him within a few weeks. In doing so, Thoreau expressed his gratitude at Greene's appreciation of *Walden*: "I should consider it a greater success to interest one wise and earnest soul, than a million unwise and frivolous" (*Correspondence*, 407). While a student at Oberlin College, Greene had been encouraged to study the ministry, an episode he later called "a narrow escape" (qtd. in Jones, 30). Although Greene did not have an opportunity to meet Thoreau before he died, he visited Concord in 1863 at the invitation of the Thoreau family.[1] In a lengthy letter in June 1862, Sophia Thoreau had also sent Greene one of the daguerreotypes taken of Thoreau at Greene's request in 1856. In 1899, Samuel Arthur Jones published Greene's correspondence with Sophia and Henry in *Some Unpublished Letters of Henry D. and Sophia E. Thoreau*. Originally published in the Free Thought organ, *The Truth Seeker*, this article clearly reflects that Thoreau's religious skepticism was a significant factor in Greene's admiration.

"WHILE I WAS at the Thoreaus in Concord, Mass., in the fall of '63," says C. H. Greene, of Rochester, Mich., who is one of the poet-naturalist's strongest admirers, "Miss Sophia Thoreau related, among others, the following anecdotes of her brother during his last illness."

Some boys of the vicinity were in the habit of bringing game for him to eat, presenting it at the kitchen door, and then gently withdrawing so as not to disturb the sick man. On one occasion he was told of it soon after their leaving, when he earnestly inquired: "Why did you not invite them in? I want to thank them for so much that they are bringing me." And then adding, thoughtfully: "Well, I declare; I don't believe they are going to let me go after all."

At another time he requested some lads who had been robbing birds' nests to be called into his sick room that he might lecture them about it. In the interview he was heard asking them if they knew what a wail of sorrow and anguish their cruelty had sent all over the fields and through the woods.

Speaking of one's hair turning gray, and to what cause it is sometimes attributed, Thoreau remarked: "I never had any trouble in all my life, or only when I was about fourteen; then I felt pretty bad a little while on account of my sins, but no trouble since that I know of. That must be the reason why my hair doesn't turn gray faster. But there is Blake; he is as gray as a rat." . . .

Still another life of Thoreau has been printed, this time by an English admirer. This makes three formal histories of a man who, when alive, could find almost no one to read his writings. Besides the lives there are innumerable essays and papers on him and his philosophy. And, true to her record, now that he is recognized as one of the men of genius, the church is claiming him for her own. But his religious status is too firmly fixed by his own words written in his own hand for their claim to be made good. He had no belief whatever in Christianity; on the contrary, his attitude toward it was almost contemptuous, as though it were too childish for serious men to talk about. He included it among the tricks and trades which he denounced by telling the story of the boy who was building the model of a church in dirt as the minister was passing. "Why, my little lad," said the minister, "why, making a meeting-house of that stuff? Why, why!" "Yes," answered the youth; "yes, I am; and I expect to have enough left over to make a Methodist minister besides." Thoreau was sometimes a trifle haughty intellectually. . . .

Thoreau's "Week" hints at a belief in immortality, and also at a deistic philosophy, but no honest person, upon reading him, could possibly conclude that he was a Christian. There is much better reason to think him a pantheist. But, pantheist or deist, he is one of the helps to the race, a philosopher and friend whom it is gratifying to see appreciated, for he can but do his readers good, encouraging them to independence of character, and urging them to set up a thinking shop for themselves, instead of taking their brains to a church to be moulded into fantastic shapes. Authority had in him an implacable foe, and liberty a stern defender. He was a virile son of the soil, rugged as the rocks and hills. He was the antithesis of the Puritans, and his works are the classics which will help clear New England's fame from the mud under which such men as the Edwardses and Mathers and other Puritans buried it.

Note

1. See Greene's diary entries describing his Concord pilgrimage in W. Barksdale Maynard's "A Pilgrim Visits Concord: The Calvin Greene Diary, Part I (1863)" and "A Pilgrim Visits Concord: The Calvin Greene Diary, Part II (1873)," in *Thoreau Society Bulletin* 243 (Spring 2003): 1–2; and 244 (Summer 2003): 1–2.

"Memories of Thoreau: Unpublished Anecdotes of New England's Anti-Puritan Author and Naturalist," *Truth Seeker* (20 November 1897): 744.

From "Thoreau's Incarceration" (1898)

S. A. J[ONES]

In 1890, homeopathic doctor and Thoreau enthusiast Samuel Arthur Jones (1834–1912) interviewed Samuel Staples (1813–1895), famous by then as the jailer who had arrested and incarcerated Henry Thoreau at the Middlesex County jail one evening late in July 1846 for continued non-payment of his poll tax. Originally from Mendon, Massachusetts, Staples settled in Concord in 1833 and married Lucinda Wesson there in 1839, with Waldo Emerson officiating. Prior to his appointment as jailer, Staples held a variety of positions in town, including clerk and bartender at the grand Middlesex Hotel. He later represented Concord in the state legislature and was a town selectman in the late 1850s. His townsman John Shepard Keyes, typically scornful of what he considered Thoreau's pretensions to principled action, claims that Staples "was very proud of locking up these silly, would-be martyrs [Bronson Alcott and Henry Thoreau], and often boasted of them as the most distinguished of his prisoners" ("Memoir," 137). But Staples himself explained Alcott's action, at least, quite differently: "It was nothing but principle, for I never heard a man talk honester" (qtd. in Sanborn, "Emerson-Thoreau Correspondence," 5/8). Preceding his rendition to Jones of Thoreau's night in jail, Staples relates a lighthearted scene when Thoreau enjoyed a joke at Waldo Emerson's expense while surveying property for Staples.

IT SEEMS THAT A question had arisen regarding the boundary line between land owned by Emerson and Mr. S. himself, which the latter told me had recently become his through a "dicker" with someone whose name I did not catch. Thoreau was employed to make the necessary survey ("and he did it right slick, I tell you"); and having finished his work, he had appointed a meeting at Emerson's house to make his report. I can never forget how Mr. S. in his statement of that meeting made me feel the bland mildness of Emerson's nature. "He was a man, sir, that wouldn't hurt a fly," said Mr. S. most emphatically. Then he went on to explain that there had been no "quarrel" between Emerson and himself; they only "just wanted to know, you know, which was which."

Thoreau was already at Emerson's house when Mr. S. arrived, and they plunged into business without delay. Much to Emerson's surprise, Thoreau said and proved by a map of the survey that his, Mr. Emerson's, partition fence intruded several feet upon the adjoining property; and without waiting for a word from the utterly unconscious intruder, he went on to declare that the appropriation of the land was intentional, only Mr. S. had proven too sharp to be imposed upon; and all these years you've been holding up your nose as an upright citizen and an example to everybody, yet every time you reset your fence you knowingly shoved it in a little farther and a little farther, until you've stolen land enough to almost feed a yearling heifer; but Mr. S. has been too smart for any of you sly fellows, and I'm glad to have a hand in exposing you; though its an awful disappointment to me.

"Why," said Mr. S., "if Emerson hed been ketched pickin' pockets at town meetin' he could n't a looked more streaked. Thoreau was talkin' in downright earnest, and you could have heard him way out on the Lexin'ton road. I felt so all-fired mean, I could n't do nothin' but look at the floor; but whilst Thoreau was a rakin' of him and had just said somthin' darned haa'sh, I just had to look at him, and when I saw his eye I laughed 'til you could a heard it up to the top of the Hill buryin' ground. You see, he was just guyin' Mr. Emerson, and when he see it, he did n't take it amiss at all. He was the nicest man that ever lived."

Surely, this surprising spirit at the expense of the "sage of Concord" will make a companion piece for that famous extemporized dance in Mr. Ricketson's parlor—and yet this was the Thoreau of whom Lowell said, "he had no humor!"

Just how the matter of Thoreau's imprisonment entered into our talk I do not remember, for the jailer's reminiscences followed each other as indiscriminately as the autumn leaves that fell at our feet that day. In the flood tide of his recollections he said: "Henry knew that I had a warrant for him, but I did n't go to hunt for him, 'cause I knew I could git him when I wanted to."

Thoreau was arrested early in the evening, while on his way to get a shoe that was being repaired preparatory to his piloting a huckleberry party on the morrow. The serving of a warrant had no novelty in it for the reminiscential jailer, so he mentioned no details of the arrest, but simply stated that he locked up Thoreau "and the rest of the boys" for the night. A little later he himself went up town on some business. During his brief absence someone rapped at the door of the jailer's private apartments. His daughter opened it, when a veiled young woman said: "Here is the money to pay Mr. Thoreau's tax," and immediately departed. The demand of the law being satisfied, Thoreau was no longer a culprit, and should have been instantly set free on the jailer's return; but when telling me of it, that worthy, in the coolest manner imaginable, said: "I had got my boots off and was sittin' by the fire when my daughter told me, and I was n't goin' to take the trouble to unlock after I'd got the boys all fixed for the night, so I kep' him in 'till after breakfast next mornin' and then I let him go."

It was indeed a surprise to learn how nearly the recalcitrant reformer had escaped his one night in prison, only for the free-and easy jailer's love of his ease we had lost the raciest experience that Thoreau has recorded. I said nothing at the time, though inwardly I questioned the jailer's statement; but on subsequently reading Thoreau's account of the event, I found that it tallied in the fact that he was discharged after having breakfasted in the Concord jail. . . .

S. A. J., "Thoreau's Incarceration," *Inlander* 9 (December 1898): 97–100.

[Recollections of Thoreau and Concord]
(1897–1898)

AMANDA P. MATHER

Amanda P. Mather (1815–1879) was married to William Mather (d. 1868), who served as minister of Concord's Trinitarian Church from 1844 to 1849 and who shared an interest in natural history with Thoreau. During these years, the Mathers became close friends of the Thoreaus. These letters respond to questions raised by Amanda's nephew Daniel Mason (1873–1953), a composer and professor of music at Columbia University, who in researching Thoreau for articles later published in the *Harvard Monthly,* had asked his aunt for her recollections of the Thoreau family. Mason's "The Idealistic Basis of Thoreau's Genius" appeared in December 1897, and "Harrison G. O. Blake, '35, and Thoreau" in May 1898. Mather's detailed, thoughtful letters to Daniel Mason and to his mother, Helen Mason, recount the facts about Thoreau's life as she experienced and remembered them. Interestingly, although a minister's wife, Mather is quite tolerant of Thoreau's unapologetic public appearances on Sunday mornings, as churchgoers returning home encountered him en route to or from his usual outdoor rambles. Thoreau "took no pains to conceal his doings," she explains, nor did he show any "spirit of defiance or scorn for others. He simply did *his way,* and was willing they should do theirs."

To Helen [Mason], 9 August 1897

You asked about my memories of Concord life, *Thoreau* &c. It's a *big subject* but interesting. If I could sit down *of an evening* with you, and your son, it would be nice. People in these days have nature revealed to them by science as they did not in Thoreau's time, and many things which he thought and felt, would not be so *strange* now as they were then. The family lived near us, and there were several reasons why we were more closely drawn together than would have been expected of persons *not sympathiz-*

ing in other things. Your Uncle Mather was fond of *scientific studies,* always took "The Scientific American," and *nature* in the common sense of the word, as it lies around us, was a favorite study with him. This interested Henry. If he, in his tramps off into the woods, found a new grass or plant, he would bring it to Mr Mather and Mr Mather the same to him. The *"Unitarian defection,"* as it was called, had divided churches a little earlier, and the old ch[urch] in Concord with the narrow creed of orthodox lines at that day, had split into separation. This separation was some *five* years before we went there. The *smaller part* came off and formed the orthodox ch[urch] of which Mr Mather was Pastor, and the old ch[urch] becoming more decided in its Unitarian creed remained. The Thoreau family remained with the old ch[urch]. But *two Aunts,* sisters of Mr Thoreau, the Father came *to our ch[urch].* They were ladies of strong character and high social position, and had almost as much influence with Henry and his *two sisters,* as their own parents. So it happened that these two sisters came to our ch[urch] with their Aunts quite often. Henry was younger, and his taste for nature, led him *I think* to look for truth and light in *it,* and in the circumstances, to *drop between the two churches.* Often times on a *Sab.* morning, as we went to ch[urch] we met him in his weekday dress going off to the river or woods, and may be on our return, again, with a bunch of plants or branches of trees in his hands. He took no pains to conceal his doings, nor was there any spirit of defiance or scorn for others. He simply did *his way,* and was willing they should do theirs. His sisters were gifted, were musical and had taste for art &c. Used their pencils and studied nature in sketching and painting. The principle or use of the *"Camera Obscura"* was described about that time, and Mr Mather was much interested in it and sent away for the lenses and made the box himself, and we had great pleasure in it, it gave very perfect pictures and the Thoreaus used to come in for it, take the view by the Camera, and then by placing an oiled paper on the glass, draw the outline. So our tastes drew us together.

It is hard to classify Henry Thoreau, to put him any where. He was *himself* and belonged to no class or creed—I think he did not reject revelation *of God* in the scriptures, but for himself sought light from nature in *His works.* There was nothing low, or with *downward* tendencies in his mental theories. This is *my impression of him.* You must take *it only for this.* When I knew him, it was *so long ago,* and what I have *read about him,* I do not lay so much stress on, for I see that the writers had *their own theories* often, rather than representing *his*. I *trust* that in "the sweet fields beyond the swelling flood," he has found the light which he sought here, or rather *its source, in the fullness of God,* Father, Son, and Holy Ghost, and that he rejoices *in the life,* which is not clouded or limited by our human weakness and ignorance. . . .

To Daniel Mason, 13 September 1897

. . . I am glad to respond to what you say of *yourself* and your *studies,* and am sympathetically moved by the subject of your present thought and research, *Thoreau.* The older I grow the more deeply I am interested in *humanity* in all its varied aspects, or perhaps I should say *subjects.* And when we find one who stands apart from his fellows as Thoreau did, and was as you say "so original, so elevated and noble," the attraction to study the character, to find if possible the springs of action, the motive is very great.

But in giving my impressions of him you will remember that my personal knowledge of him dates *far back.* He was but two *years younger than I.* And when I knew him at Concord he was just starting out in his peculiar life. Of course I did not judge of him then, as I might now. Though I think my memory keeps persons and things for the most part correctly. But I knew but little then about life, what its highest aims should be, or how they could best be attained. And I have read but little of what has been written of him or indeed of his own books latterly. In my changful life, my books have been scattered and I have but *very few* now by me. I will just say here, that *my son* came in as I was reading your letter and he says "tell cousin Dan when you write that when I was young, I read '*Walden,*' with the greatest delight, I believe it was *next* to my *Bible* to me." (And if you knew how *close* a *Student of the Bible* he was, and is, not for *form's sake,* but from fresh interest in it, you would appreciate the remark.)

Now I will take *your questions* as they came. 1. "Did your neighbors, and friends at Concord, consider Thoreau in any sense misanthropic, embittered &c?" *I think not.* They thought him *odd* in following his bent, finding society in nature apart from his fellows, but *if there was wrong* in it, it was in his *disregard of his fellows,* taking his own enjoyment as his *highest aim.* He was *kindly* to others when *it came in his way,* but it was not *an object to him.* I do not think he thought living *for others* was what his life was for he took life *slowly* was then in *childhood* so to speak—.

2. Did he laugh etc. when you met him in the village or parlor? Was he genial and pleasant?"

He was *pleasant always* and genial in the sense of being responsive to the interest you might express in any subject we had before us. But for our own intercourse with him we always talked of the matters in which we knew his line of thought wasnt ours—*Music* was always a delight to him. Animal life, as well as plant, was a study. The forces of nature as revealed at the present day, were then still unknown mostly, or only some of them conjectured. The scientists were searching for the causes of things, & any hints which were given of more light & knowledge interested my husband & Thoreau mutually. *Common talk,* a *general conversation entertainment* would have been a *great bore* to him.

III. His personal appearance.

It was peculiar and not easy to describe. *Plain* in face and feature one might say, and yet there was an *ernestness,* that took hold of you, and affected you favorably. Something you would wish to see again.—I did not know then as I do now, that we *Palmers* were almost *akin,* the Thoreaus were of Norman descent that the same brave old *Norman blood* runs in our veins! Did you know that we have the *Palmer line* distinctly traced back to "William of Normandy?" I think it is one of best of all the [*Received*] inheritances. Am proud of it.— —I have never seen *any* of Thoreaus portraits.

IIII. I have never attended any of his lectures. He was yet living at Walden, when I left Concord and after a residence of a few years there, I went west.

My impressions of him will be of little value to you, they are so far off. I very distinctly remember his true and devoted affection for his parents and sisters—A very touching incident to me was his part at the funeral of his eldest sister who died before I left Concord. She was a gifted person in music painting &c had I think more sympathy in his peculiar ways perhaps than any other. The funeral service was in the parlor of his Father's house. Both of the ministers the Unitarian, and Mr Mather, were there for the service. Henry sat unmoved with his kindred, till the service was through. (he never went to ch[urch] at that time or any other religious occasion). In the moments of interval while they were preparing outside to remove the bier, he arose and taking a *music box* from the table set it by winding, to a *particular tune* of the *sweetest tenderest* minor strains, that seemed like no earthly tone! All sat quietly till it was through.— — —

It is not possible to tell what his own soul felt in regard to death, but he was respectful, and tender to his kindred who found consolation in religious ministration at such a time. In one place he writes "for joy I could embrace the earth. I shall delight to be *buried in it.*" It seems impossible that one who loved the beauty of the outward world, and the wonderful skill and wisdom and love every where manifest, should not be led by it, to the loving Father who made it. And all see that *this life* is but the *starting point,* for endless better life when this earthly shall no longer clog and hinder if we are prepared to enjoy that more blessed state. I cannot think but that he did "look through nature up to nature's God." Wish there might have been some more expression of his religious life for *others' sakes.* But I can see a good many reasons why there was not. He on account of the peculiar circumstances of his earlier thinking years, perhaps came to confound *theology* with *christian life* and practice. About the *first,* his best friends *differed,* "how should he know?" If he *could have* with Bryant and Longfellow, Whittier, and Lowell, found God *in nature* as they did, it would have been a joy greater than all he found in the beautiful earth itself. Again I say *perhaps he did.* — — — — —

I shall be much pleased to see your essay. I dare say it will help me in my ideas of Thoreau for he was so youthful when I knew him. . . .

To Daniel Mason, n.d.

Your good letter with the "Harvard Monthly," was most gratefully received and I have read your paper on Thoreau with ernest thought, more than *once.* I am interested in it because of *its subject,* and because *you wrote it.* I do think you had much courage to undertake the portrayal of a character so unlike the usual types of humanity which we meet with. As you say, he was *"egregious* in the primary sense of the word," *one by himself* and the little care he had whether the herd he had left, understood him or not, doubtless hindered him some times from understanding them. . . .

Some day as you say, you may write something more about Thoreau. I have many thoughts about him which it would not be easy to express. Had he lived *at the present time* I think he would have been different from what he was. He took nature, the material world, as it *then was.* What a development of all natural forces there has been since that time! With his traits of character entire sincerity, truthfulness, taking the *good* of all things around him, or *satisfaction* in it, without restless worry for something

[164]

else and other virtues if he should now wake to present things as they are, what a revelation *humanity* as well as *the material world about us* would be to him! . . .

To Daniel Mason, 23 February 1898

Bringing Concord up again reminds me of Thoreau, your paper &c. The latter I *received*—I don't know if I mentioned in my letter that Wallace my son said to me, on returning the mag. "that is a *very ably written paper.*"

In Mr Hale's introduction to James Russell Lowell and his friends, he speaks of the difficulty of representing a *past* generation to the present.— Of the "careful consideration of the atmosphere in which a writer or author lived, in order to understand him." I applied these remarks to your paper on Thoreau, and thought how remarkably you had met these difficulties in your writing. And *Concord is* a *very* interesting place! I am glad I ever lived there, and felt the inspiration of its mind and soul atmosphere. If you decide to try a biographical sketch of Thoreau at some time, I think it would help you to go to Concord, and spend a day or two rambling about in the naturalist's old haunts along the river and in *Walden woods*. The River, "winding at its own sweet will" the "*Rustic Bridge,*" the *meadows* where Thoreau used to wander so often along its banks for the wonderful variety and beauties of the *grasses* which grew there—

And with all the *war clouds* now rising in our horizon, it might be well to pause at the spot where the gun "heard round the world" was fired! . . .

I write hastily now, but if you take up Thoreau farther, I should try to recall some more things of his life and habits than I did in the letter which I wrote you. Had he lived at *this day* with the great advance in science, and almost weekly revelations which are made of the wonderful, and before unknown forces in nature about us, with such a mind as his of research, and seeking the *real* and *true* about him what an enlargement to his soul and fullness of life it would have given! I hope it has come to him in the Spirit world. . . .

To Daniel Mason, 3 August 1899

As to my "*impressions*" of Thoreau, he seems to me to have been *like himself,* and *no* one else, I have known or read of. As in the material world of nature we find sporadic specimens sometimes, of which, *only one* can be found so it seems it was with him. As to his "*taking life slowly,*" it was as if a child were brought for the first time into a room, or museum, where there were many things seen for the first time and instead of running from one wonder to another, should *stop at the first,* be wholly absorbed in its properties, make a study of it. Most children would pass hastily from object to object, knowing after but little of any. This is what I meant by "taking life slowly."—Of music he was *very fond,* as his sisters were. In "Emerson at Concord" by his son, allusion is made to his *love for children* and the useful help he often rendered when living with the Emerson's by amusing the children. I know this letter will be of little service to you, but am delighted to think of the great pleasure you will find in the papers which come from Mr Russell. . . .

Amanda Mather to Helen [Mason], 9 August 1897; and Amanda Mather to Daniel Mason, n.d., 13 September 1897, 23 February 1898, and 3 August 1899, Raymond Adams Collection, Thoreau Society, Henley Library, Thoreau Institute, Lincoln, MA. Ampersands in the original source have been silently emended to "and" in this piece.

From "Reminiscences of Thoreau" (1899)

Anonymous

> When published at the turn of the twentieth century, this article was prefaced by a note identifying the author as "an intimate personal friend of the late Miss Sophia E. Thoreau, . . . [who] made frequent visits to the Thoreau home in Concord." It is representative of several late nineteenth-century anecdotal reminiscences of Concord and Thoreau and includes most of the well-known "stories" of Thoreau's life, both the historically accurate and the apocryphal (e.g., Emerson's visit to a jailed Thoreau). In contrast to many such recollections, however, this author adds dialogue and a keen sense of narrative to recount both comical episodes (as when Thoreau helps capture a neighbor's escaped pig) and relaxing moments with Thoreau as community nature guide.

HENRY USUALLY RETIRED to his study after breakfast, and later would reappear ready for a jaunt through field or forest, or by the river, or, if in winter, for a long skate on its frozen surface, once going sixteen miles before turning homeward—this was, however, an exceptional achievement. But wherever he wandered, on his return he always had some new and instructive fact to relate, often all aglow with enthusiasm over some discovery he had made or treasure he had found.

Henry seemed to regard Concord and its vicinity as an epitome of the universe; it was said that on his returning to Mr. Emerson a borrowed volume of Dr. Kane's "Arctic Journey," he remarked that "most of the phenomena noted could have been observed in Concord." Nature revealed its secrets to his sympathetic soul; his searching eyes saw far, wide, and deep; he heard, nay, knew when to expect to hear, the first bluebird's note; indeed, no harbinger of the seasons escaped his alert observation. Before we had begun to think of spring flowers Henry came in from a ramble and surprised us with a handful of early violets. Sophia with her gifted pencil made a drawing of them for me, appending Henry's poem, suggested years before by precisely such a bunch tied round by a wisp of straw. . . .

Henry and Sophia were in perfect accord (as indeed were all the family), and her thorough knowledge of botany formed a special bond of sympathy between them. Henry placed great reliance—as did all who knew her—on his sister's rare judgment and ability in practical matters, and he was himself a shrewd, practical man in affairs of every-day life; he once said, "I have as many trades as fingers." A comical illustration of his readiness to cope with sudden emergencies occurred late one warm afternoon in summer, just as a short, sharp thunder-storm had passed and the sun was breaking through the dispersing clouds. We had finished supper, but were lingering at the table, when the servant threw open the door, exclaiming, with wild excitement, "Faith! th' pig's out o' th' pin, an' th' way he's tearin' roun' Jege Hoore's fluer-bids es enuf ter scare er budy." Henry and his father at once rushed out in pursuit of the marauder, and the ladies flew to the windows to see the fray. Never was practical strategy more in evidence; plotting and counter-plotting on both sides, repeated circumvention of well-laid plans, and a final cornering and capture of the perverse beast, who, after his delicious taste of freedom, protested loudly and vigorously against being forced to return to his prison pen. It was truly a triumph of the intellectual over the animal nature, whose brief enjoyment of wild destructive liberty was suddenly ended by the power of a superior will. It was remarked at the time how much mental and physical strength had to be expended to subdue so inferior an animal.

Henry was equally prompt and victorious when he found that the rules and regulations intended for a past generation hindered the progress of his own. I was told that a few years after his graduation from Harvard he wished to obtain the loan of certain volumes from its library, and made application to President Sparks for them; he was informed that the ancient statutes of the University permitted "clergymen and graduates who lived within twelve miles of Cambridge" to take books from its library. "And," said the President, "while very desirous of accommodating you, I have no right to do so unless you can show that you come within the rule." "As to that," said Henry, "I am not a clergyman; but when the rule of which you speak was made, twelve miles was a two hours' journey, and I live much nearer than that." The President recognized the ingenuity and justice of the plea by allowing him to take the books.

Henry often showed playful instincts, yet he *was* serious. Life was no play-day for himself or others; he seemed tremendously in earnest in trying to find the key to right living. He impressed one as being interested in all humanity and its work in the world, provided it was not sordid. Low expedients, no matter what they accomplished in the making of fame or fortune, were utterly repugnant to him. There was a conspicuous Spartan fortitude in the family character; the mother had taught it both by precept and example. They took high ground on every subject, had stern views of duty, and tolerated no vacillating or compromising measures in disposing of moral questions. This attribute of the family character was strikingly manifested when Henry submitted to be imprisoned for refusing to pay taxes during the Mexican war. He believed all war to be wrong, and that the then existing struggle was for the extension of slavery, which he abhorred. Soon after his incarceration, Mr. Emerson, whom he had always supposed was of like sentiments with himself, called at the jail, and on meeting his friend exclaimed, "Henry, why are you here?" and received for answer, "Mr. Emerson, why are *you* not here?" . . .

Occasionally Henry would invite us to go with him in his boat. One of these excursions was in late November, and the weather was of almost unearthly beauty; bees in great multitudes hummed loudly as they lazily floated in the golden slumberous haze only seen in the true Indian summer. At a particular spot Henry turned the boat toward the bank, saying: "We will make a call upon a wild flower that is not ordinarily at home at this date, but the unusually warm days and nights of the past fortnight may have prevented its departure; so we will knock at its door," tapping at the upper leaves of a low-growing plant; and, verily, there was the shy, dainty little blossom underneath—welcomed by at least one pair of alert, sympathetic eyes. . . .

It was often amusing to observe Henry's want of gallantry; in getting in or out of a boat, or if a fence or wall were to be surmounted, no hand did he stretch forth; he assumed that a woman should be able to help herself in all such matters; but if she were defenseless, his inborn chivalry could be relied on; as in the case of a terrified girl pursued through the woods by a couple of young ruffians, sons of influential parents, Henry's valiant rescue was most timely; and by his persistent efforts due punishment was inflicted upon the shameless offenders. Again, when a weary mother with a heavy child in her arms was struggling to reach the station, where the train had already arrived, her feet sinking in the hot sand at every step, with one glance Henry took in the situation. He bounded over the fence, transferred the child to his own arms, and, with strides that seemed to disdain the shifting sand, he moved over the ground with a conquering air that appeared to impress the inanimate engine and compel it to tarry till the belated mother and child were safely aboard the train.

No one could more heartily enjoy his family life than Henry. He invariably came down from his study for a while in the evening for conversation; the sound of the piano was sure to draw him. . . .

Once, after a day so stormy that he had not taken his customary outdoor exercise, Henry came flying down from his study when the evening was half spent. His face was unusually animated; he sang with zest, but evidently needed an unrestricted outlet for his pent-up vitality, and soon began to dance, all by himself, spinning airily round, displaying most remarkable litheness and agility; growing more and more inspirited, he finally sprang over the center-table, alighting like a feather on the other side—then, not in the least out of breath, continued his waltz until his enthusiasm abated. . . .

In sad contrast to the memory of Henry in his strength arises another, some years later—of him in his decline; he had returned from the West, whither he had been in search of health, and by evening a flush had come to his cheeks and an ominous brightness and beauty to his eyes, painful to behold. His conversation was unusually brilliant, and we listened with a charmed attention which perhaps stimulated him to continue talking until the weak voice could no longer articulate.

This was the autumn before his death; in a few months his life on earth was ended. I was told that he retained his splendid courage and fortitude to the last.

"Reminiscences of Thoreau," *Outlook* 63 (2 December 1899): 815–17, 819–20.

From "Sketch of Henry D. Thoreau" (1902)

DANIEL RICKETSON

Daniel Ricketson (1813–1898), a wealthy Quaker and abolitionist from New Bedford, first met Thoreau after becoming enamored of *Walden* and inviting him to visit. A minor author, Ricketson published a few books, including *A History of New Bedford, New Bedford of the Past*, and two collections of poems, *An Autumn Sheaf* and *Factory Bell and Other Poems*. Like Thoreau, Ricketson was a nonconformist. As a young man, he had studied law, but his primary interest became establishing a literary and solitary life. To that end he settled with his wife and family on a small farm near New Bedford, where, inspired by Thoreau, he eventually built a "shanty" on the back of his property. There he often entertained Thoreau as well as their mutual friends Ellery Channing and Bronson Alcott. At Ricketson's urging, Thoreau had his ambrotype taken during a visit to New Bedford in the summer of 1861, the year before he died. The gaunt image pleased Sophia Thoreau, who regarded it as "one of the most successful likenesses we ever saw" (qtd. in Harding, *Days*, 452). Ricketson's detailed sketch, composed as it is by a close friend of Thoreau's and ardent devotee of his ideas, is especially valuable.

"Thoreau"

My first interview with him was so peculiar that I will venture to state it. The season was winter, a snow had lately fallen, and I was engaged in shovelling the accumulated mass from the entrance to my house, when I perceived a man walking towards me bearing an umbrella in one hand and a leather travelling-bag in the other. So unlike my ideal Thoreau, whom I had fancied, from the robust nature of his mind and habits of life, to be a man of unusual vigor and size, that I did not suspect, although I had expected him in the morning, that the slight, quaint-looking person before me was the Walden philosopher. There are few persons who had previously read his works that were not disappointed by his personal appearance. As he came near to me I gave him the usual salutation, and supposing him to be either a pedler or some way-traveller, he at once remarked, "You don't know me."

The truth flashed on my mind, and concealing my own surprise I at once took him by the hand and led him to the room already prepared for him, feeling a kind of disappointment—a disappointment, however, which soon passed off, and never again obtruded itself to the philosopher's disadvantage. In fact, I soon began to see that Nature had dealt kindly by him, and that this apparently slender personage was physically capable of enduring far more than the ordinary class of men, although he had then begun to show signs of failure of strength in his knees.

"Henry D. Thoreau"

The names of Thoreau and Emerson are not properly placed together on account of any great similarity in the character of the two men; yet from some cause, probably from their being fellow-townsmen more than any other, they are in many minds associated as of the same class. Although Thoreau was many years younger than Emerson, his mind was equally as mature, and I place his name first out of respect to the dead. While Emerson is the product of New England institutions, the ripest fruit and the best specimen, perhaps, Thoreau is one of those remarkable instances of wisdom and philosophy that grow out, as it were, of the order of nature, and may be born in any age or nation. They who drink at the fountain-head of knowledge and truth need not the artificial training of the schools. Still Henry Thoreau had the best advantages of New England in his education. He was a graduate of Harvard College, a good classical scholar, well versed in the mathematics, had been a teacher of youth, and a land surveyor in his own town, which brought him into an intimate acquaintance with the topography of the surrounding country.

He was an excellent naturalist, particularly in his knowledge of plants and birds. In fact, nothing escaped his notice or interest. He was, indeed, a most consummate observer and recorder of the works of nature and the ways of men.

It was my privilege to know him during the last eight years of his life, when in the full maturity of his powers. The relationship between Thoreau and his most intimate friends was not that of great warmth of affection, but rather of respect for manly virtues. If affection were wanting, a strong and abiding attachment took its place, and his friendship was one not liable to the usual ruptions of more ardent and emotional minds.

He was in its strictest sense a good man, sternly virtuous and temperate

in all his habits; in fact, one who did not know how little he valued the ordinary manifestations of religion would have said that he was a real Christian, indeed a Bishop of the Church could not have comported himself with
more dignity or propriety of conduct than he. His tastes and pursuits were
all of a manly character. The morning hours were usually devoted to study
or writing, and the afternoon to walking, or boating on his favorite river, the
Musketaquid or Concord, with an occasional pedestrian tour to the mountains or Cape Cod, many of his experiences in which are recorded in his
published works. Many a long ramble have I taken with him, and although
I am a pretty good walker, he usually quite fatigued me before he had accomplished his object, perhaps the pursuit of some rare plant. In a boat of
his own construction I have sailed with him up and down the slow gliding
Concord River, and found him a good boatman, both in sailing and scull-
ing. Once, during a winter visit to him, we took a tramp through the snow
to White Pond, some two or three miles beyond Walden, then surrounded
by heavy wood, and frequented by huntsmen. He was fond of hardy enterprises, and few of his companions could compete with him. In fact I have
heard that he quite tired out an Indian guide, on one of his excursions in
Maine. I do not remember of ever seeing him laugh outright, but he was
ever ready to smile at anything that pleased him; and I never knew him to
betray any tender emotion except on one occasion, when he was narrating
to me the death of his only brother, John Thoreau, from lockjaw, strong
symptoms of which, from his sympathy with the sufferer, he himself experienced. At this time his voice was choked, and he shed tears, and went to
the door for air. The subject was of course dropped, and never recurred to
again.

In person he was rather below the medium stature, though not decidedly short,—of rather slender than robust habit of body, and marked for
his drooping shoulders. Still he was vigorous and active, and when in
good health could perform a good deal of physical labor. His head was of
medium size, . . . his brow was full, and his forehead rather broad than
prominent; his eyes grayish blue, his nose long and aquiline, and his hair
inclined to sandy. When interested in conversation, and standing, he had a
decidedly dignified bearing.

At first Thoreau was far from being understood by the public; a few there
were, and but a few, who accepted him; he lived, however, long enough to
create a public for himself, and if not among the most scholarly, at least it

comprised the more thoughtful portion of the reading class of our people. I never heard him lecture or speak in public, but I believe he was not generally successful except, perhaps, in his more private readings. His thoughts were often too subtle to be readily interpreted, requiring a deliberate reading to fully understand them. He won for himself a name and fame, which had before his death reached the other side of the water, where his works are by a chosen few still known and cherished. . . .

As well as Thoreau wrote, only those whose privilege it was to listen to one of his long discursive conversations by the evening fireside know how full of interest and instruction he made the subject of his disquisition, apparently enjoying himself as much as interesting his hearers. Judging from my own relationship with him, I would say that he won rather the respect and admiration of his friends than their love. He was so superior to almost all other men that he inspired a certain amount of awe. "Why," said his eccentric friend, C———, in his own peculiar manner, which of course implied no irreverence, "Thoreau is a god!" Whether a god or saint it matters not, he was, in almost every walk of life that makes a man honored and respected by his friends, a rare example. As a son and brother he was much beloved, in temperance and frugality an example worthy of following; and though no politician he was by no means an uninterested looker-on of the state of affairs in ours as well as other countries. Few men in any age of the world have more fully rounded their lives than he.

If he had any fault, it was that he was too true to nature and himself to become a decided Christian; but in most that is excellent in Christianity he possessed a large share, and I am too much a believer in the doctrine of the light within not to recognize the divine unction in the soul even if the form of sound words be wanting. But it was in the closing scenes of his life, and when confined to his room and bed, that this truly good and brave man showed the depth and power of divine wisdom in his soul, giving him strength in his weakness, and making the sick-room and the chamber of death resplendent in beauty and hopefulness.

His inquisitive mind still found an interest in the change he was experiencing, and regarding death to be as natural as life, he accepted it with gracefulness, and investigated its approach with more than philosophic composure.

As a writer Thoreau was sententious rather than graceful or elegant; his style was his own, and well adapted to his subject-matter. Originality perhaps more than other quality marked his thought; yet at times he uttered old truths in a new dress so well adapted to his object of conveying practical ideas, that they have the charm of novelty, and are calculated to edify the attentive reader. More than any writer perhaps of his time does he require a careful reading to fully arrive at the pith of his matter, which is often marked by a subtlety that he appears to have chosen to conceal a too glaring expression of his meaning. He could, however, at will execute his thought in the most graceful and poetic manner, and a judicious selection of these passages from his works would form a volume of remarkable beauty. He was a voluminous writer; and although since his death several volumes have been added to his former works, it is probable that a large amount of manuscript yet remains. . . .

Although the life of Thoreau was mostly within himself, or rather with the company he entertained there, as he would probably have expressed it, still few men have found a keener relish for innocent out of door amusements than he. His boat, his spy-glass, and staff, though he rarely used the latter about home, comprised his equipage. So thoroughly had he learned the characteristics of his own neighborhood for miles around, that he probably knew more about its history than the proprietors themselves, even as to boundaries and titles tracing back to the days of the native Indians.

Few men have accomplished more than our late friend, or lived to better purpose.

Peace to his memory.

Daniel Ricketson, "Sketch of Henry D. Thoreau," *Daniel Ricketson and His Friends: Letters Poems Sketches Etc.*, ed. Anna and Walton Ricketson (Boston: Houghton, Mifflin, 1902), 11–19.

[Reminiscences of Henry Thoreau] (1903)

George F. Hoar

> Brother of Thoreau's friends Edward and Elizabeth, George Frisbie Hoar
> (1826–1904) graduated from Harvard College in 1846 and became a lawyer
> in Concord. From 1869 through 1877, he served in the United States House
> of Representatives; he was elected in 1877 to the U.S. Senate, in which he
> served until his death. This brief recollection illustrates Hoar's respect for
> Thoreau's creative process and intellectual curiosity.

I KNEW HENRY THOREAU very intimately. I went to school with him when
I was a little boy and he was a big one. Afterward I was a scholar in his
school. . . .

He knew the best places to find huckleberries and blackberries and
chestnuts and lilies and cardinal and other rare flowers. We used to call
him Trainer Thoreau, because the boys called the soldiers the "trainers,"
and he had a long, measured stride and an erect carriage which made him
seem something like a soldier, although he was short and rather ungainly
in figure. He had a curved nose which reminded one a little of the beak of
a parrot.

His real name was David Henry Thoreau, although he changed the order of his first two names afterward. He was a great finder of Indian arrow-
heads, spear-heads, pestles, and other stone implements which the Indians
had left behind them, of which there was great abundance in the Concord
fields and meadows.

He knew the rare forest birds and all the ways of birds and wild animals. Naturalists commonly know birds and beasts and flowers as a sur-
geon who has dissected the human body, or perhaps sometimes a painter
who has made pictures of them knows men and women. But he knew birds
and beasts as one boy knows another—all their delightful little habits and
fashions. He had the most wonderful good fortune. We used to say that if
anything happened in the deep woods which only came about once in a

hundred years, Henry Thoreau would be sure to be on the spot at the time and know the whole story. . . .

I retained his friendship to his death. I have taken many a long walk with him. I used to go down to see him in the winter days in my vacations in his hut near Walden. He was capital company. He was a capital guide in the wood. He liked to take out the boys in his boat. He was fond of discoursing. I do not think he was vain. But he liked to do his thinking out loud, and expected that you should be an auditor rather than a companion.

I have heard Thoreau say in private a good many things which afterward appeared in his writings. One day when we were walking, he leaned his back against a rail fence and discoursed of the shortness of the time since the date fixed for the creation, measured by human lives. "Why," he said, "sixty old women like Nabby Kettle" (a very old woman in Concord), "taking hold of hands, would span the whole of it." He repeats this in one of his books, adding, "They would be but a small tea-party, but their gossip would make universal history."

George F. Hoar, *Autobiography of Seventy Years,* vol. 1 (New York: Charles Scribner's Sons, 1903), 70–72.

[Thoreau's Visit to Plymouth in 1851] (1894)

ELLEN WATSON

Author and teacher Ellen Watson (1855–1926) was the daughter of Thoreau's friends Benjamin Marston Watson (1820–1896) and Mary Russell Watson (1820–1906), who lived in Plymouth, Massachusetts. In this essay, Ellen Watson revises and improves on her mother's account of Thoreau's visit to Plymouth in 1851. Her description of an animated, chatty Thoreau enjoying his informal audience brings to mind similar scenes in *Cape Cod*.

WHEN THOREAU WAS A young man he visited Plymouth and Duxbury, and as enthusiastic pedestrians never tire of walking, he attempted to continue his stroll around Captain's Hill to the north shore of Clark's Island. When the tide is at its lowest ebb this does not look so impossible! The sand flats even invite one to pace their shining surface! The channel looks narrow enough to be jumped across, and the three miles, which at high tide are a foaming sea or a level blue sheet of water, look but a short stretch to traverse. Mr. Thoreau gauged everything by his beloved Concord River:—there, an island could be walked to: here was evidently an island:—let us wade over there! But there are islands and islands, channels and channels! And a rising tide on a flat in Plymouth harbour is a swift river full of danger. Fortunately for our Concord guest a small fishing boat was at hand just at the nick of time to save him for his task of writing many volumes for the future joy of all lovers of nature! The skipper landed him at the North End—the back door of the "Island," so to speak, and there he was greeted by the "Lord of the Isle" known to all his friends as "Uncle Ed"—Edward Winslow Watson, and a worthy representative of the Pilgrims who spent their first Sunday on this Island. Bluff and hearty was his welcome, and his first question was "Where d'ye hail from?" Mr. Thoreau, fresh from the rescue, must have been breathless from climbing the cliff, and overcome with the mighty clap on his slender back that welcomed his answer: "From Concord, Sir . . . My name is Thoreau, and . . ." "You don't say so! Well, I've read some where in one of your books that you 'lost a friend, a horse and a dove! Now: What d'yer mean by it?'"—Mr. Thoreau looked up with shy, dark blue eyes:—as someone said, he looked like a wild woodchuck ready to run back to his hole—and he was very ruddy of complexion, with reddish brown hair and wore a green coat—he looked up then in shy astonishment at this breezy broad-shouldered, white-haired sea-farmer, reader of his books! "Well Sir, I suppose we have all had our losses!" "That's a pretty way to answer a fellow," replied the unsatisfied student of a fellow-poet and lover of nature.

Mr. Thoreau meekly followed him to the hospitable "Old House" where so many Concord philosophers have eaten the asparagus, turnips, clams and lobsters that are better there than in any other dining room even in New England, where those fruits of the sea and the soil are always good.

After he had borne patiently the well-deserved reproofs for his great rashness—"Where would you have been now if Sam Burgess hadn't happened to get belated hauling in his lobster pots, I'd like to know, eh?!"—the talk turned to tales of Norsemen, of adventure by sea and land,—the wood-fire was blazing to dry our wet and weary traveler—the lamps were lighted, and from the depths of the big old-fashioned arm-chair rose and fell the long arms of the teller of tales. Excited by his ever increasing audience, who peered in at the open windows and stopped to listen, until all the Island flocked to hear what "that man that thought he could wade across from Duxbury" had to say for himself—and egged on by "Uncle Ed's" questions and unreserved criticism, he talked far into the night,—a night never-to-be forgotten by those who were there to see and to hear! "The Watson boys," four in number, tall, stalwart followers of the sea, and all handsome, fresh and ready listeners, sat round in fascinated silence, their blue eyes getting bigger and bigger as Mr. Thoreau launched out into tales of ancient sea-adventures of the times of the Vikings and of his own French ancestors. The shy woodchuck, under the inspiration of such an audience, forgot how far he was from his hole, so to speak, and held them by his eloquence, breathless and spellbound.

And he returned by high tide, having gained, let us hope, a respect for Plymouth harbour with its ebb and flow of mighty waters—as his hearers *had gained insight* into a wider *world of travel and adventure.*

Ellen Watson, typescript, Hillside Collection, B. IX. XIX, Pilgrim Hall Museum Archives, Pilgrim Society Library, Plymouth, MA.

From "Thoreau's 'Maine Woods'" (1908)

[FANNY HARDY ECKSTORM]

Graduate of Smith College, where she founded the school's Audubon Society, Fanny Hardy Eckstorm (1865–1946) was the daughter of a Maine lumberman and fur trader who had worked with Thoreau's cousin George Thatcher, who accompanied Thoreau on two of his Maine excursions. She married Jacob A. Eckstorm in 1893. During her life, Eckstorm was an author, a naturalist, a school administrator, a wilderness guide, and a taxidermist; additionally, she was highly regarded as an authority on Maine's Penobscot people. In addition to books on ornithology, she published articles in *Forest and Stream* supporting fish and game protection laws in Maine. Her astute observations in this review praise the authenticity of Thoreau's *Maine Woods* with a sharp dismissiveness toward Thoreau as a woodsman and a scientist. Near the end of her life, however, and assured of Thoreau's centrality to American literature, Eckstorm significantly revised her opinion of Thoreau: He was "a prophet—like that earlier race of prophets of the Bible, Elijah and Elisha, who did not foretell but who *saw* what was about them and the trend of coming events" (qtd. in Williams, 32).

IT MUST BE ADMITTED in the beginning that *The Maine Woods* is not a masterpiece. Robert Louis Stevenson discards it as not literature. It is, however, a very good substitute, and had Robert Louis worn it next the skin he might perhaps have absorbed enough of the spirit of the American forest to avoid the gaudy melodrama which closes *The Master of Ballantrae*. *The Maine Woods* is of another world. Literature it may not be, nor one of "the three books of his that will be read with much pleasure;" but it is—the Maine woods. Since Thoreau's day, whoever has looked at these woods to advantage has to some extent seen them through Thoreau's eyes. Certain it is that no other man has ever put the coniferous forest between the leaves of a book.

For that he came—for that and the Indian. Open it where you will—and the little old first edition is by all odds to be chosen if one is fastidious about the printed page, to get the full savor of it; open where you will and these two speak to you. He finds water "too civilizing"; he wishes to become "selvaggia"; he turns woodworm in his metamorphosis, and loves to hear himself crunching nearer and nearer to the heart of the tree. He is tireless in his efforts to wrench their secrets from the woods; and, in every trial, he endeavors, not to talk *about* them, but to flash them with lightning vividness into the mind of the reader. "It was the opportunity to be ignorant that I improved. It suggested to me that there was something to be seen if one had eyes. It made a believer of me more than before. I believed that the woods were not tenantless, but choke-full of honest spirits as good as myself any day."

It is sometimes the advantage of a second-rate book that it endears the writer to us. The Thoreau of *Walden,* with his housekeeping all opened up for inspection, refusing the gift of a rug rather than shake it, throwing away his paperweight to avoid dusting it—where's the woman believes he *would* have dusted it?—parades his economies priggishly, like some pious anchoret with a business eye fixed on Heaven. But when he tells us in the appendix to the *Woods* that for a cruise three men need only one large knife and one iron spoon (for all), a four-quart tin pail for kettle, two tin dippers, three tin plates and a fry pan, his economy, if extreme, is manly and convincing. We meet him here among men whom we have known ourselves; we see how he treated them and how they treated him, and he appears to better advantage than when skied among the lesser gods of Concord.

Here is Joe Polis, whose judgment of a man would be as shrewd as any mere literary fellow's, and Joe talks freely, which in those days an Indian rarely did with whites. Here is the late Hiram L. Leonard, "the gentlemanly hunter of the stage," known to all anglers by his famous fishing rods. Those who remember his retiring ways will not doubt that it was Thoreau who prolonged the conversation. Here is Deacon George A. Thatcher, the "companion" of the first two trips. That second invitation and the deacon's cordial appreciation of "Henry" bespeak agreeable relations outside those of kinship. The Thoreau whom we meet here smiles at us. We see him, a shortish, squarish, brown-bearded, blue-eyed man, in a check shirt, with a black string tie, thick waistcoat, thick trousers, an old Kossuth hat,—for the costume that he recommends for woods wear must needs have been his own,—and over all a brown linen sack, on which, indelible, is the ugly smutch that he got when he hugged the sooty kettle to his side as he raced Polis across Grindstone Carry.

To every man his own Thoreau! But why is not this laughing runner, scattering boots and tinware, as true to life as any? Brusque, rude, repellant no doubt he often was, and beyond the degree excusable; affecting an unnecessary disdain of the comfortable, harmless goods of life; more proud, like Socrates, of the holes in his pockets than young Alciabiades of his whole, new coat; wrong very often, and most wrong upon his points of pride; yet he still had his southerly side, more open to the sun than to the wind. It is not easy to travel an unstaked course, against the advice and wishes and in the teeth of the prophecies of all one's friends, when it would be sweet and easy to win their approval—and, Himmel! to stop their mouths!—by burning one's faggot. A fighting faith, sleeping on its arms, often has to be stubborn and ungenial. What Henry Thoreau needed was to be believed in through thick and thin, and then let alone; and the very crabbedness, so often complained of, indicates that, like his own wild apples, in order to get a chance to grow, he had to protect himself by thorny underbrush from his too solicitous friends. . . .

It was not as an observer that Thoreau surpassed other men, but as an interpreter. He had the art—and how much of an art it is no one can realize until he has seated himself before an oak or a pine tree and has tried by the hour to write out its equation in terms of humanity—he had the art to see the human values of natural objects, to perceive the ideal elements of unreasoning nature and the service of those ideals to the soul of man. "The greatest delight which the fields and woods minister, is the suggestion of an occult relation between man and the vegetable," wrote Emerson; and it became Thoreau's chief text. It is the philosophy behind Thoreau's words, his attempt to reveal the Me through the Not Me, reversing the ordinary method, which makes his observations of such interest and value. . . .

So, though he was neither woodsman nor scientist, Thoreau stood at the gateway of the woods and opened them to all future comers with the key of poetic insight. And after the woods shall have passed away, the vision of them as he saw them will remain. In all that was best in him Thoreau was a poet. The finest passages in this book are poetical, and he is continually striking out some glowing phrase, like a spark out of flint. . . .

Indeed, this whole description of Katahdin is unequaled. "Chesuncook" is the best paper of the three, taken as a whole, but these few pages on Katahdin are incomparable. Happily he knew the traditions of the place, the awe and veneration with which the Indians regarded it as the dwelling-place of Pamola, their god of thunder, who was angry at any invasion of his home and resented it in fogs and sudden storms. . . . Thoreau's Katahdin was a realm of his own, in which for a few hours he lived in primeval solitude above the clouds, invading the throne of Pamola the Thunderer, as Prometheus harried Zeus of his lightnings. The gloomy grandeur of Aeschylus rises before him to give him countenance, and he speaks himself as if he wore the buskin. But it is not windy declamation. He does not explode into exclamation points. Katahdin is a strange, lone, savage hill, unlike all others,—a very Indian among mountains. It does not need superlatives to set it off. Better by far is Thoreau's grim humor, his calling it a "cloud factory," where they made their bed "in the nest of a young whirlwind," and lined it with "feathers plucked from the live tree." Had he been one of the Stonish men, those giants with flinty eyebrows, fabled to dwell within the granite vitals of Katahdin, he could not have dealt more stout-heartedly by the home of the Thunder-God.

The best of Thoreau's utterances in this volume are like these, tuned to the rapid and high vibration of the poetic string, but not resolved into rhythm. It is poetry, but not verse. Thoreau's prose stands in a class by itself. There is an honest hardness about it. We may accept or deny Buffon's dictum that the style is the man; but the man of soft and slippery make-up would strive in vain to acquire the granitic integrity of structure which marks Thoreau's writing. It is not poetical prose in the ordinary scope of that flowery term; but, as the granite rock is rifted and threaded with veins of glistening quartz, this prose is fused at white heat with poetical insights and interpretations. Judged by ordinary standards, he was a poet who failed. He had no grace at metres; he had no aesthetic softness; his sense always overruled the sound of his stanzas. The fragments of verse which litter his workshop remind one of the chips of flint about an Indian encampment. They might have been the heads of arrows, flying high and singing in their flight, but that the stone was obdurate or the maker's hand was unequal to the shaping of it. But the waste is nothing; there is behind them the Kineo that they came from, this prose of his, a whole mountain of the same stuff, every bit capable of being wrought to ideal uses.

[Fanny Hardy Eckstorm], "Thoreau's 'Maine Woods,'" *Atlantic Monthly* 52 (August 1908): 243–44, 246, 249–50.

From "Henry D. Thoreau" (1909)

Thomas Wentworth Higginson

Published two years before Higginson died, this assessment reflects his case for the importance of Thoreau in the twentieth century. In the *Atlantic Monthly* a few years earlier, Higginson had found it difficult to believe that Thoreau, "eccentric and unsuccessful" in his own time, was then "still growing in international fame"; by 1900, however, he described Thoreau and Margaret Fuller as "our most original authors" (*Cheerful Yesterdays*, 170; *Studies*, 235). In this article, Higginson criticizes Sophia Thoreau for "repress[ing] the publication" of Thoreau's journals, although he was likely far more piqued by her refusal to allow him to edit them. Higginson opens this assessment by comparing Thoreau's reputation at the turn of the century to that of Poe and Whitman, a strategy that allows him another opportunity to impugn Whitman, whose work he found "nausea[ting]" (*Part of a Man's Life*, 164).

THERE HAS BEEN IN America no such instance of posthumous reputation as in the case of Thoreau. Poe and Whitman may be claimed as parallels, but not justly. Poe, even during his life, rode often on the very wave of success, until it subsided presently beneath him, always to rise again, had he but made it possible. Whitman gathered almost immediately a small but stanch band of followers, who have held by him with such vehemence and such flagrant imitation as to keep his name defiantly in evidence, while perhaps enhancing the antagonism of his critics. Thoreau could be egotistical enough, but was always high-minded; all was open and aboveboard; one could as soon conceive of self-advertising by a deer in the woods or an otter of the brook. He had no organized clique of admirers, nor did he possess even what is called personal charm,—or at least only that piquant attraction which he himself found in wild apples. As a rule, he kept men at a distance, being busy with his own affairs. He left neither wife nor children to attend to his memory; and his sister seemed for a time to repress the publication of his manuscripts. Yet this plain, shy, retired student, who when thirty-two years old carried the unsold edition of his first book upon his back to his attic chamber; who died at forty-four still unknown to the general public; this child of obscurity, who printed but two volumes during his lifetime, has had ten volumes of his writings published by others since his death, while four biographies of him have been issued in America. . . .

When I was endeavoring, about 1870, to persuade Thoreau's sister to let some one edit his journals, I invoked the aid of Judge Hoar, then lord of the manor in Concord, who heard me patiently through, and then said: "Whereunto? You have not established the preliminary point. Why should any one wish to have Thoreau's journals printed?" Ten years later, four successive volumes were made out of these journals by the late H. G. O. Blake, and it became a question if the whole might not be published. I hear from a local photograph dealer in Concord that the demand for Thoreau's pictures now exceeds that for any other local celebrity. In the last sale catalogue of autographs which I have encountered, I find a letter from Thoreau priced at $17.50, one from Hawthorne valued at the same, one from Longfellow at $4.50 only, and one from Holmes at $3, each of these being guaranteed as an especially good autograph letter. Now the value of such memorials during a man's life affords but a slight test of his permanent standing,—since almost any man's autograph can be obtained for two postage-stamps if the request be put with sufficient ingenuity;—but when this financial standard can be safely applied more than thirty years after a man's death, it comes pretty near to a permanent fame. . . .

The real and human Thoreau, who often whimsically veiled himself . . . was plainly enough seen by any careful observer. That he was abrupt and repressive to bores and pedants, that he grudged his time to them and frequently withdrew himself, was as true of him as of Wordsworth or Tennyson. If they were allowed their privacy, though in the heart of England, an American who never left his own broad continent might at least be allowed his privilege of stepping out of doors. The Concord schoolchildren never quarreled with this habit, for he took them out of doors with him and taught them where the best whortleberries grew. . . .

His especial greatness is that he gives us standing-ground below the surface, a basis not to be washed away. A hundred sentences might be quoted from him which make common observers seem superficial and professed philosophers trivial, but which, if accepted, place the realities of life beyond the reach of danger. He was a spiritual ascetic, to whom the simplicity of nature was luxury enough; and this, in an age of growing expenditure, gave him an unspeakable value. To him, life itself was a source of joy so great that it was only weakened by diluting it with meaner joys. This was the standard to which he constantly held his contemporaries. . . .

Thomas Wentworth Higginson, *Carlyle's Laugh and Other Surprises* (Boston: Houghton, Mifflin, 1909), 67–69, 72–74.

From *Henry Thoreau as Remembered by a Young Friend* (1917)

EDWARD WALDO EMERSON

Edward Waldo Emerson (1844–1930), the son of Waldo and Lidian Emerson, graduated from Harvard College in 1866 and Harvard Medical School in 1874, in which year he married Concord native Annie Shepard Keyes; the couple had seven children. Although predominantly interested in art and literature, Emerson practiced medicine in Concord, where he never truly overcame living in the large shadow cast by his father. Thomas Wortham contends that "the burden of being his father's son rested heavily upon Edward's shoulders, and circumstances and family expectations often thwarted his ambitions and personal desires" (vii). After Waldo Emerson died in 1882, Edward gave up his medical practice and began lecturing, painting, and writing as well as assisting his sister, Ellen, and James Elliot Cabot in compiling and editing his father's manuscripts.

From the time they were born, Henry Thoreau was a reliable, trusted friend to all the Emerson children. During his extended stay with the family during Waldo's visit abroad in 1847, Thoreau reported to Waldo a recent conversation he'd had with three-year-old Edward: "He very seriously asked me, the other day, 'Mr. Thoreau, will you be my father?' . . . So you must come back soon, or you will be superseded" (*Correspondence*, 189). Not only does this example evidence the mutual affection between Thoreau and Emerson's young son, it may also reflect both Thoreau's yearning to fulfill a paternal role and desire to chastise Emerson for his extended stay away from his family. Concord neighbor and historian Allen French affirms the value of Thoreau's friendship with Edward: "Thoreau had a marked respect for children and with his varied entertainment and instruction did much to develop Edward's mind and character. In the household all the interests of the day were discussed. Edward learned to think for himself and, when necessary, to say his say" (1). Before leaving home to take his Harvard College entrance exams, Edward valued Thoreau's supportive advice: "He had divined my suppressed state of mind and remembered that first crisis in his own life. . . . With serious face, but with a very quiet, friendly tone of voice, he reassured me, told me that I should be really close to home; very likely should pass my life in Concord. It was a great relief" (*Henry Thoreau*, 147).

As an adult, Edward likely realized that he and Thoreau had shared the plight of disappointing Waldo Emerson's expectations. But he waited until after his father's death to publish *Henry Thoreau as Remembered by a Young Friend* (1917), in which he overturns his father's contention that Thoreau lacked ambition: "This man . . . is better known and prized more nearly at his worth each year, and to-day is giving freedom and joy in life to fellowmen in the far parts of this country, and beyond the ocean. Let us not misprize him, and regret that he did not make pencils and money." Moreover, Edward reestablishes Thoreau as a writer, a crucial missing component from Waldo's "Thoreau." Edward Emerson explains that he began to lecture on Thoreau in the 1890s "because I was troubled at the want of knowledge and understanding, both in Concord and among his readers at large, not only of his character, but of the events of his life,—which he did not tell to everybody,—and by the false impressions given by accredited writers who really knew him hardly at all" (*Henry Thoreau*, v–vi). One audience member who attended Emerson's 10 December 1890 lecture in Concord was Maria S. Porter. Her report on the talk for the *Boston Transcript* makes plain that Emerson met his objective: "The remarkable intellectual power and originality of Thoreau as a writer were not so much dwelt upon by the lecturer as was the practical side of his life among them in Concord, his love of Nature, also of music; and his great helpfulness in the family of the Emersons, of which for some time he was an inmate, was spoken of, and illustrated by facts and incidents that were of real interest to the audience and of great value to know. Many pleasant recollections of the lecturer's childhood were given; also of Thoreau's delightful stories told the children, of his walks with them in the woods and fields; also of his making musical instruments, that they called trombones, from the stalks of the pumpkin vines or sometimes from those of the odorous onion. . . . Many little things relating to Thoreau's life in Concord were told and the lecture seemed to greatly interest the large audience of his townspeople and friends there assembled. . . . all the notable Concord worthies, were there to listen to the lecture from the son of Emerson, who seemed thoroughly to appreciate the originality and strength of Thoreau as a writer and ardent lover of nature, and who was able to see and prove that there was another side of his character that had not always been recognized; namely, the practical one." The finale to Emerson's lecture was his reading of Louisa May Alcott's poem, "Thoreau's Flute" ("A Day at Concord").

The Thoreau who emerges from Edward Emerson's thoughtful treatment is a nurturing and inspiring friend whose worth intrinsically and directly counters his father's version of a "classic statue."

IN CHILDHOOD I had a friend,—not a house friend, domestic, stuffy in association; nor yet herdsman, or horseman, or farmer, or slave of bench, or shop, or office; nor of letters, nor art, nor society; but a free, friendly, youthful-seeming man, who wandered in from unknown woods or fields without knocking,—

> Between the night and day
> When the fairy king has power,—

as the ballad says, passed by the elders' doors, but straightway sought out the children, brightened up the wood-fire forthwith; and it seemed as if it were the effect of a wholesome brave north wind, more than of the armful of "cat-sticks" which he would bring in from the yard. His type was Northern,—strong features, light brown hair, an open-air complexion with suggestion of a seafaring race; the mouth pleasant and flexible when he spoke, aquiline nose, deep-set but very wide-open eyes of clear blue grey, sincere, but capable of a twinkle, and again of austerity, but not of softness. Those eyes could not be made to rest on what was unworthy, saw much and keenly (but yet in certain worthy directions hardly at all), and did not fear the face of clay. A figure short and narrow, but thick; a carriage assuring of sturdy strength and endurance. When he walked to get over the ground one thought of a tireless machine, seeing his long, direct, uniform pace; but his body was active and well balanced, and his step could be light, as of one who could leap or dance or skate well at will. . . .

This youthful, cheery figure was a familiar one in our house, and when he, like the "Pied Piper of Hamelin," sounded his note in the hall, the children must needs come and hug his knees, and he struggled with them, nothing loath, to the fireplace, sat down and told stories, sometimes of the strange adventures of his childhood, or more often of squirrels, muskrats, hawks, he had seen that day, the Monitor-and-Merrimac duel of mud-turtles in the river, or the great Homeric battle of the red and black ants. Then he would make our pencils and knives disappear, and redeem them presently from our ears and noses; and last, would bring down the heavy copper warming-pan from the oblivion of the garret and unweariedly shake it over the blaze till reverberations arose within, and then opening it, let a white-blossoming explosion of popcorn fall over the little people on the rug. . . .

This youth, who could pipe and sing himself, made for children pipes of all sorts, of grass, of leaf-stalk of squash and pumpkin, handsome but fragrant flageolets of onion tops, but chiefly of the golden willow-shoot, when the rising sap in spring loosens the bark. As the children grew older, he led them to choice huckleberry hills, swamps where the great high-bush blueberries grew, guided to the land of the chestnut and barberry, and more than all, opened that land of enchantment into which, among dark hemlocks, blood-red maples, and yellowing birches, we floated in his boat, and freighted it with leaves and blue gentians and fragrant grapes from the festooning vines. . . .

He taught us also the decorum and manners of the wood, which gives no treasures or knowledge to the boisterous and careless; the humanity not to kill a harmless snake because it was ugly, or in revenge for a start; and that the most zealous collector of eggs must always leave the mother-bird most of her eggs, and not go too often to watch the nest. . . .

Then I went away from home, and began to read his books; but in the light of the man I knew. I met persons who asked questions about him, had heard strange rumours and made severe criticisms; then I read essays and satires, even by one whose gifts render such obtuseness well-nigh unpardonable, in which he was held lightly or ridiculed—heard that he was pompous, rustic, conceited, that his thoughts were not original, that he strove to imitate another; that even his observations on natural history were of no value, and not even new.

Even in Concord among persons who had known him slightly at school or in the young society of his day, or had some acquaintance with him in village relations, I found that, while his manifest integrity commanded respect, he was regarded unsympathetically by many, and not only the purposes, but many of the events of his life were unknown. The indictments are numerous, but of varying importance:—When a school-teacher, he once flogged several pupils at school without just cause. Once some wood-lots were burned through his carelessness. He carried a tree through the town while the folks came home from meeting. He, while living at Walden, actually often went out to tea, and carried pies home from his mother's larder. He let others pay his taxes. He was lazy. He was selfish. He did not make money, as he might have done for himself and family by attending to his business. He did not believe in Government and was unpatriotic. He was irreligious.

What, then, was Thoreau?

The man of whom I speak was the friend of my childhood and early youth, and living and dead has helped me, and in no common way. It is a natural duty, then, to acknowledge thankfully this help and render homage to his memory, because his name and fame, his life and lesson, have become part of America's property and are not merely the inheritance of the children who dwell by the Musketaquid. . . .

His thoughtfulness in childhood, his independent course in college themes and early journals, prove that Thoreau was Thoreau and not the copy of another. His close association, under the same roof, for months, with the maturer Emerson may, not unnaturally, have tinged his early writings, and some superficial trick of manner or of speech been unconsciously acquired, as often happens. But this is all that can be granted. Entire independence, strong individuality were Thoreau's distinguishing traits, and his foible was not subserviency, but combativeness in conversation, as his friends knew almost too well. Conscious imitation is not to be thought of as a possibility of this strong spirit. . . .

He could do all sorts of jobbing and tinkering well at home and for other people. One or two fences were standing until lately, in town, which he built; he planted for his friend Emerson his barren pasture by Walden with pines. He especially loved to raise melons. I once went to a melon-party at his mother's with various people, young and old, where his work had furnished the handsome and fragrant pink or salmon fruit on which alone we were regaled; and he, the gardener, came in to help entertain the guests.

He wrote articles for magazines which brought him some money, and books, now classics, but hardly saleable in his day.

But his leading profession was that of a land-surveyor. In this, as in his mechanics, he did the best possible work. I remember his showing me some brass instrument which he had made or improved, with his own hands. Those who assisted him tell me that he was exceedingly particular, took more offsets than any other surveyor in these parts, often rectified bounds carelessly placed before. . . .

When the spirit clearly shows a man of high purpose what his gift is, or may be, his neighbours must not insist on harnessing him into a team,—just one more to pull through their crude or experimental reform,—or require of him exact following of village ways or city fashion. We all know persons whose quiet light shining apart from public action has more illuminated and guided our lives. . . .

His sojourn in Walden woods, as seen by his townsmen, told by himself, and rumoured abroad, made a stronger impression, and more obvious, than any part of his strong and original life. He is more thought of as a hermit, preaching by life and word a breach with society, than in any other way; and this notion is so widespread that it seems to require a few words here.

And, first, it must be remembered that the part of his life lived in the Walden house was from July 4, 1845, to September 6, 1847, just two years and two months of his forty-four years of life. They were happy, wholesome years, helping his whole future by their teachings. He did not go there as a Jonah crying out on Nineveh, but simply for his own purposes, to get advantageous conditions to do his work, exactly as a lawyer or banker or any man whose work requires concentration is sure to leave his home to do it. He prepared there his first and perhaps best book, the "Week on the Concord and Merrimack Rivers," for publication; he tried his spiritual, intellectual, social and economic experiment, and recorded it; and incidentally made an interesting survey and history of one of the most beautiful and remarkable ponds in Massachusetts. Meantime he earned the few dollars that it took to keep him.

Unlike the prophet at Nineveh, he went to the woods to mind his own business in the strictest sense, and there found the freedom, joy, and blessed influences that came of so simple and harmless a life, nearer the flowers and stars, and the God that the child had looked for behind the stars, free from the millstones, even the carved and gilded ones, which customary town life hangs around the necks of most of us. . . .

They err entirely who suppose that he counselled every one to build hermitages in the woods, break with society and live on meal. This he distinctly disavows, but makes a plea for simple and brave living, not drowned in the details, not merely of cooking, sweeping, and dusting, but of politics, whether parish, town, state, or federal, and even of societies, religious, professional, charitable, or social, for, after all, these are but preparatory,—police regulations on a larger or smaller scale,—designed as means to make life possible, and not to be pursued as ends. . . .

And now as to the belief that he was hard, stern, selfish, or misanthropic. Truly he was undemonstrative, . . . but under this oak-bark was friendship and loyalty in the tough grain, through and through. He was a friend, "even to the altars," too sincere and true to stoop to weakness from his noble ideal. . . .

I can bring my own witness and that of many others to his quiet, dutiful, loyal attitude to his mother and father, how respectfully he listened to them, whether he agreed with them or not; how in his quiet way he rendered all sorts of useful and skillful help in domestic and household matters. . . . His family were a little anxious and troubled when he went to Walden, fearing danger and hardship in this life, and they missed him; but they sympathized with his desire and wanted him to carry it out as pleased him. He came constantly home to see them and to help them in garden or house, and also dropped in at other friendly homes in the village, where he was always welcome at table or fireside.

The mighty indictment that he was not honest in his experiment, for he did not live exclusively on his own meal and rice, but often accepted one of his mother's pies, or chanced in at a friend's at supper-time, seems too frivolous to notice, but since it is so often made, I will say that Henry Thoreau, while he could have lived uncomplainingly where an Esquimau could, on *tripe de roche* lichen and blubber, if need were (for never was man less the slave of appetite and luxury), was not a prig, nor a man of so small pattern as to be tied to a rule-of-thumb in diet, and ungraciously thrust back on his loving mother her gift. Nor was there the slightest reason that he should forgo his long-established habit of appearing from time to time at nightfall, a welcome guest at the fireside of friends. He came for friendship, not for food. . . . And, fully to satisfy cavil, it is certain that he overpaid his keep in mere handiwork, which he convinced all friends that it was a favour to him to allow him to do for them (such as burning out chimneys, setting stoves, door-knobs, or shutters to right), to make no mention of higher service. . . .

To the criticism, Why did he allow his tax to be paid? the simple answer is, He could n't help it, and did not know who did it. Why, then, did he go out of jail? Because they would not keep him there. . . .

Thoreau by no means neglected all civic duties. The low moral tone of his country stirred him, so that again and again he left the quiet, consoling woods and meadows to speak in Concord and elsewhere for freedom of person, of thought, and of conscience. He gave the countenance of his presence and speech to the meetings for the relief and self-protection against murder and outrage of the Free State settlers in Kansas, and contributed money. He admired John Brown, the sturdy farmer with whom he had talked on his visits to Concord, as a liberator of men, and one who dared to defend the settlers' rights. But, later, when two successive administrations ignored the outrages, and steadily favoured the party which were committing them, Thoreau, hopeless of any good coming of the United States Government, thoroughly sympathized with a man who had courage to break its bonds in the cause of natural right. In the first days of the Harper's Ferry raid, when Brown's friends and backers, hitherto, were in doubt as to their attitude in this crisis, Thoreau, taking counsel of none, announced that he should speak in the church vestry, on John Brown, to whoever came. It was as if he spoke for his own brother, so deeply stirred was he, so searching and brave his speech. Agree or disagree,—all were moved. . . .

Thoreau was a good talker, but a certain enjoyment in taking the other side for the joy of intellectual fencing, and a pleasure of startling his companions by a paradoxical statement of his highly original way of looking at things, sometimes, were baffling to his friends. . . . This fatal tendency to parry and hit with the tongue . . . for no object but the fun of intellectual fence, as such, was a temperamental fault standing in the way of relations that would otherwise have been perfect with his friends. One could sometimes only think of his Uncle Charles Dunbar, once well known in the neighbourhood for his friendly desire to "burst" his acquaintances in wrestling. Thoreau held this trait in check with women and children, and with humble people who were no match for him. With them he was simple, gentle, friendly, and amusing; and all testify his desire to share all the pleasant things he learned in his excursions. But to a conceited gentleman from the city, or a dogmatic or patronizing clergyman or editor, he would, as Emerson said, appear as a "gendarme, good to knock down cockneys with and go on his way smiling." . . .

He could afford to be a philosopher, for he was first a good common man. It takes good iron to receive a fine polish. His simple, direct speech and look and bearing were such that no plain, common man would put him down in his books as a fool, or visionary, or helpless, as the scholar, writer, or reformer would often be regarded by him. Much of Alcibiades's description of Socrates in Plato's "Symposium" would apply to Thoreau. He loved to talk with all kinds and conditions of men if they had no hypocrisy or pretence about them, and though high in his standard of virtue, and most severe with himself, could be charitable to the failings of humble fellow-men. His interest in the Indian was partly one of natural history, and the human interest was because of the genuineness of the Indian's knowledge and his freedom from cant. . . .

One of the young men who helped him survey had pleasant recollection of his wealth of entertainment by instruction given afield, opening the way to studies of his own; and also of his good humour and fun. One who made collections for Agassiz and the Smithsonian was thus first led to natural history; but said that, were he in trouble and need of help, he thought he should as soon have turned to Henry Thoreau as any man in town. Another, born on a farm, who knew and had worked in the black-lead mill many years, said, when I asked what he thought of Thoreau: "Why, he was the best friend I ever had. He was always straight in his ways: and was very particular to make himself agreeable. Yes, he was always straight and true: you could depend upon him: all was satisfactory." Was he a kindly and helpful man? "Yes, he was all of that: what we call solid and true, but he could n't bear any gouge-game and dishonesty. When I saw him crossing my field I always wanted to go and have a talk with him. He was more company for me than the general run of neighbours. I liked to hear his ideas and get information from him. He liked to talk as long as you did, and what he said was new; mostly about Nature. I think he went down to Walden to pry into the arts of Nature and get something that was n't open to the public. He liked the creatures. He seemed to think their nature could be improved. Some people called him lazy: I did n't deem it so. I called him industrious, and he was a first-rate mechanic. He was a good neighbor and very entertaining. I found him a particular friend." . . .

Just before Thoreau built his Walden house the Fitchburg Railroad was being laid through Concord, and a small army of Irishmen had their rough shanties in the woods along the deep cuts, and some of them, later good

Concord citizens, had their wives and little children in these rude abodes; the remains of excavation and banking can still be traced near Walden. These people seemed a greater innovation than Samoans would to-day. Thoreau talked with them in his walks and took some kindly interest. I well remember the unusual wrath and indignation he felt a few years later when one of these, a poor neighbour, industrious but ignorant, had his spading-match prize at Cattle Show taken by his employer, on the plea, "Well, as I pay for his time, what he gets in the time I pay for nat'rally comes to me," and I know that Thoreau raised the money to make good the poor man's loss, and, I think, made the farmer's ears burn.

Once or twice I knew of the kindling of that anger, and reproof bravely given, as when an acquaintance, who had a faithful dog, discarded and drove him away out of caprice; and again, when a buyer of hens set a dog to catch them. His remarks in his book about the man getting faithful work out of the horse day by day, but doing nothing whatever to help the horse's condition, is suggestive reading for any horse-owner. He felt real respect for the personality and character of animals, and could never have been guilty of asking with Paul, "Doth God care for oxen?" The humble little neighbours in house or wood whose characters he thus respected, rewarded his regard by some measure of friendly confidence. He felt that until men showed higher behaviour, the less they said about the "lower animals" the better. . . .

Some naturalists of the Dry as-dust School are critical of him because he was not, like them, a cataloguer, and mere student of dead plants and animals. . . . Thoreau considered that one living bird for study, in its proper haunts, was worth more than a sackful of bird-skins and skeletons. A brown, brittle plant in a portfolio gave him little comfort, but he knew the day in March when it would show signs of life, the days in August when it would be in flower, and what birds would come in January from far Labrador to winter on those particular seeds that its capsule held stored for them above the snow. . . .

He stopped once on the street and made me hear, clear, but far above, the red-eyed vireo's note and, rarely coming, that of his little white-eyed cousin. I had not known—I venture to say few persons know—that the little olive-brown bird whom we associate with her delicate nest hanging between two twigs in the woods, is one of the commonest singers on our main street in July, . . . Many a boy and girl owed to him the opening of the gate of this almost fairy knowledge, . . .

Our hero was a born story-teller, and of the Norseman type in many ways, a right Saga-man and Scald like them, telling of woods and waters and the dwarf-kin that peopled them—and ever he knew what he saw for a symbol, and looked through it for a truth. "Even the facts of science," said he, "may dust the mind by their dryness, unless they are in a sense effaced by the dews of fresh and living truth." . . .

Mr. Emerson was chafing at the waste of this youth in the pencil mill, and impatient for his fruiting time, surely to come. And yet he did not quite see that Thoreau was steering a course true to his compass with happy result to his voyage, a course that would for him, Emerson, have been quite unfit. . . .

When Thoreau came, rather unwillingly, by invitation to dine with company, it often happened that he was in a captious mood, amusing himself by throwing paradoxes in the way of the smooth current of the conversation. It was like having Pan at a dinner party. Even when he "dropped in" to the study at the end of the afternoon, and had told the last news from the river or Fairhaven Hill, Mr. Emerson, at a later period, complained that Thoreau baulked his effort "to hold intercourse with his mind." With all their honour for one another, and their Spartan affection, satisfactory talks then seem to have been rare. But a long afternoon's ramble with Pan guiding to each sight, or sound, or fragrance, perhaps to be found only on that day, was dear privilege, and celebrated as such by Emerson in his journals. . . .

When "Walden" appeared Mr. Emerson seems to have felt as much pleasure as if his brother had written it. But when the Thoreau family, after Henry's death, submitted the journals to his friend's consideration, he, coming from his study, day by day, would tell his children his joyful surprise in the merit and the beauty which he found everywhere in those daily chronicles of Nature and of thought. . . .

Make allowance for strong statement due to any original, vigorous man, trying to arouse his neighbours from lethargy to freedom and happiness that he believed within their reach, and then, with the perspective of years to help us, look fairly at the main lines of his life and thought, which have been considered so strange and *outré*.

Consider the standards of education and religion in New England in Thoreau's youth,—the position of the churches, their distrust of the right of the individual to question the words of the Bible as interpreted by the Sects; the horror that Theodore Parker inspired, the shyness of the so-called Pagan Scriptures, the difficulty with which any one who spoke for the slave could get a hearing, the ridicule of the so-called Transcendentalists, the general practice of what is now called "pauperizing Mediaeval Charity," the indignant rejection of Evolution theories, the slight taste for Natural History, and the astonishment that a rich family "camping out" would have excited. . . .

This rare and happy venture of Thoreau's,—bringing his soul face to face with Nature as wondrous artist, as healer, teacher, as mediator between us and the Creator, has slowly spread its wide beneficence. Look at out-of-door life, and love of plant and tree, and sympathy with animals, now, as compared with these seventy years ago. Yet to-day the inestimable value of frequent solitude is much overlooked.

He devoutly listened. . . .

His friend and companion, Edward Hoar, said to me, "With Thoreau's life something went out of Concord woods and fields and river that never will return. He so loved Nature, delighted in her every aspect and seemed to infuse himself into her." Yes, something went. But our woods and waters will always be different because of this man. Something of him abides and truly "for good" in his town. Here he was born, and within its borders he found a wealth of beauty and interest—all that he asked—and shared it with us all. . . .

Edward Waldo Emerson, *Henry Thoreau as Remembered by a Young Friend* (Boston: Houghton, Mifflin, 1917), 1–2, 3–4, 5–6, 7, 9–11, 28–29, 39–40, 45, 49–51, 55–56, 57–58, 60–62, 66, 70–71, 72–73, 74, 77–78, 80–82, 83–84, 90, 92, 105–6, 107–8, 109–10, 112–13, 114–15, 118.

From *Memories of Concord* (1926)

MARY HOSMER BROWN

Mary Hosmer Brown (1856–1929) was the granddaughter of Concord farmer Edmund Hosmer, one of the friends who helped Thoreau erect his Walden cabin. Born and raised in Detroit, as a child Brown often visited her grandparents in Concord. Her sympathetic reminiscences cast familiar stories in a personal and genuine sketch that avoids sentimentalizing Thoreau himself. Brown's description that "Thoreau was tall and straight and gave the impression of an independent pine tree" is ironically apt in light of editor James Russell Lowell's censoring of Thoreau's "blasphemous" statement in "Chesuncook" that a pine tree "is as immortal as I am, and perchance will go to as high a heaven" (*Maine Woods,* 122).

ONE OF THE MOST welcome visitors to the Hosmer farm was Henry D. Thoreau. There have been many opinions of this quiet man who wore coarse shoes and homespun raiment, which he considered best fitted for his long walks and close study of nature. Some said that because except to make a few lead pencils, survey a neighbor's field, or teach a term of school he had no regular occupation, he was an idle, lazy sort of fellow. Others, that he was an eccentric citizen who refused to pay his poll tax. His friends knew him as a rare soul, of feminine purity and of keen intellect. A few readers found in him an original and daring thinker, bringing them into touch with those things which make for the soul's eternal progress. Some discovered in him the closest of observers, a wonderful painter of things he had seen, so accurate a describer of bird or flower that the description needed no name to enlighten it.

His intense love of nature was like a sixth sense which won from her secrets hidden from others. As Velasquez reproduced the life of his time, so Concord has been reproduced in his writings. Concord's gentle landscapes are painted with colors that glow with the intensity of his love for the town. He used to say that he had been born in just the right place at just the right time. Again, he wrote, "Concord is my old coat, my morning gown, my study gown, my working dress, and at last will be my night gown." It has also become a monument to him. As long as Walden Pond remains or Concord River flows, the name of Thoreau will be associated with them. He taught hearing to those who before had only ears, and sight to those who had never seen. He said he would not know the river or the fields if he awoke some morning with someone else's eyes. Channing called Concord a bare town, but Thoreau made it teem on every side with beauty. . . .

Graduated from Harvard, in after years the only part of college life he appears to have remembered with joy were the hours he spent at the library. He won and kept a scholarship and earned some money while an undergraduate by teaching school in Canton, Massachusetts. His life at Cambridge was interrupted by a serious illness, although he went back to college for his senior year. Whether on account of this illness or not, we find him more and more determined to travel his own path, unmindful of the broad highway made popular by usage. In discrediting the value of study for the sake of high rank we note the beginning of that distrust for the learning acquired in college which grew more intense in later years.

On finishing his course he taught school in Concord. His pupils always testified to the excellence of his discipline, but the story is that the school committee were not satisfied because he never resorted to corporal punishment. Thoreau therefore flogged six boys one afternoon, but resigned the next day from a profession too brutal to suit him.

He and John then opened a private school in their own home. Henry taught French, Greek and Latin, physics, and mathematics. The school prospered, outgrew the house, and they moved to larger quarters. They were much beloved by the pupils, who were managed without resort to flogging or threats. They were original in their methods; surveying was taught and open air walks taken for nature studies. The non-resident pupils boarded with the Thoreaus. The school had twenty-five pupils enrolled when John's illness became too serious and Henry refused to go on alone.

Mr. Thoreau, senior, being financially embarrassed, Henry came to his aid in the manufacture of lead pencils. My aunts well remembered the parcels of these pencils with the label, "Thoreau and Son, Concord, Mass." These were peddled from Boston to New York and Thoreau speaks of his satisfaction in knowing that their pencils were the finest on the market. Our family used them and I still have several of them among my treasures. Afterwards he invented a machine for making a fine lead dust to be used in electrotyping, which brought in considerable money for the family. This machine spun round like a top inside of a box set on a table. It was wound up to run itself and was easily operated by a woman. After Henry's death Sophia kept on with the business and orders came directed to S. Thoreau, Esq., customers supposing her to be a man.

The family being provided for, Henry was free to carry on his true business, that of "Living." Now, surveying a neighbor's field, or doing some odd job for a farmer was sufficient to supply his personal needs while off on a tramp or a boating cruise, or for acquiring leisure to write.

From boyhood the river had a strong attraction for him. When sixteen he built a boat called "The Rover," of the style or seaworthiness of which we have no record. While in college, the Red Jacket was made, not much of a craft according to his own notes. He writes in his log book of its casting him ashore on Nashawtuc Beach, whence he says, "Got her off at twenty minutes of four, and after a pleasant passage of ten minutes, arrived safely in port with a valuable cargo,"—the precious cargo being himself.

After leaving college his brother John and he built on land near the present public library a fifteen foot dory, which they named "The Musketaquid" after the Indian name of the river. This was, he said, "strongly built but heavy," and was painted green with a border of blue. . . .

Those who thought of Thoreau as cold or indifferent little understood the depth of feeling that lay beneath his undemonstrative exterior. During his father's illness his devotion was such that Mrs. Thoreau in recalling it said, "If it hadn't been for my husband's illness, I should never have known what a tender heart Henry had." He mourned deeply for this beloved brother. He laid aside his flute and for years refused to speak his name. A friend told me that twelve years later Thoreau started, turned pale, and could hardly overcome his emotion when some reference to John was made.

For nearly two years after John's death he lived with the Emersons. Mr. Emerson, who was away much of the time on lecture tours, liked to leave Thoreau in charge. There was a strong tie of grief that joined Mrs. Emerson, who had lost little Waldo, and this young man who mourned so deeply his beloved brother, and a warm affection arose between them. Henry's capable ways were a great comfort to her. The loose bolts were tightened, the hens well cared for, the garden bloomed in luxuriant beauty, the vegetables and fruit trees were tended by skillful hands. The children held him as a boon companion and recognized the youthful heart that could make evenings pass in merriment. No wonder that Mrs. Emerson loved him or that he found an abiding corner in the heart of that spinster as uncompromising as himself, Emerson's Aunt Mary. . . .

For some years he had vaguely dreamed of having a sylvan shelter fitted for his purpose. He made some attempts to buy an isolated farm, but finally decided to build a hut at Walden on land owned by Emerson, the latter at the time planning to erect a similar one across the pond to be used for himself as a "literary retreat." With a borrowed axe he felled "some tall, arrowy white pines, still in their youth" for the cabin, which he planned to be ten feet wide and fifteen feet long.

Early in the morning of July fourth, Thoreau stopped at the farm, for this was the day chosen for the raising. Grandfather shouldered his axe and together with his three oldest sons, John, Edmund, and Andrew, went down the turnpike to Emerson's and across the fields and woods to the chosen site. By dint of hard work the shack was raised by nightfall and Thoreau's dream of a woodland study was made a reality. Here he lived for two years and another name was added to Concord's calendar of famous places, that of Walden Pond. . . .

His life at Walden was never intended by him to be that of a hermit, nor was his sojourn there a very lonely one. When actually writing he refused to be disturbed; otherwise a chair set outside the door proclaimed his readiness for company. He went into the woods to live near nature, to be a neighbor to the birds, "not," as he says, "by having imprisoned them, but having caged myself near them."

Being such an adept at tramping, the distance to the village meant moderate exertion for him and he was a frequent visitor at his own house, sometimes to please his mother carrying back a homemade pie, which doubtless was not included in his cost of living accounts, but was considered an unessential luxury. Often, also, he walked over to the Emerson's. On stormy days his familiar step was wont to be heard on our doorstep. He knew that if the weather was bad farm duties must be suspended and that Grandfather would probably be at leisure.

The children hailed his coming with delight. It was better than any fairy tale to listen to his stories of the woods or the river. To hear him talk they would gather around as still as mice. What marvelous ways the birds and squirrels had which no one else had discovered. Who but Mr. Thoreau could tame the fishes in the pond, feed the little mice from his fingers, keep up a whistling fire of conversation with the birds till they alighted on his head and shoulders, wondering what friend could be so very familiar with bird language. Who else received calls from the moles,—and how the children's eyes would brighten as he told them of the tamed partridge so proud of her family that she brought them all to show him and how in return for her kindness he shared his breakfast with the brood. He knew every spot where the wild flowers grew, every sheltered nook where the maidenhair or climbing fern hid their treasures of gracefulness. One day he came in with a rare nettle which he could not place. Aunt Abby was immediately sent for the botany. Nothing could be said till the nettle problem was settled.

He liked to read to the children from the *Canterbury Tales*. Often he would stop and think about a line, saying, "You can sometimes catch the sense better by listening than by reading."

In later life when my Aunt Jane became a teacher and read these same tales to her pupils, she said she could distinctly recall that melodious voice and the wonderful sense of rhythm he could impart as he read.

Unlike Emerson, Thoreau was a natural musician. He played the flute well and had a musical voice for singing. His ears were so keenly attuned to the various melodies of nature that sounds unheard by others were easily distinguished by him. It was this musical sense that enabled him to discern so accurately the notes of birds and the calls of other animals.

He had fitted a lyre in one of his windows and he noticed that in a deep cut in the woods certain trees formed a natural aeolian lyre when the wind blew through them. Aunt Eliza, when a small girl, tried to make an aeolian lyre and was quite disconsolate because it wouldn't work as the one at the Thoreau home did. . . .

On a Sunday afternoon the children loved to go to the Walden shack. Thoreau sat at his desk, Grandfather was given a chair, while they arranged themselves along the edge of the cot bed, the youngest child still remembering that her feet couldn't quite reach the floor. If the conversation grew too abstruse or they were tired of sitting still, one by one they slipped out to amuse themselves in the woods. They might be rewarded later by a glimpse of friendly animals, or Mr. Thoreau would give them a row on the pond.

To take a walk with Thoreau, one must rigidly adhere to the manners of the woods. He could lead one to the ripest berries, the hidden nest, the rarest flowers, but no plant life could be carelessly destroyed, no mother bird lose her eggs.

First he would give a curious whistle and a woodchuck would appear—a different whistle and two squirrels would run to him. A different note yet and birds would fly and even so shy a bird as a crow would alight on his shoulder. The children must be mute and very motionless till each pet was fed from his pocket and had departed. Thus the children were introduced to his family, as he called them.

When boating, he could name all the lilies of the pond or the wood lilies, and he could delight them with stories of the Indians who once lived around Walden.

When someone asked him why he did not shoot the birds and make a collection of them if he wished to study them, "If I wanted to study you would I shoot you?" was the quick reply. "A gun gives you the body only, but the field glass gives you the bird."

The tenderness of his heart was shown in this unvarying love for all life. St. Francis of Assissi admitted that the destinies of animals required our Christian sympathy. Thoreau said, "The best part of an animal is its anima (its soul), but the scientists never get any further than its shell." . . .

Sometimes the owner of that familiar grey homespun suit, made by his aunt to suit the needs of a perennial tramper, would appear at the farm late in the afternoon. That meant a simple supper with the ten children and a long evening for talk.

Aunt Jane said that Thoreau and her father discussed Scandinavian mythology so much that she became an adept in those legends. Such a deep impression was made on her mind that in later life she was compelled to translate Greek and Roman myths back into her early models of Thor, Woden, and Igdrasil. Grandmother told me that sometimes the two men would get into a lively discussion over some vital question. Neither would give in, each could well sustain his own side of the argument, time would pass unheeded and the hour of midnight strike before they realized it. If however Thoreau departed unconvinced or unconvincing and could think during the following day of a fresh argument wherewith to overwhelm Grandfather's point of view, he would come back and they would go at it again the next night.

After the trips to Maine or Canada there were fascinating evenings when no child wanted to go to bed, so interesting were the new experiences in forest lore and the stories about the Indians.

There was one Indian expression, current in the family, which I often say silently to myself when I hear anyone stretching the truth. The Maine campers would invite the Indians to come over and have a supper of deer meat around the camp fire. Sometimes, though, the hunting was poor and other meat was substituted, the deer not being available. After a while the Indians became suspicious and when they were asked to have deer meat one Indian would grunt to another, "Mebbe so, mebbe woodchuck."

The children all loved Mr. Thoreau and had no fear of him. Doubtless no liberties were taken, for "seen and not heard" was Grandfather's motto for them. Thoreau himself resented too great familiarity. . . .

His love for simplicity may have been a legacy from his Quaker great-grandmother who refused to marry her lover until he had laid aside his too foppish ruffles. In his quiet way he was always deferential at home and courteous to all who met him sincerely. . . .

The Puritan flavor was so strong in Concord in the early years of the nineteenth century that the habits of Thoreau were disapproved by many. All must go to the meeting house twice if possible on Sunday. No horse was taken out except for church or a funeral. That a young man, just out of college, should not choose a profession but prefer to spend his Sabbaths in a boat on the river seemed to the good villagers quite sacrilegious. In these days of Sunday golf and canoeing it would have attracted little notice. . . .

The desire to carve his own way produced an intense egotism by which he sought to discover the greatest assets to be added to man's supreme possession, "his own personality." Yet having found them he writes, "I would fain communicate the wealth of my life to men, would really give them what is most precious in my gift."

Indifferent he might seem on the exterior but how close to the surface lay his warm sympathy for the runaway slave, his courageous facing of ostracism in publicly defending John Brown and the anxiety of those sleepless nights when Brown lay in prison. Did those things betoken the indifference of a cold heart?

He refused to pay state taxes as a protest against Massachusetts' adoption of the infamous fugitive slave law, but he gladly paid his road tax, for that was for a worthy purpose.

An instance of his kindness of heart was his observance of a ragged boy: "Leonidas and the Spartans dared at Thermopylae to die, but this little Irish boy dares to face the bitter cold in ragged clothes for a schooling." Mrs. Thoreau took pity on this boy and made him a suit out of an old one of Henry's. She evidently was not much of a seamstress for the neighbors declared that the clothes sat on Johnny as if fitted to a tea kettle.

Thoreau was a skillful gardener, often supplementing Emerson's lack of ability. He planted trees and shrubs around the house and also beautified the terraces back of the Orchard House with fruit trees to suit Alcott's vegetarian taste.

If he seemed different from other men it was because, as he wrote, "If a man does not keep pace with his companions, perhaps it is because he hears a different drummer." It was just this that gave value to his contributions to the world. Whatever notes he heard from that "different drummer" he listened to intently and recorded honestly.

Once the Chicago speculator, known then as "Old Hutch," came to the house to talk with Grandmother about Thoreau. That was after Grandfather's death. He seemed deeply interested in all she told him. Soon after the press was full of the account of some deal whereby he had cleaned up millions. When Grandmother read of it she shook her head and said, "He had better read his Thoreau all over again." . . .

He kept on with his manuscripts up to the last days. When very weak, he was found by a neighbor writing. "You know it is the fashion to leave an estate behind you," he said.

The afternoon before he died, as one of my aunts was passing the house, Sophia called her in. "Mr. B—," she said, "has offered to sit up with my brother tonight, but Henry wants your father." So after supper Grandfather walked over to spend the night with him.

The next day he passed on, trustfully expectant of renewed vision. When Grandfather said, "I heard the robins sing as I came along," Thoreau answered, "This is a beautiful world, but soon I shall see one that is fairer," and again he said to him, "I have so loved nature." . . .

Thoreau never pretended to analyze nature technically, but it was this deep love, human, intuitive, subtle rather than scientific, that made him the pioneer naturalist of his country. When a well known writer made a remark about Thoreau to John Burroughs, the latter replied, "But I couldn't hold a candle to Thoreau." . . .

Of the Thoreau relics, his chair, writing desk, quill pen, buckskin suit, and walking stick, thought lingers longest over the stick. A plain but sturdy stick, like its owner unadorned with trappings of vanity. A cane for use not only in walking, but for measuring, since it was notched on a flat surface to twenty-four inches.

Could it speak, what a medley of deep mystical musings and practical knowledge it could reveal, from its long wanderings with such a combination of seer and surveyor, scholar and naturalist as was Thoreau. What marvellous commingling of the spirit of nature and the soul of that intrepid seeker for truth who listened so closely to Mother Earth's revelations and pondered so deeply on their meanings. We might discover just how much of the real Thoreau is still lost to us; we might learn more of the wondrous glory of the near by and familiar and perceive in greater degree "just how much civilization is necessary for the serenity of the soul."

The portrait expressing best the real man is the crayon by Rawse. The artist was staying at Thoreau's house while making a portrait of Emerson. He became fascinated by Henry's face and wished to make one of him, but what he wanted eluded him. Over and over he would say, "I can't get it; I can't get it." Finally one day he jumped up from the dinner table exclaiming, "Now I have it!" and went to work with a satisfied spirit. Rawse liked best to work as much as possible away from the sitter.

Thoreau was tall and straight and gave the impression of an independent pine tree. The kindness of his eye and the strong nose added to this impression of self reliance and strength. . . .

No one who understood Thoreau could possibly think of him as an idler, as some have done. All that we know about him contradicts that idea.

The beautiful accuracy of his drawings, the exactness of his writing, the excellent quality of his pencils, and his masterly skill at gardening testify to his industry. As a scholar most justice has been done him by Channing the poet. He amused himself by translating two dramas of Aeschylus and parts of Homer, to which he added a number of lesser Greek poets. He was familiar with all the early English poets, read Latin as easily as English, and read Greek classics in the original. He was also a student of oriental literature, extracting from it, as did Emerson, whatever appealed to him as true.

From his seemingly inactive hours, many have learned how to find glory in the near by and familiar. Well for us all if we listened more to his ideas of life and men, for that dauntless apostle of truth was not mild as to our shortcomings.

Mary Hosmer Brown, *Memories of Concord* (Boston: Four Seas, 1926), 88–93, 94–97, 98–101, 102–106, 107–108, 109–110.

From *The Thoreau Family*
Two Generations Ago (1958)

MABEL LOOMIS TODD

Author and editor Mabel Loomis Todd (1856–1932) was the daughter of Thoreau family friends Mary Alden Wilder and Eben Loomis, and the grand-daughter of Mary Wales Fobes Jones Wilder, a close friend of Maria Thoreau and Prudence Ward. With her husband, David Peck Todd, Mabel Todd lived most of her adult life in Amherst, Massachusetts, where her husband was a professor of astronomy at Amherst College. With Thomas Wentworth Higginson, Todd later coedited the first volumes of Emily Dickinson's poems. Her reminiscence of the Thoreau family, including observations about Henry, derives largely from her mother and father's recollections. Especially insightful are Todd's comments on Thoreau as a natural historian, likely drawn from Eben Loomis, who had often accompanied Thoreau on outdoor excursions. Loomis regarded Thoreau as "the most remarkable man in that Concord co-terie . . . with a mind uniquely original, [who] faced the problems of life with a fixed determination to find a satisfactory solution" (1–2). Here Todd reflects Loomis's admiration as she recalls Thoreau's ability to imagine the full range of history and science offered through the study of a single leaf, tree, or berry.

MY MEMORY GOES back a long way, but it does not quite reach that day in Cambridge when my mother invited Henry Thoreau to come to the house to see her wonderful new baby. He came in, boldly enough, and so remained until, with mistaken zeal, the nurse placed me in his arms, doubtless thinking it would be an especial treat to the shy recluse. Far from it—he did not know which end was which! My terrified mother caught sight of two wildly waving little pink feet sticking out at the top, poor little head quite lost in the lower invisible end of the bundle. After one agonized moment the bewildered man, with a groan of relief, relinquished me to the giver. Apparently babies bore no large part in Henry's scheme of life.

Henry Thoreau was an especial friend of my father and mother. They spent the first two or three summers after their marriage in 1853 at his mother's house in Concord. One afternoon the three were taking a quiet rowing trip on the placid Concord River, a diversion to which they were greatly devoted when, as they were approaching a fine old oak on the river bank, Henry ceased rowing, stood up suddenly in the tiny skiff, looked up into the huge tree with something akin to adoration and said, as one inspired, "Why, there is enough in that tree alone to keep one man happily busy all his life!" His face was alight with fervour as he went on to tell of the rich reward awaiting him who would take the oak-tree for his lifework. "The whole story of creation and all of natural history is in that one tree! Why does anyone want to take long journeys to study anything? It is all here." My mother was deeply impressed by his shining face turned upward, and often spoke of that rare evening when she had caught an instant glimpse of all futurity.

Henry was wont to say that he had travelled a great deal—"in Concord," he would add with a whimsical expression. Of genuine journeys he had taken few. One along the Concord and Merrimack Rivers, one down the length of Cape Cod, one through Maine,[1] and one trip into Canada comprised most of his wanderings. But from those short journeys what a wealth of material afterward used in essays and his delightful journals—whole volumes of careful and accurate observation!

All through my childhood when my father wished to impress upon my mind some bit of bird or butterfly or flower lore, he was apt to quote Henry, and incidents from their many rambles were part of my happy training. He and my father were both interested in Indian relics still to be found all over the country. My father once said to him as they walked along a country road, that it was unfortunate these reminders of the past were being gathered up by the general run of persons neither interested in them nor properly instructed.

"Oh, well, there are always plenty left," said Henry, stooping over at the moment to pick up a perfect stone arrow-head.

During one of their happy and prolific summers with him, my parents became acquainted with [Samuel] Rowse, who was also spending some weeks at the Thoreaus', drawing in crayon the portrait of Henry, although to "sit for a portrait" was as much outside his plan as holding a friend's baby right end up. Sometimes the artist would leave the table abruptly in the midst

[211]

of a meal, excusing himself afterward by explaining to his hostess—small, vivid and alert Mrs. Thoreau —that a sudden turn of Henry's head had given him new insight. He had just seen an expression cross his face which must be recorded else one aspect of his mind and changing thought would be lost. Rowse would rush to his easel to put on paper at once the glimpse into Henry's real personality. That portrait, many times reproduced, was the only one which his intimate old friends cared to keep as the permanent representation of the shy naturalist, and it became the one most liked by his family, until all had died and there is no one left to judge. It used to be said that Rowse greatly desired to marry Sophia, Henry's brilliant sister.

A surveyor and a pencil-maker like his father, John Thoreau, Henry David even as a child began his minute observation of birds and insects, of flowers and leaves, indeed of every aspect of nature, animate and inanimate. He even made a collection of these things for Agassiz who had but recently come to the United States, and who became later my father's preceptor in Cambridge. Henry, after his graduation from Harvard in 1837 tried tutoring, even lecturing, but he ultimately fell back upon surveying and the parental pencil-making.

Deciding that rigid economy was a necessity, particularly for a brainworker, and that a few days' labour in the month were all that even necessity could demand, he put his theories to practical test by retiring from even the simple life in Concord, and the society of his best friend Emerson, to live in virtual seclusion on the shores of Walden Pond. The little cabin and its furnishings were made by his own hands, and the potatoes and beans and corn upon which he was supposed to live were raised by himself in the tiny garden surrounding this picturesque domain. But Mrs. Thoreau—a noteworthy housekeeper—used to tell us gleefully that Henry was by no means so utterly indifferent to the good things of life as he liked to believe himself, and that regularly every week of his self-enforced retirement he came home to eat a deliciously prepared dinner which their old family cook took pains to have as perfect as she knew how, and which he very evidently enjoyed to the full after his abstemious days at Walden. My mother's humourous account of Henry's intense satisfaction in coming home for those wonderful dinners during the "hermitage" was a new angle of the naturalist's life and likings. It was while half living at Walden that he was writing such memorable sentences as, "The light which puts out our eyes is darkness to us.

Only that day dawns to which we are awake. There is more to day than dawn. The sun is but a morning star." . . .

This "bachelor of nature," as well as Bronson Alcott, refused to pay taxes to a "slave-holding government," but one of Henry's dear aunts paid them for him. He was thought an oddity, but was nevertheless besought for free lectures for the Lyceum. The villagers rather despised both Alcott and Thoreau, as well as Hawthorne and Channing. But Thoreau, unfailingly honest and upright, for years supporting himself only by hard manual labour, won their respect. If he worked faithfully for one month out of the twelve, however, that supported him for the other eleven. He thus gained time for his own occupations and his dearly loved writing. He used to say that "a broad margin of leisure is as beautiful in a man's life as in a book."

Years afterward when my happiest experiences as a little child in Cambridge were daily walks with my handsome and adored father, he sometimes took me across the College Yard to point out to me the entry of the ancient dormitory which led to Henry's room, enlivening my day with quaint tales of their adventures. During those years shortly after his death (May, 1862) his memory was held fresh and dear in my father's heart—as, indeed, it was ever afterward. Their long rambles together about the Concord woods and fields had cemented their affection through love for the same poets and writers as well as for the marvelous revelations of nature. . . .

Note

1. Todd is mistaken here; Thoreau took three trips to the Maine woods: in 1846, 1853, and 1857.

Mabel Loomis Todd, *The Thoreau Family Two Generations Ago* (Berkeley Heights, NJ: Oriole Press for the Thoreau Society, 1958), 1–6.

Permissions

*Permission statements for items in the Introduction
are included in its endnotes, rather than here.*

Abigail May Alcott to Samuel J. May, 8 February and 18 March 1847, MS Am
1130.9 (25), courtesy of the Houghton Library, Harvard University.

Amos Bronson Alcott, Journals and Diaries of Amos Bronson Alcott, 9 March
1859, MS Am 1130.12 (29), courtesy of the Houghton Library, Harvard
University.

Caroline Healey Dall to [Sophia] Thoreau, 26 July 1862, Thoreau-Sewall
Papers, Scrapbook HM 64967 (HT-25), courtesy of the Huntington Library,
San Marino, California.

The Letters of Ellen Tucker Emerson, vol. 1, ed. Edith E. W. Gregg (Kent,
OH: Kent State University Press, 1982), reprinted by permission of the Ralph
Waldo Emerson Memorial Association.

Lidian Jackson Emerson to Ralph Waldo Emerson, [17 May 1848], bMS Am
1280.235 (619), courtesy of the Houghton Library, Harvard University.

The Selected Letters of Lidian Jackson Emerson, ed. Delores Bird Carpenter
(Columbia: University of Missouri Press, 1987), reprinted by permission of
the Ralph Waldo Emerson Memorial Association.

The Journals and Miscellaneous Notebooks of Ralph Waldo Emerson, ed. William H. Gilman et al., 16 vols. (Cambridge, MA: Belknap Press of Harvard
University Press, 1960–1982), reprinted by permission of Harvard University
Library.

The Letters of Ralph Waldo Emerson, 10 vols., ed. Ralph L. Rusk and Eleanor M. Tilton (New York: Columbia University Press, 1939–95), reprinted by
permission of the Ralph Waldo Emerson Memorial Foundation.

Mabel Loomis Todd, *The Thoreau Family Two Generations Ago* (Berkeley Heights, NJ: Oriole Press for the Thoreau Society, 1958), reprinted by permission of the Thoreau Society.

Ellen Watson, typescript in Hillside Collection, B. IX. XIX, Pilgrim Hall Museum Archives, reprinted by permission of the Pilgrim Society Library, Plymouth, Massachusetts.

Bibliography

Adams, Raymond. "Thoreau and His Neighbors." *Thoreau Society Bulletin* 44 (Summer 1953): 1.

Alcott, Bronson. *The Journals of Bronson Alcott*. Ed. Odell Shepard. Boston: Little, Brown, 1938.

[Amos Bronson Alcott]. "The Forester." *Atlantic Monthly* 9 (April 1862): 443–45.

Alcott, Louisa May. "In Memoriam." *Springfield Republican,* 3 April 1878.

———. *The Selected Letters of Louisa May Alcott*. Ed. Joel Myerson, Daniel Shealy, and Madeleine B. Stern. Boston: Little, Brown, 1987.

Allen, Irving. "American Women to Whom the World Is Indebted: Sophia Peabody, Nathaniel Hawthorne's Wife—Her Influence on the Great Author—Thoreau's Mother and Sister." *Independent* 47 (25 July 1895): 987–88.

———. "Of the Thoreaus and of Other Notable People in Concord." *Boston Daily Advertiser,* 23 April 1894.

Bartlett, George B. *The Concord Guide Book*. Boston: D. Lothrop, 1880.

———. Letter to Edward Jarvis Bartlett, 17 July 1865. Vault A45, Bartlett, Unit 2, series 1, folder 1. Special Collections. Concord Free Public Library. Concord, MA.

Bellin, Joshua David. "Native American Rights." *The Oxford Handbook of Transcendentalism*. Ed. Joel Myerson, Sandra Harbert Petrulionis, and Laura Dassow Walls. New York: Oxford University Press, 2010.

Blake, H. G. O. Letter to H. S. Salt, 25–26 November 1889. Walter Harding Collection. Henley Library, Thoreau Institute, Lincoln, MA.

———. "Thoreau, The Poet-Philosopher." *Springfield Daily Republican,* 14 August 1880.

Blanding, Thomas, and Edmund A. Schofield. "E. Harlow Russell's Reminiscences of Thoreau." *Concord Saunterer* 17 (August 1984): 6–14.

Block, Louis J. "Thoreau's Letters." *Dial* 27 (16 October 1894): 228–30.

"Books Notices." *Portland Transcript,* 19 August 1854.

Bosco, Ronald A., and Joel Myerson, eds. *Emerson In His Own Time*. Iowa City: University of Iowa Press, 2003.

Buell, Lawrence. *The Environmental Imagination: Thoreau, Nature Writing, and the Formation of American Culture.* Cambridge, MA: Belknap Press of Harvard University Press, 1995.

———. "Henry Thoreau Enters the American Canon." *New Essays on* Walden. Ed. Robert F. Sayre. New York: Cambridge University Press, 1992.

Burkholder, Robert E. "Franklin Benjamin Sanborn." *The Transcendentalists: A Review of Research and Criticism.* Ed. Joel Myerson. New York: MLA, 1984.

Burroughs, John. "Henry D. Thoreau." *Century* 24 (July 1882): 368–79.

———. "Thoreau's Wildness." *Critic* 1 (26 March 1881): 74.

Cameron, Kenneth Walter. "Thoreau at Harvard: Diligent, Bright and Cheerful." *Emerson Society Quarterly (ESQ)* 42 (1st quarter 1966): 1.

———, ed. *The New England Writers and the Press.* Hartford: Transcendental Books, 1980.

Capper, Charles. *Margaret Fuller: An American Romantic Life.* 2 vols. New York: Oxford University Press, 2007.

Carpenter, Delores Bird. "Introduction." *The Life of Lidian Jackson Emerson.* Ellen Tucker Emerson. Ed. Delores Bird Carpenter. Lansing: Michigan State University Press, 1992.

Carpenter, Nan Cooke. "Louisa May Alcott and 'Thoreau's Flute': Two Letters." *Huntington Library Quarterly* 24 (November 1960): 71–74.

[Child, Lydia Maria]. "Review of A Week and Walden." *Recognition of Henry David Thoreau: Selected Criticism Since 1848.* Ed. Wendell Glick. Ann Arbor: University of Michigan Press, 1969.

C. K. W. "Fifth Fraternity Lecture." *Liberator,* 4 November 1859.

A Complete Manual of English Literature. New York: Shelden and Company, 1868.

"Contemporary Literature." *Universalist Quarterly and General Review* 22 (October 1865): 530–31.

Conway, Moncure Daniel. *Autobiography Memories and Experiences.* 2 vols. Boston: Houghton Mifflin, 1904.

[———]. "Thoreau." *Fraser's Magazine for Town and Country* 73 (April 1866): 447–65.

Cooke, George Willis. "The Two Thoreaus." *Independent* 48 (10 December 1896): 1671–72.

[Curtis, George William]. "Editor's Easy Chair." *Harper's Monthly* 25 (July 1862): 270–75.

———. "Editor's Easy Chair." *Harper's Monthly* 38 (February 1869): 415–20.

———. "Editor's Easy Chair." *Harper's Monthly* 56 (March 1878): 621–25.

———. "Editor's Easy Chair." *Harper's Monthly* 65 (September 1882): 629–41.

Dall, Caroline Healey. *Daughter of Boston: The Extraordinary Diary of a Nineteenth-Century Woman*. Ed. Helen R. Deese. Boston: Beacon Press, 2005.

———. *Selected Journals of Caroline Healey Dall. Volume 1: 1838–1855*. Ed. Helen R. Deese. Boston: Massachusetts Historical Society, 2006.

Davis, Rebecca Harding. *Bits of Gossip*. Boston: Houghton, Mifflin, 1904.

Dean, Bradley P. "Introduction." *Letters to a Spiritual Seeker*. Ed. Bradley P. Dean. New York: Norton, 2004.

———, ed. "A Rare Reminiscence of Thoreau as a Child." *Thoreau Society Bulletin* 245 (Fall 2003): 1–2.

———, and Ronald Wesley Hoag. "Thoreau's Lectures after *Walden:* An Annotated Calendar." *Studies in the American Renaissance 1996*. Ed. Joel Myerson. Charlottesville: University of Virginia Press, 1996.

———, and Ronald Wesley Hoag. "Thoreau's Lectures before *Walden:* An Annotated Calendar." *Studies in the American Renaissance 1995*. Ed. Joel Myerson. Charlottesville: University of Virginia Press, 1995.

Dedmond, Francis B. "Letters of Caroline Sturgis to Margaret Fuller." *Studies in the American Renaissance 1988*. Ed. Joel Myerson. Charlottesville: University of Virginia Press, 1988.

Deese, Helen R. "Introduction." *Daughter of Boston: The Extraordinary Diary of a Nineteenth-Century Woman, Caroline Healey Dall*. Ed. Helen R. Deese. Boston: Beacon Press, 2005.

———. "Sophia Thoreau to Caroline Dall." *Thoreau Society Bulletin* 178 (Winter 1987): 6–7.

Dickinson, Ellen E. "A Morning with Mr. Longfellow." *New York Evangelist*, 7 April 1881.

Downs, Annie Sawyer. "Mr. Hawthorne, Mr. Thoreau, Miss Alcott, Mr. Emerson, and Me." Ed. Walter Harding. *American Heritage* 30 (December 1978): 100–1.

Dunton, Edith Kellogg. "An Old and a New Estimate of Thoreau." *Dial* 33 (16 December 1902): 465.

[Eckstorm, Fanny Hardy]. "Thoreau's 'Maine Woods.'" *Atlantic Monthly* 52 (August 1908): 242–50.

Ellis, Havelock. "Thoreau." *Thoreau: A Century of Criticism*. Ed. Walter Harding. Dallas: Southern Methodist University Press, 1954.

Emerson, Edward Waldo. Edward W. Emerson Papers, unpublished notes from interview with Elizabeth J. Weir, Vault A45, Emerson, Unit 3, series 1, box 1, folder 20. Special Collections. Concord Free Public Library. Concord, MA.

———. *Henry Thoreau as Remembered by a Young Friend*. Boston: Houghton, Mifflin, 1917.

Emerson, Ellen Tucker. *The Letters of Ellen Tucker Emerson*. 2 vols. Ed. Edith E. W. Gregg. Kent, OH: Kent State University Press, 1982.

———. *The Life of Lidian Jackson Emerson*. Ed. Delores Bird Carpenter. Lansing: Michigan State University Press, 1992.

Emerson, Lidian Jackson. *Selected Letters of Lidian Jackson Emerson*. Ed. Delores Bird Carpenter. Columbia: University of Missouri Press, 1987.

Emerson, Mary Moody. *The Selected Letters of Mary Moody Emerson*. Ed. Nancy Craig Simmons. Athens: University of Georgia Press, 1993.

Emerson, Ralph Waldo. *The Journals and Miscellaneous Notebooks (JMN)*. 16 vols. Ed. William H. Gilman et al. Cambridge, MA: Harvard University Press, 1960–82.

———. *The Letters of Ralph Waldo Emerson*. 10 vols. Ed. Ralph L. Rusk and Eleanor M. Tilton. New York: Columbia University Press, 1939.

———. *Uncollected Prose Writings: Addresses, Essays, and Reviews*. Vol. 10. Ed. Ronald A. Bosco and Joel Myerson. Cambridge, MA: Harvard University Press, forthcoming.

E[merson], [Ralph Waldo]. "Henry D. Thoreau." *Boston Daily Advertiser*, 8 May 1862.

Fields, James T. *Biographical Notes and Personal Sketches*. Boston: Houghton, Mifflin, 1882.

Fink, Steven. "Thoreau and His Audience." *The Cambridge Companion to Henry David Thoreau*. Cambridge, MA: Cambridge University Press, 1995.

French, Allen. "Edward Waldo Emerson: A Memoir." *Massachusetts Historical Society Proceedings* 65 (1931): 1–4.

Fuller, Margaret. Letter to Thoreau, 31 August 1854. *Correspondence*. Vol. 2. Ed. Robert N. Hudspeth. Princeton: Princeton University Press, forthcoming.

———. *The Letters of Margaret Fuller*. 6 vols. Ed. Robert N. Hudspeth. Ithaca: Cornell University Press, 1983.

Gifford, Terry. "Introduction." *John Muir: His Life and Letters and Other Writings*. Ed. Terry Gifford. Seattle: Mountaineers, 1996.

Glick, Wendell. "Preface." *Recognition of Henry David Thoreau: Selected Criticism Since 1848*. Ed. Wendell Glick. Ann Arbor: University of Michigan Press, 1969.

Goodwin, Joan W. *The Remarkable Mrs. Ripley: The Life of Sarah Alden Bradford Ripley*. Boston: Northeastern University Press, 1998.

Gower, Joseph F., and Richard M. Leliaert, eds. *The Brownson-Hecker Correspondence*. Notre Dame, IN: University of Notre Dame Press, 1979.

Gross, Robert A. "'That Terrible Thoreau': Concord and Its Hermit." *A Historical Guide to Henry David Thoreau*. Ed. William E. Cain. New York: Oxford University Press, 2000.

Harding, Walter. *The Days of Henry Thoreau*. Rev. and corr. ed. Princeton: Princeton University Press, 1982.

——. "Edward Hoar on Thoreau." *Thoreau Society Bulletin* 198 (Winter 1992): 6–7.

——. "John Shepard Keyes on Thoreau." *Thoreau Society Bulletin* 103 (Spring 1968): 2–3.

——. "Thoreau's Sexuality." *Journal of Homosexuality* 21, no. 3 (1991): 23–45.

——, and Michael Meyer. *The New Thoreau Handbook*. New York: New York University Press, 1980.

Haskins, David Greene. "The Maternal Ancestors of Ralph Waldo Emerson." *Literary World* 17 (4 September 1886): 297–99.

Hawthorne, Nathaniel. *The American Notebooks*. Ed. Claude M. Simpson. Columbus: Ohio State University Press, 1972.

——. *The Letters*. 6 vols. Ed. Thomas Woodson et al. Columbus: Ohio State University Press, 1984–88.

Hendrick, George, ed. *Remembrances of Concord and the Thoreaus: Letters of Horace Hosmer to Dr. S. A. Jones*. Urbana: University of Illinois Press, 1977.

"Henry Thoreau, the Poet-Naturalist." *Eclectic Magazine* 19 (March 1874): 305–12.

Higginson, Mary Thacher. *Thomas Wentworth Higginson: The Story of His Life*. Boston: Houghton, Mifflin, 1914.

[Higginson, Samuel Storrow]. "Henry D. Thoreau." *Harvard Magazine* 8 (May 1862): 313–18.

Higginson, Thomas Wentworth. *Carlyle's Laugh and Other Surprises*. Boston: Houghton, Mifflin, 1909.

——. *Cheerful Yesterdays*. Boston: Houghton, Mifflin, 1898.

——. Letter to Sophia E. Thoreau, 21 September 1865. Vault A45, Thoreau, Unit 3, Letter File 3a, H35, CAS D-2030i. Special Collections. Concord Free Public Library. Concord, MA.

——. *Letters and Journals of Thomas Wentworth Higginson, 1846–1906*. Ed. Mary Thacher Higginson. Boston: Houghton, Mifflin, 1921.

——. *Part of a Man's Life*. 1905. Reprint, Port Washington, NY: Kennikat Press, 1971.

————. "Reviews and Literary Notices." *Atlantic Monthly* 14 (September 1864): 386.

————. "Reviews and Literary Notices." *Atlantic Monthly* 16 (October 1865): 504.

————. "Short Studies of American Authors. III." *Literary World* (24 May 1879): 169–70.

————. *Studies in History and Letters.* Boston: Houghton, Mifflin, 1900.

Hoar, Edward Sherman. Letter to Edward Sandford Burgess, 4 January [18]93. Vault A45, Burgess Unit 1. Special Collections. Concord Free Public Library. Concord, MA.

Holley, Sallie. *A Life for Liberty: Anti-Slavery and Other Letters of Sallie Holley.* Ed. John White Chadwick. New York: G. P. Putnam's Sons, 1899.

Holmes, Oliver Wendell. *Ralph Waldo Emerson.* Boston: Houghton, Mifflin, 1884.

Howe, M. A. DeWolfe. *Memories of a Hostess: A Chronicle of Eminent Friendships Drawn Chiefly from the Diaries of Mrs. James T. Fields.* Boston: Atlantic Monthly, 1922.

Hudspeth, Robert N. "A Perennial Springtime: Channing's Friendship with Emerson and Thoreau." *ESQ* 54 (1969): 30–36.

Jackson, Charles T. *Proceedings of the Boston Society of Natural History* 9 (1865): 71–72.

James, Henry, Jr. *Hawthorne.* New York: Harper and Brothers, 1879.

"John Burroughs's 'Pepacton.'" *Scribner's Monthly* 22 (August 1881): 634–35.

Johnson, Linck. "Historical Introduction." *A Week on the Concord and Merrimack Rivers.* Ed. Carl F. Hovde. Princeton: Princeton University Press, 1980.

Jones, Samuel Arthur, ed. *Some Unpublished Letters of Henry D. and Sophia E. Thoreau: A Chapter of a Still-born Book.* Queensborough, NY: Marion, 1899.

————. "Thoreau and His Biographers." *Lippincott's* 48 (August 1891): 224–28.

Keyes, John S. Diary entries for 2 August 1839 and 27 January and 15 September 1841. Vault A45, Keyes, Unit 2. Special Collections. Concord Free Public Library. Concord, MA.

————. "Memoir of Samuel Staples." *Memoirs of Members of the Social Circle in Concord.* Fourth Series. Cambridge: Privately printed, Riverside, 1909.

Kopley, Richard. "Naysayers: Poe, Hawthorne, and Melville." *The Oxford Handbook of Transcendentalism.* Ed. Joel Myerson, Sandra Harbert Petrulionis, and Laura Dassow Walls. New York: Oxford University Press, 2010.

Lathrop, Rose Hawthorne. *Memories of Hawthorne.* Boston: Houghton, Mifflin, 1897.

Loomis, Eben Jenks. Typescript, ["On Concord, Emerson, and Thoreau"].

MS 496A, series 2, box 12, folder 198. Loomis Wilder Papers. Manuscripts and Archives. Yale University Library. New Haven, CT.

Lowell, James Russell. "Letters to Various Persons." *North American Review* 101 (October 1865): 597–608.

———. *The Poetical Works of James Russell Lowell.* Boston: Houghton Mifflin, 1978.

[———]. *"A Week on the Concord and Merrimack Rivers." Massachusetts Quarterly Review* 9 (December 1849): 40–51.

Lunt, Sarah Hosmer. "Memories of Concord." Unpublished typescript, series 2, Sarah Hosmer Lunt Papers, folder 3, p. 18. Special Collections. Concord Free Public Library. Concord, MA.

Lysaker, John T., and William Rossi, eds. *Emerson and Thoreau: Figures of Friendship.* Bloomington: Indiana University Press, 2010.

"The Magazines." *New Hampshire Patriot and State Gazette,* 15 July 1862.

Mann, Mary Peabody. Letter to Horace Mann Jr., 24 April 1864, Robert L. Straker Collection of Peabody Letters. Antiochana. Antioch College Library. Yellow Springs, OH.

Marx, Leo. "Introduction." *Henry David Thoreau.* By Frank B. Sanborn. New York: Chelsea House, 1980.

Mason, Daniel Gregory. "Harrison G. O. Blake, '35, and Thoreau." *Harvard Monthly* 26 (May 1898): 87–95.

———. "The Idealistic Basis of Thoreau's Genius." *Harvard Monthly* 25 (December 1897): 82–93.

Maxfield-Miller, Elizabeth. "Emerson and Elizabeth of Concord." *Harvard Library Bulletin* 19 (July 1971): 290–306.

May, Samuel, Jr. "Annual Statement of the General Agent of the Massachusetts Anti-Slavery Society." *Liberator,* 2 February 1855.

Meyer, Michael. *Several More Lives to Live: Thoreau's Political Reputation in America.* Westport, CT: Greenwood, 1977.

Moller, Mary Elkins. *Thoreau in the Human Community.* Amherst: University of Massachusetts Press, 1980.

———. "Thoreau, Womankind, and Sexuality." *ESQ* 22 (third quarter 1976): 123–48.

Myerson, Joel. "Eight Lowell Letters from Concord in 1838." *Illinois Quarterly* 38 (1975): 20–42.

———. "Emerson's 'Thoreau': A New Edition from Manuscript." *Studies in the American Renaissance 1979.* Ed. Joel Myerson. Boston: Twayne, 1979. 17–92.

———. "Thoreau Receives a Fan Letter for *A Week*." *Thoreau Society Bulletin* 208 (Summer 1994): 10.

Neufeldt, Leonard N. "'We Never Agreed . . . in Hardly Anything': Henry Thoreau and Joseph Hosmer." *ESQ* 35.2 (2nd quarter, 1989): 85–107.

"New Publications." *Salem Register.* 10 August 1854.

"Notices of New Books." *New Englander* 125 (October 1873): 765–66.

O'Connor, J. V. *Catholic World* 27 (June 1878): 289–300.

Oehlschlaeger, Fritz, and George Hendrick, eds. *Toward the Making of Thoreau's Reputation: Selected Correspondence of S. A. Jones, A. W. Hosmer, H. S. Salt, H. G. O. Blake, and D. Ricketson.* Urbana: University of Illinois Press, 1979.

Page, H. A. [Alexander H. Japp]. *Thoreau: His Life and Aims.* Boston: Osgood, 1877.

Petrulionis, Sandra Harbert. *To Set This World Right: The Antislavery Movement in Henry Thoreau's Concord.* Ithaca: Cornell University Press, 2006.

Porter, Maria S. "A Day at Concord." *Boston Evening Transcript,* 22 December 1890.

Powers, H. N. "Thoreau." *Dial* 3 (August 1882): 70–71.

"Recent Publications." *Western Christian Advocate,* 6 September 1882.

"Reminiscences of the Thoreaus by Edward Jarvis." *Thoreau Society Bulletin* 167 (Spring 1984): 5.

Ricketson, Anna, and Walton Ricketson, eds. *Daniel Ricketson and His Friends: Letters Poems Sketches Etc.* Boston: Houghton, Mifflin, 1902.

Robinson, Mrs. W. S. [Harriet Hanson], ed. *"Warrington" Pen-Portraits: A Collection of Personal and Political Reminiscences from 1848 to 1876 from the Writings of William S. Robinson.* Boston: Mrs. W. S. Robinson, 1877.

Rogin, Michael Paul. *Subversive Genealogy: The Politics and Art of Herman Melville.* 1979. Reprint, Berkeley: University of California Press, 1985.

Rosenblum, Joseph. "A Cock Fight Between Melville and Thoreau." *Studies in Short Fiction* 23 (Spring 1986): 159–67.

Rossi, William. "'In Dreams Awake': Loss, Transcendental Friendship, and Elegy." *Emerson and Thoreau: Figures of Friendship.* Ed. John T. Lysaker and William Rossi. Bloomington: Indiana University Press, 2010.

Salt, Henry S. *The Life of Henry Thoreau.* London: Bentley and Son, 1890.

Sanborn, Franklin Benjamin. "Hawthorne and His Friends: Reminiscence and Tribute." *ATQ* 9 (1971): 5–24.

———. "The Emerson-Thoreau Correspondence. The Dial Period." *Atlantic Monthly* 69 (May 1892): 577–96.

———. *Recollections of Seventy Years.* 2 vols. Boston: Richard G. Badger, 1909.

———. "Thoreau and Emerson." *Forum* 23 (April 1897): 218–27.

Sattelmeyer, Robert. "General Introduction." *Journal.* Henry D. Thoreau. 8 vols. to date. Ed. John C. Broderick, Elizabeth Hall Witherell, William L. Howarth, Robert Sattlemeyer, and Thomas Blanding. Princeton: Princeton University Press, 1981–.

———. "Thoreau and Emerson." *Cambridge Companion to Henry David Thoreau.* Ed. Joel Myerson. Cambridge: Cambridge University Press, 1995.

———. *Thoreau's Reading: A Study in Intellectual History with Bibliographical Catalogue.* Princeton: Princeton University Press, 1988.

———. "'When He Became My Enemy': Emerson and Thoreau 1848–49." *New England Quarterly* 62 (June 1989): 187–204.

Scharnhorst, Gary. *Henry David Thoreau: A Case Study in Canonization.* Columbia, SC: Camden House, 1993.

———. *Henry David Thoreau: An Annotated Bibliography of Comment and Criticism Before 1900.* New York: Garland, 1992.

———. "'The Most Dismal Fraud of the New England Transcendental Group': Julian Hawthorne on Thoreau." *Concord Saunterer* n.s. 17 (2009): 125–36.

Scholnick, Robert J. "Between Realism and Romanticism: The Curious Career of Eugene Benson." *American Literary Realism* 14 (Autumn 1981): 242–61.

Seaburg, Alan. "A Thoreau Document." *Thoreau Society Bulletin* 109 (Fall 1969): 5.

Simmons, Edward. *From Seven to Seventy: Memories of a Painter and a Yankee.* New York: Harper and Brothers, 1922.

Smith, Harmon. *My Friend, My Friend: The Story of Thoreau's Relationship with Emerson.* Amherst: University of Massachusetts Press, 2001.

"Sophia Thoreau, T. W. Higginson, and the Journal." *Thoreau Society Bulletin* 181 (Fall 1987): 2.

Stern, Madeleine B. "Introduction." *The Selected Letters of Louisa May Alcott.* Ed. Joel Myerson, Daniel Shealy, and Madeleine B. Stern. Boston: Little, Brown, 1987.

S[tevenson], R[obert] L[ouis]. "Henry David Thoreau: His Character and His Opinions." *Cornhill Magazine* 41 (June 1880): 665–82.

———. "Preface." *Familiar Studies of Men and Books Criticisms.* New York: Charles Scribner's Sons, 1925.

Stowell, Robert F. "Poetry about Thoreau: 19th Century." *Thoreau Society Bulletin* 112 (Summer 1970): 1–3.

Thoreau, Henry D. *The Correspondence of Henry David Thoreau.* Ed. Walter Harding and Carl Bode. New York: New York University Press, 1958.

———. *Journal.* 14 vols bound as 2. Ed. Bradford Torrey and Francis H. Allen. 1906. New York: Dover, 1962.

———. *Journal (PEJ).* Ed. John C. Broderick, Elizabeth Hall Witherell, William L. Howarth, Robert Sattelmeyer, Thomas Blanding. 8 vols. to date. Princeton: Princeton University Press, 1981–.

———. *The Maine Woods.* Ed. Joseph J. Moldenhauer. Princeton: Princeton University Press, 1972.

———. "To Edith." *Collected Essays and Poems.* Ed. Elizabeth Hall Witherell. New York: Library of America, 2001.

———. *Walden.* Ed. J. Lyndon Shanley. Princeton: Princeton University Press, 1971.

Thoreau, Maria. Letters to Prudence Ward, 25 September 1847, 15 March 1849, and 17 December 1849. HM 64963–64966 and 64930–64938. Thoreau-Sewall Papers. Huntington Library, San Marino, CA.

"Thoreau and His Writings." *The New England Writers and the Press.* Ed. Kenneth Walter Cameron. Hartford, CT: Transcendental Books, 1980.

"Thoreau and Sophia Dobson Collet." *Thoreau Society Bulletin* 179 (Spring 1987): 4–5.

Todd, Mabel Loomis. *The Thoreau Family Two Generations Ago.* Berkeley Heights, NJ: Oriole Press for the Thoreau Society, 1958.

"Topics of the Month." *Holden's Dollar Magazine* 4 (July 1849): 441–48.

Torrey, Bradford. "Thoreau." *The Recognition of Henry David Thoreau: Selected Criticism Since 1848.* Ed. Wendell Glick. Ann Arbor: University of Michigan Press, 1969.

Traubel, Horace. *With Walt Whitman in Camden.* Vol. 1. New York: D. Appleton, 1908.

———. *With Walt Whitman in Camden.* Vol. 3. New York: Mitchell Kennerley, 1914.

Wade, J. S. "The Friendship of Two Old-Time Naturalists." *Scientific Monthly* 23 (August 1926): 152–60.

Ward, Prudence. Letters to Caroline Sewall, 25 September [1837] and 26 February 1847, HM 64930–64938 and 64963–64966. Thoreau-Sewall Papers. Huntington Library, San Marino, CA.

Wasson, David A. "Modern Speculative Radicalism." *The Radical* (July 1867): 1–22.

[Weiss, John]. "Thoreau." *Christian Examiner* 79 (July 1865): 96–117.

Wells, David A., ed. *Annual of Scientific Discovery* . . . Boston: Gould and Lincoln, 1863.

Wendell, Barrett. *The Literary History of America.* New York: Charles Scribner's Sons, 1905.

Whittier, John Greenleaf. *The Letters of John Greenleaf Whittier.* 3 vols. Ed. John B. Pickard. Cambridge, MA: Belknap Press of Harvard University Press, 1975.

Williams, Donald H. "T. W. Higginson on Thoreau and Maine." *Colby Library Quarterly* 7 (March 1965): 29–32.

[Williams, Henry]. "Henry D. Thoreau." *Memorials of the Class of 1837 of Harvard University.* Boston: George H. Ellis, 1887.

Willis, Frederick H. L. *Alcott Memoirs.* Boston: Richard G. Badger, 1915.

Winslow, Richard E., III. "Thoreau Reviews in the *New England Farmer* (1863–1866)." *Thoreau Society Bulletin* 203 (Spring 1993): 5–6.

"Words That Burn." *National Anti-Slavery Standard,* 12 August 1854.

Wollstonecraft, Mary. *A Vindication of the Rights of Woman.* Ed. Deirdre Lynch. New York: Norton, 2009.

Wortham, Thomas. "Introduction." *Henry Thoreau as Remembered by a Young Friend.* Edward Emerson. 1917. New York: Dover, 1999.

Index